Web Scraping with Python

Collecting Data from the Modern Web

Ryan Mitchell

Beijing · Boston · Farnham · Sebastopol · Tokyo

Web Scraping with Python

by Ryan Mitchell

Copyright © 2015 Ryan Mitchell. All rights reserved.

Printed in the United States of America.

Published by O'Reilly Media, Inc., 1005 Gravenstein Highway North, Sebastopol, CA 95472.

O'Reilly books may be purchased for educational, business, or sales promotional use. Online editions are also available for most titles (*http://safaribooksonline.com*). For more information, contact our corporate/institutional sales department: 800-998-9938 or *corporate@oreilly.com*.

Editors: Simon St. Laurent and Allyson MacDonald
Production Editor: Shiny Kalapurakkel
Copyeditor: Jasmine Kwityn
Proofreader: Carla Thornton

Indexer: Lucie Haskins
Interior Designer: David Futato
Cover Designer: Karen Montgomery
Illustrator: Rebecca Demarest

June 2015:   First Edition

Revision History for the First Edition
2015-06-10:   First Release

See *http://oreilly.com/catalog/errata.csp?isbn=9781491910276* for release details.

978-1-491-91027-6

[LSI]

Table of Contents

Preface. vii

Part I. Building Scrapers

1. Your First Web Scraper. 3
Connecting   3
An Introduction to BeautifulSoup   6
Installing BeautifulSoup   6
Running BeautifulSoup   8
Connecting Reliably   9

2. Advanced HTML Parsing. 13
You Don't Always Need a Hammer   13
Another Serving of BeautifulSoup   14
find() and findAll() with BeautifulSoup   16
Other BeautifulSoup Objects   18
Navigating Trees   18
Regular Expressions   22
Regular Expressions and BeautifulSoup   27
Accessing Attributes   28
Lambda Expressions   28
Beyond BeautifulSoup   29

3. Starting to Crawl. 31
Traversing a Single Domain   31
Crawling an Entire Site   35
Collecting Data Across an Entire Site   38
Crawling Across the Internet   40
Crawling with Scrapy   45

4. Using APIs. 49
How APIs Work   50

Common Conventions 50
   Methods 51
   Authentication 52
Responses 52
   API Calls 53
Echo Nest 54
   A Few Examples 54
Twitter 55
   Getting Started 56
   A Few Examples 57
Google APIs 60
   Getting Started 60
   A Few Examples 61
Parsing JSON 63
Bringing It All Back Home 64
More About APIs 68

5. Storing Data. **71**
Media Files 71
Storing Data to CSV 74
MySQL 76
   Installing MySQL 77
   Some Basic Commands 79
   Integrating with Python 82
   Database Techniques and Good Practice 85
   "Six Degrees" in MySQL 87
Email 90

6. Reading Documents. **93**
Document Encoding 93
Text 94
   Text Encoding and the Global Internet 94
CSV 98
   Reading CSV Files 98
PDF 100
Microsoft Word and .docx 102

Part II.   Advanced Scraping

7. Cleaning Your Dirty Data. **109**
Cleaning in Code 109

    Data Normalization   112
    Cleaning After the Fact   114
      OpenRefine   114

8. Reading and Writing Natural Languages. 119
    Summarizing Data   120
    Markov Models   123
      Six Degrees of Wikipedia: Conclusion   126
    Natural Language Toolkit   129
      Installation and Setup   129
      Statistical Analysis with NLTK   130
      Lexicographical Analysis with NLTK   132
    Additional Resources   136

9. Crawling Through Forms and Logins. 137
    Python Requests Library   137
    Submitting a Basic Form   138
    Radio Buttons, Checkboxes, and Other Inputs   140
    Submitting Files and Images   141
    Handling Logins and Cookies   142
      HTTP Basic Access Authentication   144
    Other Form Problems   144

10. Scraping JavaScript. 147
    A Brief Introduction to JavaScript   148
      Common JavaScript Libraries   149
    Ajax and Dynamic HTML   151
      Executing JavaScript in Python with Selenium   152
    Handling Redirects   158

11. Image Processing and Text Recognition. 161
    Overview of Libraries   162
      Pillow   162
      Tesseract   163
      NumPy   164
    Processing Well-Formatted Text   164
      Scraping Text from Images on Websites   167
    Reading CAPTCHAs and Training Tesseract   169
      Training Tesseract   171
    Retrieving CAPTCHAs and Submitting Solutions   174

12. Avoiding Scraping Traps... 177

A Note on Ethics   177
Looking Like a Human   178
    Adjust Your Headers   179
    Handling Cookies   181
    Timing Is Everything   182
Common Form Security Features   183
    Hidden Input Field Values   183
    Avoiding Honeypots   184
The Human Checklist   186

13. Testing Your Website with Scrapers.. 189

An Introduction to Testing   189
    What Are Unit Tests?   190
Python unittest   190
    Testing Wikipedia   191
Testing with Selenium   193
    Interacting with the Site   194
Unittest or Selenium?   197

14. Scraping Remotely... 199

Why Use Remote Servers?   199
    Avoiding IP Address Blocking   199
    Portability and Extensibility   200
Tor   201
    PySocks   202
Remote Hosting   203
    Running from a Website Hosting Account   203
    Running from the Cloud   204
Additional Resources   206
Moving Forward   206

A. Python at a Glance... 209

B. The Internet at a Glance... 213

C. The Legalities and Ethics of Web Scraping.................................. 217

Index.. 231

Preface

To those who have not developed the skill, computer programming can seem like a kind of magic. If programming is magic, then *web scraping* is wizardry; that is, the application of magic for particularly impressive and useful—yet surprisingly effortless —feats.

In fact, in my years as a software engineer, I've found that very few programming practices capture the excitement of both programmers and laymen alike quite like web scraping. The ability to write a simple bot that collects data and streams it down a terminal or stores it in a database, while not difficult, never fails to provide a certain thrill and sense of possibility, no matter how many times you might have done it before.

It's unfortunate that when I speak to other programmers about web scraping, there's a lot of misunderstanding and confusion about the practice. Some people aren't sure if it's legal (it is), or how to handle the modern Web, with all its JavaScript, multimedia, and cookies. Some get confused about the distinction between APIs and web scrapers.

This book seeks to put an end to many of these common questions and misconceptions about web scraping, while providing a comprehensive guide to most common web-scraping tasks.

Beginning in Chapter 1, I'll provide code samples periodically to demonstrate concepts. These code samples are in the public domain, and can be used with or without attribution (although acknowledgment is always appreciated). All code samples also will be available on the website (*http://www.pythonscraping.com/code/*) for viewing and downloading.

What Is Web Scraping?

The automated gathering of data from the Internet is nearly as old as the Internet itself. Although *web scraping* is not a new term, in years past the practice has been more commonly known as *screen scraping*, *data mining*, *web harvesting*, or similar variations. General consensus today seems to favor *web scraping*, so that is the term I'll use throughout the book, although I will occasionally refer to the web-scraping programs themselves as *bots*.

In theory, web scraping is the practice of gathering data through any means other than a program interacting with an API (or, obviously, through a human using a web browser). This is most commonly accomplished by writing an automated program that queries a web server, requests data (usually in the form of the HTML and other files that comprise web pages), and then parses that data to extract needed information.

In practice, web scraping encompasses a wide variety of programming techniques and technologies, such as data analysis and information security. This book will cover the basics of web scraping and crawling (Part I), and delve into some of the advanced topics in Part II.

Why Web Scraping?

If the only way you access the Internet is through a browser, you're missing out on a huge range of possibilities. Although browsers are handy for executing JavaScript, displaying images, and arranging objects in a more human-readable format (among other things), web scrapers are excellent at gathering and processing large amounts of data (among other things). Rather than viewing one page at a time through the narrow window of a monitor, you can view databases spanning thousands or even millions of pages at once.

In addition, web scrapers can go places that traditional search engines cannot. A Google search for "cheapest flights to Boston" will result in a slew of advertisements and popular flight search sites. Google only knows what these websites say on their content pages, not the exact results of various queries entered into a flight search application. However, a well-developed web scraper can chart the cost of a flight to Boston over time, across a variety of websites, and tell you the best time to buy your ticket.

You might be asking: "Isn't data gathering what APIs are for?" (If you're unfamiliar with APIs, see Chapter 4.) Well, APIs can be fantastic, if you find one that suits your purposes. They can provide a convenient stream of well-formatted data from one server to another. You can find an API for many different types of data you might want to use such as Twitter posts or Wikipedia pages. In general, it is preferable to use an API (if one exists), rather than build a bot to get the same data. However, there are several reasons why an API might not exist:

- You are gathering data across a collection of sites that do not have a cohesive API.
- The data you want is a fairly small, finite set that the webmaster did not think warranted an API.
- The source does not have the infrastructure or technical ability to create an API.

Even when an API *does* exist, request volume and rate limits, the types of data, or the format of data that it provides might be insufficient for your purposes.

This is where web scraping steps in. With few exceptions, if you can view it in your browser, you can access it via a Python script. If you can access it in a script, you can store it in a database. And if you can store it in a database, you can do virtually anything with that data.

There are obviously many extremely practical applications of having access to nearly unlimited data: market forecasting, machine language translation, and even medical diagnostics have benefited tremendously from the ability to retrieve and analyze data from news sites, translated texts, and health forums, respectively.

Even in the art world, web scraping has opened up new frontiers for creation. The 2006 project "We Feel Fine" (*http://wefeelfine.org/*) by Jonathan Harris and Sep Kamvar, scraped a variety of English-language blog sites for phrases starting with "I feel" or "I am feeling." This led to a popular data visualization, describing how the world was feeling day by day and minute by minute.

Regardless of your field, there is almost always a way web scraping can guide business practices more effectively, improve productivity, or even branch off into a brand-new field entirely.

About This Book

This book is designed to serve not only as an introduction to web scraping, but as a comprehensive guide to scraping almost every type of data from the modern Web. Although it uses the Python programming language, and covers many Python basics, it should not be used as an introduction to the language.

If you are not an expert programmer and don't know any Python at all, this book might be a bit of a challenge. If, however, you are an experienced programmer, you should find the material easy to pick up. Appendix A covers installing and working with Python 3.x, which is used throughout this book. If you have only used Python 2.x, or do not have 3.x installed, you might want to review Appendix A.

If you're looking for a more comprehensive Python resource, the book *Introducing Python* by Bill Lubanovic is a very good, if lengthy, guide. For those with shorter attention spans, the video series *Introduction to Python* (*http://shop.oreilly.com/product/110000448.do*) by Jessika McKeller is an excellent resource.

Appendix C includes case studies, as well as a breakdown of key issues that might affect how you can legally run scrapers in the United States and use the data that they produce.

Technical books are often able to focus on a single language or technology, but web scraping is a relatively disparate subject, with practices that require the use of databases, web servers, HTTP, HTML, Internet security, image processing, data science, and other tools. This book attempts to cover all of these to an extent for the purpose of gathering data from remote sources across the Internet.

Part I covers the subject of web scraping and web crawling in depth, with a strong focus on a small handful of libraries used throughout the book. Part I can easily be used as a comprehensive reference for these libraries and techniques (with certain exceptions, where additional references will be provided).

Part II covers additional subjects that the reader might find useful when writing web scrapers. These subjects are, unfortunately, too broad to be neatly wrapped up in a single chapter. Because of this, frequent references will be made to other resources for additional information.

The structure of this book is arranged to be easy to jump around among chapters to find only the web-scraping technique or information that you are looking for. When a concept or piece of code builds on another mentioned in a previous chapter, I will explicitly reference the section that it was addressed in.

Conventions Used in This Book

The following typographical conventions are used in this book:

Italic
:   Indicates new terms, URLs, email addresses, filenames, and file extensions.

`Constant width`
:   Used for program listings, as well as within paragraphs to refer to program elements such as variable or function names, databases, data types, environment variables, statements, and keywords.

`Constant width bold`
:   Shows commands or other text that should be typed by the user.

Constant width italic

Shows text that should be replaced with user-supplied values or by values determined by context.

This element signifies a tip or suggestion.

This element signifies a general note.

This element indicates a warning or caution.

Using Code Examples

Supplemental material (code examples, exercises, etc.) is available for download at *http://pythonscraping.com/code/*.

This book is here to help you get your job done. In general, if example code is offered with this book, you may use it in your programs and documentation. You do not need to contact us for permission unless you're reproducing a significant portion of the code. For example, writing a program that uses several chunks of code from this book does not require permission. Selling or distributing a CD-ROM of examples from O'Reilly books does require permission. Answering a question by citing this book and quoting example code does not require permission. Incorporating a significant amount of example code from this book into your product's documentation does require permission.

We appreciate, but do not require, attribution. An attribution usually includes the title, author, publisher, and ISBN. For example: "*Web Scraping with Python* by Ryan Mitchell (O'Reilly). Copyright 2015 Ryan Mitchell, 978-1-491-91029-0."

If you feel your use of code examples falls outside fair use or the permission given here, feel free to contact us at *permissions@oreilly.com*.

Safari® Books Online

 Safari Books Online is an on-demand digital library that delivers expert content in both book and video form from the world's leading authors in technology and business.

Technology professionals, software developers, web designers, and business and creative professionals use Safari Books Online as their primary resource for research, problem solving, learning, and certification training.

Safari Books Online offers a range of product mixes and pricing programs for organizations, government agencies, and individuals. Subscribers have access to thousands of books, training videos, and prepublication manuscripts in one fully searchable database from publishers like O'Reilly Media, Prentice Hall Professional, Addison-Wesley Professional, Microsoft Press, Sams, Que, Peachpit Press, Focal Press, Cisco Press, John Wiley & Sons, Syngress, Morgan Kaufmann, IBM Redbooks, Packt, Adobe Press, FT Press, Apress, Manning, New Riders, McGraw-Hill, Jones & Bartlett, Course Technology, and dozens more. For more information about Safari Books Online, please visit us online.

How to Contact Us

Please address comments and questions concerning this book to the publisher:

O'Reilly Media, Inc.
1005 Gravenstein Highway North
Sebastopol, CA 95472
800-998-9938 (in the United States or Canada)
707-829-0515 (international or local)
707-829-0104 (fax)

We have a web page for this book, where we list errata, examples, and any additional information. You can access this page at *http://oreil.ly/1ePG2Uj*.

To comment or ask technical questions about this book, send email to *bookquestions@oreilly.com*.

For more information about our books, courses, conferences, and news, see our website at *http://www.oreilly.com*.

Find us on Facebook: *http://facebook.com/oreilly*

Follow us on Twitter: *http://twitter.com/oreillymedia*

Watch us on YouTube: *http://www.youtube.com/oreillymedia*

Acknowledgments

Just like some of the best products arise out of a sea of user feedback, this book could have never existed in any useful form without the help of many collaborators, cheerleaders, and editors. Thank you to the O'Reilly staff and their amazing support for this somewhat unconventional subject, to my friends and family who have offered advice and put up with impromptu readings, and to my coworkers at LinkeDrive who I now likely owe many hours of work to.

Thank you, in particular, to Allyson MacDonald, Brian Anderson, Miguel Grinberg, and Eric VanWyk for their feedback, guidance, and occasional tough love. Quite a few sections and code samples were written as a direct result of their inspirational suggestions.

Thank you to Yale Specht for his limitless patience throughout the past nine months, providing the initial encouragement to pursue this project, and stylistic feedback during the writing process. Without him, this book would have been written in half the time but would not be nearly as useful.

Finally, thanks to Jim Waldo, who really started this whole thing many years ago when he mailed a Linux box and *The Art and Science of C* to a young and impressionable teenager.

## PART I

Building Scrapers

This section focuses on the basic mechanics of web scraping: how to use Python to request information from a web server, how to perform basic handling of the server's response, and how to begin interacting with a website in an automated fashion. By the end, you'll be cruising around the Internet with ease, building scrapers that can hop from one domain to another, gather information, and store that information for later use.

To be honest, web scraping is a fantastic field to get into if you want a huge payout for relatively little upfront investment. In all likelihood, 90% of web scraping projects you'll encounter will draw on techniques used in just the next six chapters. This section covers what the general (albeit technically savvy) public tends to think of when they think of "web scrapers":

- Retrieving HTML data from a domain name
- Parsing that data for target information
- Storing the target information
- Optionally, moving to another page to repeat the process

This will give you a solid foundation before moving on to more complex projects in part II. Don't be fooled into thinking that this first section isn't as important as some of the more advanced projects in the second half. You will use nearly all the information in the first half of this book on a daily basis while writing web scrapers.

## CHAPTER 1

Your First Web Scraper

Once you start web scraping, you start to appreciate all the little things that browsers do for us. The Web, without a layer of HTML formatting, CSS styling, JavaScript execution, and image rendering, can look a little intimidating at first, but in this chapter, as well as the next one, we'll cover how to format and interpret data without the help of a browser.

This chapter will start with the basics of sending a GET request to a web server for a specific page, reading the HTML output from that page, and doing some simple data extraction in order to isolate the content that we are looking for.

Connecting

If you haven't spent much time in networking, or network security, the mechanics of the Internet might seem a little mysterious. We don't want to think about what, exactly, the network is doing every time we open a browser and go to *http://google.com*, and, these days, we don't have to. In fact, I would argue that it's fantastic that computer interfaces have advanced to the point where most people who use the Internet don't have the faintest idea about how it works.

However, web scraping requires stripping away some of this shroud of interface, not just at the browser level (how it interprets all of this HTML, CSS, and JavaScript), but occasionally at the level of the network connection.

To give you some idea of the infrastructure required to get information to your browser, let's use the following example. Alice owns a web server. Bob uses a desktop computer, which is trying to connect to Alice's server. When one machine wants to talk to another machine, something like the following exchange takes place:

1. Bob's computer sends along a stream of 1 and 0 bits, indicated by high and low voltages on a wire. These bits form some information, containing a header and body. The header contains an immediate destination of his local router's MAC address, with a final destination of Alice's IP address. The body contains his request for Alice's server application.
2. Bob's local router receives all these 1's and 0's and interprets them as a packet, from Bob's own MAC address, and destined for Alice's IP address. His router stamps its own IP address on the packet as the "from" IP address, and sends it off across the Internet.
3. Bob's packet traverses several intermediary servers, which direct his packet toward the correct physical/wired path, on to Alice's server.
4. Alice's server receives the packet, at her IP address.
5. Alice's server reads the packet port destination (almost always port 80 for web applications, this can be thought of as something like an "apartment number" for packet data, where the IP address is the "street address"), in the header, and passes it off to the appropriate application – the web server application.
6. The web server application receives a stream of data from the server processor. This data says something like:
   - This is a GET request
   - The following file is requested: index.html
7. The web server locates the correct HTML file, bundles it up into a new packet to send to Bob, and sends it through to its local router, for transport back to Bob's machine, through the same process.

And *voilà*! We have The Internet.

So, where in this exchange did the web browser come into play? Absolutely nowhere. In fact, browsers are a relatively recent invention in the history of the Internet, when Nexus was released in 1990.

Yes, the web browser is a very useful application for creating these packets of information, sending them off, and interpreting the data you get back as pretty pictures, sounds, videos, and text. However, a web browser is just code, and code can be taken apart, broken into its basic components, re-written, re-used, and made to do anything we want. A web browser can tell the processor to send some data to the application that handles your wireless (or wired) interface, but many languages have libraries that can do that just as well.

Let's take a look at how this is done in Python:

```
from urllib.request import urlopen
html = urlopen("http://pythonscraping.com/pages/page1.html")
print(html.read())
```

You can save this code as *scrapetest.py* and run it in your terminal using the command:

```
$python scrapetest.py
```

Note that if you also have Python 2.x installed on your machine, you may need to explicitly call Python 3.x by running the command this way:

```
$python3 scrapetest.py
```

This will output the complete HTML code for the page at *http://bit.ly/1QjYgcd*. More accurately, this outputs the HTML file *page1.html*, found in the directory *<web root>/ pages*, on the server located at the domain name *http://pythonscraping.com*.

What's the difference? Most modern web pages have many resource files associated with them. These could be image files, JavaScript files, CSS files, or any other content that the page you are requesting is linked to. When a web browser hits a tag such as `<img src="cuteKitten.jpg">`, the browser knows that it needs to make another request to the server to get the data at the file *cuteKitten.jpg* in order to fully render the page for the user. Keep in mind that our Python script doesn't have the logic to go back and request multiple files (yet);it can only read the single HTML file that we've requested.

So how does it do this? Thanks to the plain-English nature of Python, the line

```
from urllib.request import urlopen
```

means what it looks like it means: it looks at the Python module request (found within the urllib library) and imports only the function `urlopen`.

urllib or urllib2?

If you've used the urllib2 library in Python 2.x, you might have noticed that things have changed somewhat between urllib2 and urllib. In Python 3.x, urllib2 was renamed urllib and was split into several submodules: `urllib.request`, `urllib.parse`, and `urllib.error`. Although function names mostly remain the same, you might want to note which functions have moved to submodules when using the new urllib.

`urllib` is a standard Python library (meaning you don't have to install anything extra to run this example) and contains functions for requesting data across the web, handling cookies, and even changing metadata such as headers and your user agent. We will be using `urllib` extensively throughout the book, so we recommend you read the Python documentation for the library (*http://bit.ly/1FncvYE*).

urlopen is used to open a remote object across a network and read it. Because it is a fairly generic library (it can read HTML files, image files, or any other file stream with ease), we will be using it quite frequently throughout the book.

An Introduction to BeautifulSoup

"Beautiful Soup, so rich and green,
Waiting in a hot tureen!
Who for such dainties would not stoop?
Soup of the evening, beautiful Soup!"

The BeautifulSoup library was named after a Lewis Carroll poem of the same name in *Alice's Adventures in Wonderland*. In the story, this poem is sung by a character called the Mock Turtle (itself a pun on the popular Victorian dish Mock Turtle Soup made not of turtle but of cow).

Like its Wonderland namesake, BeautifulSoup tries to make sense of the nonsensical; it helps format and organize the messy web by fixing bad HTML and presenting us with easily-traversible Python objects representing XML structures.

Installing BeautifulSoup

Because the BeautifulSoup library is not a default Python library, it must be installed. We will be using the BeautifulSoup 4 library (also known as BS4) throughout this book. The complete instructions for installing BeautifulSoup 4 can be found at Crummy.com (*http://bit.ly/1FjBSJN*); however, the basic method for Linux is:

```
$sudo apt-get install python-bs4
```

and for Macs:

```
$sudo easy_install pip
```

This installs the Python package manager *pip*. Then run the following:

```
$pip install beautifulsoup4
```

to install the library.

Again, note that if you have both Python 2.x and 3.x installed on your machine, you might need to call `python3` explicitly:

```
$python3 myScript.py
```

Make sure to also use this when installing packages, or the packages might be installed under Python 2.x, but not Python 3.x:

```
$sudo python3 setup.py install
```

If using pip, you can also call `pip3` to install the Python 3.x versions of packages:

```
$pip3 install beautifulsoup4
```

Installing packages in Windows is nearly identical to the process for the Mac and Linux. Download the most recent BeautifulSoup 4 release from the download URL above, navigate to the directory you unzipped it to, and run:

```
>python setup.py install
```

And that's it! BeautifulSoup will now be recognized as a Python library on your machine. You can test this out by opening a Python terminal and importing it:

```
$python
> from bs4 import BeautifulSoup
```

The import should complete without errors.

In addition, there is an .exe installer for pip on Windows (*http://bit.ly/1dF0W8z*), so you can easily install and manage packages:

```
>pip install beautifulsoup4
```

Keeping Libraries Straight with Virtual Environments

If you intend to work on multiple Python projects or you need a way to easily bundle projects with all associated libraries, or you're worried about potential conflicts between installed libraries, you can install a Python virtual environment to keep everything separated and easy to manage.

When you install a Python library without a virtual environment, you are installing it *globally*. This usually requires that you be an administrator, or run as root, and that Python library exists for every user and every project on the machine. Fortunately, creating a virtual environment is easy:

```
$ virtualenv scrapingEnv
```

This creates a new environment called *scrapingEnv*, which you must activate in order to use:

```
$ cd scrapingEnv/
$ source bin/activate
```

After you have activated the environment, you will see that environment's name in your command line prompt, reminding you that you're currently working with it. Any libraries you install or scripts you run will be under that virtual environment only.

Working in the newly-created scrapingEnv environment, I can install and use BeautifulSoup, for instance:

```
(scrapingEnv)ryan$ pip install beautifulsoup4
(scrapingEnv)ryan$ python
> from bs4 import BeautifulSoup
>
```

I can leave the environment with the deactivate command, after which I can no longer access any libraries that were installed inside the virtual environment:

```
(scrapingEnv)ryan$ deactivate
ryan$ python
> from bs4 import BeautifulSoup
Traceback (most recent call last):
  File "<stdin>", line 1, in <module>
ImportError: No module named 'bs4'
```

Keeping all your libraries separated by project also makes it easy to zip up the entire environment folder and send it to someone else. As long as they have the same version of Python installed on their machine, your code will work from the virtual environment without requiring them to install any libraries themselves.

Although we won't explicitly instruct you to use a virtual environment in all of this book's examples, keep in mind that you can apply virtual environment any time simply by activating it beforehand.

Running BeautifulSoup

The most commonly used object in the BeautifulSoup library is, appropriately, the BeautifulSoup object. Let's take a look at it in action, modifying the example found in the beginning of this chapter:

```
from urllib.request import urlopen
from bs4 import BeautifulSoup
html = urlopen("http://www.pythonscraping.com/exercises/exercise1.html")
bsObj = BeautifulSoup(html.read());
print(bsObj.h1)
```

The output is:

```
<h1>An Interesting Title</h1>
```

As in the example before, we are importing the urlopen library and calling html.read() in order to get the HTML content of the page. This HTML content is then transformed into a BeautifulSoup object, with the following structure:

- **html** → *<html><head>...</head><body>...</body></html>*
  - **head** → *<head><title>A Useful Page<title></head>*
    - **title** → *<title>A Useful Page</title>*
  - **body** → *<body><h1>An Int...</h1> Lorem ip... </body>*
    - **h1** → *<h1>An Interesting Title</h1>*
    - **div** → *<div>Lorem Ipsum dolor...</div>*

Note that the <h1> tag that we extracted from the page was nested two layers deep into our BeautifulSoup object structure (html → body → h1). However, when we actually fetched it from the object, we called the h1 tag directly:

```
bsObj.h1
```

In fact, any of the following function calls would produce the same output:

```
bsObj.html.body.h1
bsObj.body.h1
bsObj.html.h1
```

We hope this small taste of BeautifulSoup has given you an idea of the power and simplicity of this library. Virtually any information can be extracted from any HTML (or XML) file, as long as it has some identifying tag surrounding it, or near it. In chapter 3, we'll delve more deeply into some more-complex BeautifulSoup function calls, as well as take a look at regular expressions and how they can be used with Beau tifulSoup in order to extract information from websites.

Connecting Reliably

The web is messy. Data is poorly formatted, websites go down, and closing tags go missing. One of the most frustrating experiences in web scraping is to go to sleep with a scraper running, dreaming of all the data you'll have in your database the next day—only to find out that the scraper hit an error on some unexpected data format and stopped execution shortly after you stopped looking at the screen. In situations like these, you might be tempted to curse the name of the developer who created the website (and the oddly formatted data), but the person you should really be kicking is yourself, for not anticipating the exception in the first place!

Let's take a look at the first line of our scraper, after the import statements, and figure out how to handle any exceptions this might throw:

```
html = urlopen("http://www.pythonscraping.com/exercises/exercise1.html")
```

There are two main things that can go wrong in this line:

- The page is not found on the server (or there was some error in retrieving it)
- The server is not found

In the first situation, an HTTP error will be returned. This HTTP error may be "404 Page Not Found," "500 Internal Server Error," etc. In all of these cases, the urlopen function will throw the generic exception "HTTPError" We can handle this exception in the following way:

```
try:
    html = urlopen("http://www.pythonscraping.com/exercises/exercise1.html")
except HTTPError as e:
    print(e)
```

```
    #return null, break, or do some other "Plan B"
else:
    #program continues. Note: If you return or break in the
    #exception catch, you do not need to use the "else" statement
```

If an HTTP error code is returned, the program now prints the error, and does not execute the rest of the program under the else statement.

If the server is not found at all (if, say, *http://www.pythonscraping.com* was down, or the URL was mistyped), urlopen returns a None object. This object is analogous to null in other programming languages. We can add a check to see if the returned html is None:

```
if html is None:
    print("URL is not found")
else:
    #program continues
```

Of course, if the page is retrieved successfully from the server, there is still the issue of the content on the page not quite being what we expected. Every time you access a tag in a BeautifulSoup object, it's smart to add a check to make sure the tag actually exists. If you attempt to access a tag that does not exist, BeautifulSoup will return a None object. The problem is, attempting to access a tag on a None object itself will result in an AttributeError being thrown.

The following line (where nonExistentTag is a made-up tag, not the name of a real BeautifulSoup function):

```
print(bsObj.nonExistentTag)
```

returns a None object. This object is perfectly reasonable to handle and check for. The trouble comes if you don't check for it, but instead go on and try to call some other function on the None object, as illustrated in the following:

```
print(bsObj.nonExistentTag.someTag)
```

which returns the exception:

```
AttributeError: 'NoneType' object has no attribute 'someTag'
```

So how can we guard against these two situations? The easiest way is to explicitly check for both situations:

```
try:
    badContent = bsObj.nonExistingTag.anotherTag
except AttributeError as e:
    print("Tag was not found")
else:
    if badContent == None:
        print ("Tag was not found")
    else:
        print(badContent)
```

This checking and handling of every error does seem laborious at first, but it's easy to add a little reorganization to this code to make it less difficult to write (and, more importantly, much less difficult to read). This code, for example, is our same scraper written in a slightly different way:

```
from urllib.request import urlopen
from urllib.error import HTTPError
from bs4 import BeautifulSoup
 def getTitle(url):
    try:
        html = urlopen(url)
    except HTTPError as e:
        return None
    try:
        bsObj = BeautifulSoup(html.read())
        title = bsObj.body.h1
    except AttributeError as e:
        return None
    return title
title = getTitle("http://www.pythonscraping.com/exercises/exercise1.html")
if title == None:
    print("Title could not be found")
else:
    print(title)
```

In this example, we're creating a function getTitle, which returns either the title of the page, or a None object if there was some problem with retrieving it. Inside getTitle, we check for an HTTPError, as in the previous example, and also encapsulate two of the BeautifulSoup lines inside one try statement. An AttributeError might be thrown from either of these lines (if the server did not exist, html would be a None object, and html.read() would throw an AttributeError). We could, in fact, encompass as many lines as we wanted inside one try statement, or call another function entirely, which can throw an AttributeError at any point.

When writing scrapers, it's important to think about the overall pattern of your code in order to handle exceptions and make it readable at the same time. You'll also likely want to heavily reuse code. Having generic functions such as getSiteHTML and getTitle (complete with thorough exception handling) makes it easy to quickly—and reliably—scrape the web.

## CHAPTER 2

Advanced HTML Parsing

When Michelangelo was asked how he could sculpt a work of art as masterful as his David, he is famously reported to have said: "It is easy. You just chip away the stone that doesn't look like David."

Although web scraping is unlike marble sculpting in most other respects, we must take a similar attitude when it comes to extracting the information we're seeking from complicated web pages. There are many techniques to chip away the content that doesn't look like the content that we're searching for, until we arrive at the information we're seeking. In this chapter, we'll take look at parsing complicated HTML pages in order to extract only the information we're looking for.

You Don't Always Need a Hammer

It can be tempting, when faced with a Gordian Knot of tags, to dive right in and use multiline statements to try to extract your information. However, keep in mind that layering the techniques used in this section with reckless abandon can lead to code that is difficult to debug, fragile, or both. Before getting started, let's take a look at some of the ways you can avoid altogether the need for advanced HTML parsing!

Let's say you have some target content. Maybe it's a name, statistic, or block of text. Maybe it's buried 20 tags deep in an HTML mush with no helpful tags or HTML attributes to be found. Let's say you dive right in and write something like the following line to attempt extraction:

```
bsObj.findAll("table")[4].findAll("tr")[2].find("td").findAll("div")[1].find("a")
```

That doesn't look so great. In addition to the aesthetics of the line, even the slightest change to the website by a site administrator might break your web scraper altogether. So what are your options?

- Look for a "print this page" link, or perhaps a mobile version of the site that has better-formatted HTML (more on presenting yourself as a mobile device—and receiving mobile site versions—in Chapter 12).
- Look for the information hidden in a JavaScript file. Remember, you might need to examine the imported JavaScript files in order to do this. For example, I once collected street addresses (along with latitude and longitude) off a website in a neatly formatted array by looking at the JavaScript for the embedded Google Map that displayed a pinpoint over each address.
- This is more common for page titles, but the information might be available in the URL of the page itself.
- If the information you are looking for is unique to this website for some reason, you're out of luck. If not, try to think of other sources you could get this information from. Is there another website with the same data? Is this website displaying data that it scraped or aggregated from another website?

Especially when faced with buried or poorly formatted data, it's important not to just start digging. Take a deep breath and think of alternatives. If you're certain no alternatives exist, the rest of this chapter is for you.

Another Serving of BeautifulSoup

In Chapter 1, we took a quick look at installing and running BeautifulSoup, as well as selecting objects one at a time. In this section, we'll discuss searching for tags by attributes, working with lists of tags, and parse tree navigation.

Nearly every website you encounter contains stylesheets. Although you might think that a layer of styling on websites that is designed specifically for browser and human interpretation might be a bad thing, the advent of CSS is actually a boon for web scrapers. CSS relies on the differentiation of HTML elements that might otherwise have the exact same markup in order to style them differently. That is, some tags might look like this:

```
<span class="green"></span>
```

while others look like this:

```
<span class="red"></span>
```

Web scrapers can easily separate these two different tags based on their class; for example, they might use BeautifulSoup to grab all of the red text but none of the green text. Because CSS relies on these identifying attributes to style sites appropriately, you are almost guaranteed that these class and ID attributes will be plentiful on most modern websites.

Let's create an example web scraper that scrapes the page located at *http://bit.ly/ 1Ge96Rw*.

On this page, the lines spoken by characters in the story are in red, whereas the names of characters themselves are in green. You can see the span tags, which reference the appropriate CSS classes, in the following sample of the page's source code:

```
"<span class="red">Heavens! what a virulent attack!</span>" replied <span class=
"green">the prince</span>, not in the least disconcerted by this reception.
```

We can grab the entire page and create a BeautifulSoup object with it using a program similar to the one used in Chapter 1:

```
from urllib.request import urlopen
from bs4 import BeautifulSoup
html = urlopen("http://www.pythonscraping.com/pages/warandpeace.html")
bsObj = BeautifulSoup(html)
```

Using this BeautifulSoup object, we can use the findAll function to extract a Python list of proper nouns found by selecting only the text within <span class="green"></span> tags (findAll is an extremely flexible function we'll be using a lot later in this book):

```
nameList = bsObj.findAll("span", {"class":"green"})
for name in nameList:
    print(name.get_text())
```

When run, it should list all the proper nouns in the text, in the order they appear in *War and Peace*. So what's going on here? Previously, we've called bsObj.tagName in order to get the first occurrence of that tag on the page. Now, we're calling bsObj.findAll(tagName, tagAttributes) in order to get a list of all of the tags on the page, rather than just the first.

After getting a list of names, the program iterates through all names in the list, and prints name.get_text() in order to separate the content from the tags.

When to get_text() and When to Preserve Tags

.get_text() strips all tags from the document you are working with and returns a string containing the text only. For example, if you are working with a large block of text that contains many hyperlinks, paragraphs, and other tags, all those will be stripped away and you'll be left with a tagless block of text.

Keep in mind that it's much easier to find what you're looking for in a BeautifulSoup object than in a block of text. Calling .get_text() should always be the last thing you do, immediately before you print, store, or manipulate your final data. In general, you should try to preserve the tag structure of a document as long as possible.

find() and findAll() with BeautifulSoup

BeautifulSoup's `find()` and `findAll()` are the two functions you will likely use the most. With them, you can easily filter HTML pages to find lists of desired tags, or a single tag, based on their various attributes.

The two functions are extremely similar, as evidenced by their definitions in the BeautifulSoup documentation:

```
findAll(tag, attributes, recursive, text, limit, keywords)
find(tag, attributes, recursive, text, keywords)
```

In all likelihood, 95% of the time you will find yourself only needing to use the first two arguments: `tag` and `attributes`. However, let's take a look at all of the arguments in greater detail.

The `tag` argument is one that we've seen before—you can pass a string name of a tag or even a Python list of string tag names. For example, the following will return a list of all the header tags in a document:[1]

```
.findAll({"h1","h2","h3","h4","h5","h6"})
```

The `attributes` argument takes a Python dictionary of attributes and matches tags that contain any one of those attributes. For example, the following function would return *both* the green and red `span` tags in the HTML document:

```
.findAll("span", {"class":"green", "class":"red"})
```

The `recursive` argument is a boolean. How deeply into the document do you want to go? If `recursion` is set to `True`, the `findAll` function looks into children, and children's children, for tags that match your parameters. If it is `false`, it will look only at the top-level tags in your document. By default, `findAll` works recursively (`recursive` is set to `True`); it's generally a good idea to leave this as is, unless you really know what you need to do and performance is an issue.

The `text` argument is unusual in that it matches based on the text content of the tags, rather than properties of the tags themselves. For instance, if we want to find the number of times "the prince" was surrounded by tags on the example page, we could replace our `.findAll()` function in the previous example with the following lines:

```
nameList = bsObj.findAll(text="the prince")
print(len(nameList))
```

The output of this is "7."

---

[1] If you're looking to get a list of all h<some_level> tags in the document, there are more succinct ways of writing this code to accomplish the same thing. We'll take a look at other ways of approaching these types of problems in the section BeautifulSoup and regular expressions.

The limit argument, of course, is only used in the findAll method; find is equivalent to the same findAll call, with a limit of 1. You might set this if you're only interested in retrieving the first *x* items from the page. Be aware, however, that this gives you the first items on the page in the order that they occur, not necessarily the first ones that you want.

The keyword argument allows you to select tags that contain a particular attribute. For example:

```
allText = bsObj.findAll(id="text")
print(allText[0].get_text())
```

A Caveat to the keyword Argument

The keyword argument can be very helpful in some situations. However, it is technically redundant as a BeautifulSoup feature. Keep in mind that anything that can be done with keyword can also be accomplished using techniques we will discuss later in this chapter (see Regular Expressions and Lambda Expressions).

For instance, the following two lines are identical:

```
bsObj.findAll(id="text")
bsObj.findAll("", {"id":"text"})
```

In addition, you might occasionally run into problems using keyword, most notably when searching for elements by their class attribute, because class is a protected keyword in Python. That is, class is a reserved word in Python that cannot be used as a variable or argument name (no relation to the BeautifulSoup.findAll() keyword argument, previously discussed).[2] For example, if you try the following call, you'll get a syntax error due to the nonstandard use of class:

```
bsObj.findAll(class="green")
```

Instead, you can use BeautifulSoup's somewhat clumsy solution, which involves adding an underscore:

```
bsObj.findAll(class_="green")
```

Alternatively, you can enclose class in quotes:

```
bsObj.findAll("", {"class":"green"}
```

At this point, you might be asking yourself, "But wait, don't I already know how to get a list of tags by attribute—by passing attributes to the function in a dictionary list?"

---

2 The Python Language Reference provides a complete list of protected keywords (*https://docs.python.org/3/ reference/lexical_analysis.html#keywords*).

Recall that passing a list of tags to .findAll() via the attributes list acts as an "or" filter (i.e., it selects a list of all tags that have tag1 or tag2 or tag3...). If you have a lengthy list of tags, you can end up with a lot of stuff you don't want. The keyword argument allows you to add an additional "and" filter to this.

Other BeautifulSoup Objects

So far in the book, you've seen two types of objects in the BeautifulSoup library:

```
bsObj.div.h1
```

BeautifulSoup *objects*
    Seen in previous code examples as bsObj

Tag *objects*
    Retrieved in lists or individually by calling find and findAll on a Beauti fulSoup object, or drilling down, as in:

However, there are two more objects in the library that, although less commonly used, are still important to know about:

NavigableString *objects*
    Used to represent text within tags, rather than the tags themselves (some functions operate on, and produce, NavigableStrings, rather than tag objects).

The Comment *object*
    Used to find HTML comments in comment tags, <!--like this one-->

These four objects are the only objects you will ever encounter (as of the time of this writing) in the BeautifulSoup library.

Navigating Trees

The findAll function is responsible for finding tags based on their name and attribute. But what if you need to find a tag based on its location in a document? That's where tree navigation comes in handy. In Chapter 1, we looked at navigating a BeautifulSoup tree in a single direction:

```
bsObj.tag.subTag.anotherSubTag
```

Now let's look at navigating up, across, and diagonally through HTML trees using our highly questionable online shopping site *http://bit.ly/1KGe2Qk* as an example page for scraping (see Figure 2-1):

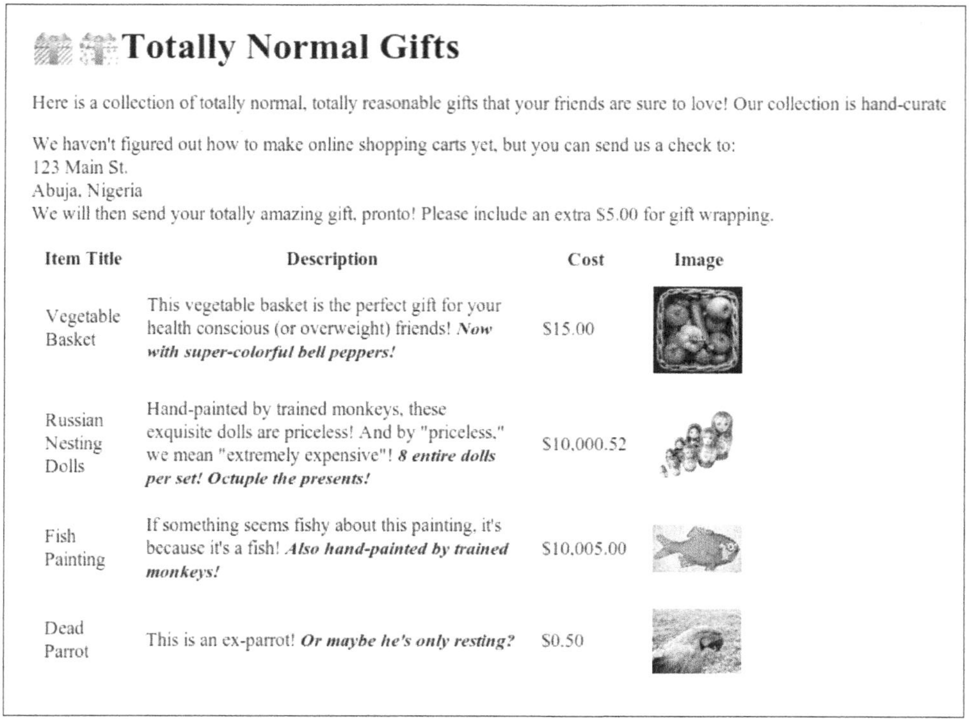

Totally Normal Gifts

Here is a collection of totally normal, totally reasonable gifts that your friends are sure to love! Our collection is hand-curate

We haven't figured out how to make online shopping carts yet, but you can send us a check to:
123 Main St.
Abuja, Nigeria
We will then send your totally amazing gift, pronto! Please include an extra $5.00 for gift wrapping.

Item Title	Description	Cost	Image
Vegetable Basket	This vegetable basket is the perfect gift for your health conscious (or overweight) friends! *Now with super-colorful bell peppers!*	$15.00	
Russian Nesting Dolls	Hand-painted by trained monkeys, these exquisite dolls are priceless! And by "priceless," we mean "extremely expensive"! *8 entire dolls per set! Octuple the presents!*	$10,000.52	
Fish Painting	If something seems fishy about this painting, it's because it's a fish! *Also hand-painted by trained monkeys!*	$10,005.00	
Dead Parrot	This is an ex-parrot! *Or maybe he's only resting?*	$0.50	

Figure 2-1. Screenshot from http://www.pythonscraping.com/pages/page3.html

The HTML for this page, mapped out as a tree (with some tags omitted for brevity), looks like:

- html
  — body
    — div.wrapper
      — h1
      — div.content
      — table#giftList
        — tr
          — th
          — th
          — th
          — th
        — tr.gift#gift1
          — td
          — td

— span.excitingNote
　　— td
　　— td
　　　— img
　— ...table rows continue...
— div.footer

We will use this same HTML structure as an example in the next few sections.

Dealing with children and other descendants

In computer science and some branches of mathematics, you often hear about horrible things done to children: moving them, storing them, removing them, and even killing them. Fortunately, in BeautifulSoup, children are treated differently.

In the BeautifulSoup library, as well as many other libraries, there is a distinction drawn between *children* and *descendants*: much like in a human family tree, children are always exactly one tag below a parent, whereas descendants can be at any level in the tree below a parent. For example, the tr tags are children of the `table` tag, whereas tr, th, td, img, and span are all descendants of the `table` tag (at least in our example page). All children are descendants, but not all descendants are children.

In general, BeautifulSoup functions will always deal with the descendants of the current tag selected. For instance, `bsObj.body.h1` selects the first h1 tag that is a descendant of the body tag. It will not find tags located outside of the body.

Similarly, `bsObj.div.findAll("img")` will find the first div tag in the document, then retrieve a list of all img tags that are descendants of that div tag.

If you want to find only descendants that are children, you can use the `.children` tag:

```
from urllib.request import urlopen
from bs4 import BeautifulSoup

html = urlopen("http://www.pythonscraping.com/pages/page3.html")
bsObj = BeautifulSoup(html)

for child in bsObj.find("table",{"id":"giftList"}).children:
    print(child)
```

This code prints out the list of product rows in the giftList table. If you were to write it using the descendants() function instead of the children() function, about two dozen tags would be found within the table and printed, including img tags, span tags, and individual td tags. It's definitely important to differentiate between children and descendants!

Dealing with siblings

The BeautifulSoup `next_siblings()` function makes it trivial to collect data from tables, especially ones with title rows:

```
from urllib.request import urlopen
from bs4 import BeautifulSoup
html = urlopen("http://www.pythonscraping.com/pages/page3.html")
bsObj = BeautifulSoup(html)

for sibling in bsObj.find("table",{"id":"giftList"}).tr.next_siblings:
    print(sibling)
```

The output of this code is to print all rows of products from the product table, except for the first title row. Why does the title row get skipped? Two reasons: first, objects cannot be siblings with themselves. Any time you get siblings of an object, the object itself will not be included in the list. Second, this function calls *next* siblings only. If we were to select a row in the middle of the list, for example, and call `next_siblings` on it, only the subsequent (next) siblings would be returned. So, by selecting the title row and calling `next_siblings`, we can select all the rows in the table, without selecting the title row itself.

Make Selections Specific

Note that the preceding code will work just as well, if we select `bsObj.table.tr` or even just `bsObj.tr` in order to select the first row of the table. However, in the code, I go through all of the trouble of writing everything out in a longer form:

```
bsObj.find("table",{"id":"giftList"}).tr
```

Even if it looks like there's just one table (or other target tag) on the page, it's easy to miss things. In addition, page layouts change all the time. What was once the first of its kind on the page, might someday be the second or third tag of that type found on the page. To make your scrapers more robust, it's best to be as specific as possible when making tag selections. Take advantage of tag attributes when they are available.

As a complement to `next_siblings`, the `previous_siblings` function can often be helpful if there is an easily selectable tag at the end of a list of sibling tags that you would like to get.

And, of course, there are the `next_sibling` and `previous_sibling` functions, which perform nearly the same function as `next_siblings` and `previous_siblings`, except they return a single tag rather than a list of them.

Dealing with your parents

When scraping pages, you will likely discover that you need to find parents of tags less frequently than you need to find their children or siblings. Typically, when we look at HTML pages with the goal of crawling them, we start by looking at the top layer of tags, and then figure out how to drill our way down into the exact piece of data that we want. Occasionally, however, you can find yourself in odd situations that require BeautifulSoup's parent-finding functions, .parent and .parents. For example:

```
from urllib.request import urlopen
from bs4 import BeautifulSoup

html = urlopen("http://www.pythonscraping.com/pages/page3.html")
bsObj = BeautifulSoup(html)
print(bsObj.find("img",{"src":"../img/gifts/img1.jpg"
                        }).parent.previous_sibling.get_text())
```

This code will print out the price of the object represented by the image at the location ../img/gifts/img1.jpg (in this case, the price is "$15.00").

How does this work? The following diagram represents the tree structure of the portion of the HTML page we are working with, with numbered steps:

- \<tr>
    — \<td>
    — \<td>
    — \<td>(**3**)
        — "$15.00" (**4**)
    — s\<td> (**2**)
        — \<img src=".../img/gifts/img1.jpg">(**1**)

1. The image tag where src="../img/gifts/img1.jpg" is first selected
2. We select the parent of that tag (in this case, the \<td> tag).
3. We select the previous_sibling of the \<td> tag (in this case, the \<td> tag that contains the dollar value of the product).
4. We select the text within that tag, "$15.00"

Regular Expressions

As the old computer-science joke goes: "Let's say you have a problem, and you decide to solve it with regular expressions. Well, now you have two problems."

Unfortunately, regular expressions (often shortened to *regex*) are often taught using large tables of random symbols, strung together to look like a lot of nonsense. This tends to drive people away, and later they get out into the workforce and write needlessly complicated searching and filtering functions, when all they needed was a one-line regular expression in the first place!

Fortunately for you, regular expressions are not all that difficult to get up and running with quickly, and can easily be learned by looking at and experimenting with a few simple examples.

Regular expressions are so called because they are used to identify regular strings; that is, they can definitively say, "Yes, this string you've given me follows the rules, and I'll return it," or "This string does not follow the rules, and I'll discard it." This can be exceptionally handy for quickly scanning large documents to look for strings that look like phone numbers or email addresses.

Notice that I used the phrase *regular string*. What is a regular string? It's any string that can be generated by a series of linear rules,[3] such as:

1. Write the letter "a" at least once.
2. Append to this the letter "b" exactly five times.
3. Append to this the letter "c" any even number of times.
4. Optionally, write the letter "d" at the end.

Strings that follow these rules are: "aaaabbbbbccccd," "aabbbbbcc," and so on (there are an infinite number of variations).

Regular expressions are merely a shorthand way of expressing these sets of rules. For instance, here's the regular expression for the series of steps just described:

```
aa*bbbbb(cc)*(d | )
```

This string might seem a little daunting at first, but it becomes clearer when we break it down into its components:

aa*

> The letter *a* is written, followed by *a** (read as *a star*) which means "any number of *a*'s, including 0 of them." In this way, we can guarantee that the letter *a* is written at least once.

bbbbb

> No special effects here—just five b's in a row.

---

3 You might be asking yourself, "Are there 'irregular' expressions?" Nonregular expressions are beyond the scope of this book, but they encompass strings such as "write a prime number of a's, followed by exactly twice that number of b's" or "write a palindrome." It's impossible to identify strings of this type with a regular expression. Fortunately, I've never been in a situation where my web scraper needed to identify these kinds of strings.

(cc)*

Any even number of things can be grouped into pairs, so in order to enforce this rule about even things, you can write two *c*'s, surround them in parentheses, and write an asterisk after it, meaning that you can have any number of *pairs* of *c*'s (note that this can mean 0 pairs, as well).

(d |)

Adding a bar in the middle of two expressions means that it can be "this thing *or* that thing." In this case, we are saying "add a *d* followed by a space *or* just add a space without a *d*." In this way we can guarantee that there is, at most, one *d*, followed by a space, completing the string.

Experimenting with RegEx

When learning how to write regular expressions, it's critical to play around with them and get a feel for how they work.

If you don't feel like firing up a code editor, writing a few lines, and running your program in order to see if a regular expression works as expected, you can go to a website such as RegexPal (*http://regexpal.com/*) and test your regular expressions on the fly.

One classic example of regular expressions can be found in the practice of identifying email addresses. Although the exact rules governing email addresses vary slightly from mail server to mail server, we can create a few general rules. The corresponding regular expression for each of these rules is shown in the second column:

Rule 1	[A-Za-z0-9\._ +]+
The first part of an email address contains at least one of the following: uppercase letters, lowercase letters, the numbers 0-9, periods (.), plus signs (+), or underscores (_).	The regular expression shorthand is pretty smart. For example, it knows that "A-Z" means "any uppercase letter, A through Z." By putting all these possible sequences and symbols in brackets (as opposed to parentheses) we are saying "this symbol can be any one of these things we've listed in the brackets." Note also that the + sign means "these characters can occur as many times as they want to, but must occur at least once."
Rule 2	@
After this, the email address contains the @ symbol.	This is fairly straightforward: the @ symbol must occur in the middle, and it must occur exactly once.

Rule 3	[A-Za-z]+
The email address then must contain at least one uppercase or lowercase letter.	We may use only letters in the first part of the domain name, after the @ symbol. Also, there must be at least one character.
Rule 4	\.
This is followed by a period (.).	You must include a period (.) before the domain name.
Rule 5	(com|org|edu|net)
Finally, the email address ends with com, org, edu, or net (in reality, there are many possible top-level domains, but, these four should suffice for the sake of example).	This lists the possible sequences of letters that can occur after the period in the second part of an email address.

By concatenating all of the rules, we arrive at the regular expression:

```
[A-Za-z0-9\._+]+@[A-Za-z]+\.(com|org|edu|net)
```

When attempting to write any regular expression from scratch, it's best to first make a list of steps that concretely outlines what your target string looks like. Pay attention to edge cases. For instance, if you're identifying phone numbers, are you considering country codes and extensions?.

Table 2-1 lists some commonly used regular expression symbols, with a brief explanation and example. This list is by no means complete, and as mentioned before, you might encounter slight variations from language to language. However, these 12 symbols are the most commonly used regular expressions in Python, and can be used to find and collect most any string type.

Table 2-1. Commonly used regular expression symbols

Symbol(s)	Meaning	Example	Example Matches
*	Matches the preceding character, subexpression, or bracketed character, 0 or more times	a*b*	aaaaaaaa, aaabbbbb, bbbbbb
+	Matches the preceding character, subexpression, or bracketed character, 1 or more times	a+b+	aaaaaaaab, aaabbbbb, abbbbbb

[]	Matches any character within the brackets (i.e., "Pick any one of these things")	[A-Z]*	APPLE, CAPITALS, QWERTY
()	A grouped subexpression (these are evaluated first, in the "order of operations" of regular expressions)	(a*b)*	aaabaab, abaaab, ababaaaaab
{m, n}	Matches the preceding character, subexpression, or bracketed character between m and n times (inclusive)	a{2,3}b{2,3}	aabbb, aaabbb, aabb
[^]	Matches any single character that is *not* in the brackets	[^A-Z]*	apple, lowercase, qwerty
|	Matches any character, string of characters, or subexpression, separated by the "|" (note that this is a vertical bar, or "pipe," not a capital "i")	b(a|i|e)d	bad, bid, bed
.	Matches any single character (including symbols, numbers, a space, etc.)	b.d	bad, bzd, b$d, b d
^	Indicates that a character or subexpression occurs at the beginning of a string	^a	apple, asdf, a
\	An escape character (this allows you to use "special" characters as their literal meaning)	\. \\| \\\\	. | \\
$	Often used at the end of a regular expression, it means "match this up to the end of the string." Without it, every regular expression has a defacto ".*" at the end of it, accepting strings where only the first part of the string matches. This can be thougt of as analogous to the ^ symbol.	[A-Z]*[a-z]*$	ABCabc, zzzyx, Bob
?!	"Does not contain." This odd pairing of symbols, immediately preceding a character (or regular expression), indicates that that character should not be found in that specific place in the larger string. This can be tricky to use; after all, the character might be found in a different part of the string. If trying to eliminate a character entirely, use in conjunction with a ^ and $ at either end.	^((?![A-Z]).)*$	no-caps-here, $ymb0ls a4e f!ne

Regular Expressions: Not Always Regular!

The standard version of regular expressions (the one we are covering in this book, and that is used by Python and BeautifulSoup) is based on syntax used by Perl. Most modern programming languages use this or one very similar to it. Be aware, however, that if you are using regular expressions in another language, you might encounter problems. Even some modern languages, such as Java, have slight differences in the way they handle regular expressions. When in doubt, read the docs!

Regular Expressions and BeautifulSoup

If the previous section on regular expressions seemed a little disjointed from the mission of this book, here's where it all ties together. BeautifulSoup and regular expressions go hand in hand when it comes to scraping the Web. In fact, most functions that take in a string argument (e.g., find(id="aTagIdHere")) will also take in a regular expression just as well.

Let's take a look at some examples, scraping the page found at *http://bit.ly/1KGe2Qk*.

Notice that there are many product images on the site—they take the following form:

```
<img src="../img/gifts/img3.jpg">
```

If we wanted to grab URLs to all of the product images, it might seem fairly straightforward at first: just grab all the image tags using .findAll("img"), right? But there's a problem. In addition to the obvious "extra" images (e.g., logos), modern websites often have hidden images, blank images used for spacing and aligning elements, and other random image tags you might not be aware of. Certainly, you can't count on the only images on the page being product images.

Let's also assume that the layout of the page might change, or that, for whatever reason, we don't want to depend on the *position* of the image in the page in order to find the correct tag. This might be the case when you are trying to grab specific elements or pieces of data that are scattered randomly throughout a website. For instance, there might be a featured product image in a special layout at the top of some pages, but not others.

The solution is to look for something identifying about the tag itself. In this case, we can look at the file path of the product images:

```
from urllib.request
import urlopenfrom bs4
import BeautifulSoupimport re

html = urlopen("http://www.pythonscraping.com/pages/page3.html")
bsObj = BeautifulSoup(html)
images = bsObj.findAll("img", {"src":re.compile("\.\.\/img\/gifts/img.*\.jpg")})
for image in images:
    print(image["src"])
```

This prints out only the relative image paths that start with *../img/gifts/img* and end in *.jpg*, the output of which is the following:

```
../img/gifts/img1.jpg
../img/gifts/img2.jpg
../img/gifts/img3.jpg
../img/gifts/img4.jpg
../img/gifts/img6.jpg
```

A regular expression can be inserted as any argument in a BeautifulSoup expression, allowing you a great deal of flexibility in finding target elements.

Accessing Attributes

So far, we've looked at how to access and filter tags and access content within them. However, very often in web scraping you're not looking for the content of a tag; you're looking for its attributes. This becomes especially useful for tags such as <a>, where the URL it is pointing to is contained within the href attribute, or the <img> tag, where the target image is contained within the src attribute.

With tag objects, a Python list of attributes can be automatically accessed by calling:

```
myTag.attrs
```

Keep in mind that this literally returns a Python dictionary object, which makes retrieval and manipulation of these attributes trivial. The source location for an image, for example, can be found using the following line:

```
myImgTag.attrs['src']
```

Lambda Expressions

If you have a formal education in computer science, you probably learned about lambda expressions once in school and then never used them again. If you don't, they might be unfamiliar to you (or familiar only as "that thing I've been meaning to learn at some point"). In this section, we won't go deeply into these extremely useful functions, but we will look at a few examples of how they can be useful in web scraping.

Essentially, a lambda expression is a function that is passed into another function as a variable; that is, instead of defining a function as f(x, y), you may define a function as f(g(x), y), or even f(g(x), h(x)).

BeautifulSoup allows us to pass certain types of functions as parameters into the fin dAll function. The only restriction is that these functions must take a tag object as an argument and return a boolean. Every tag object that BeautifulSoup encounters is evaluated in this function, and tags that evaluate to "true" are returned while the rest are discarded.

For example, the following retrieves all tags that have exactly two attributes:

```
soup.findAll(lambda tag: len(tag.attrs) == 2)
```

That is, it will find tags such as the following:

```
<div class="body" id="content"></div>
<span style="color:red" class="title"></span>
```

Using lambda functions in BeautifulSoup, selectors can act as a great substitute for writing a regular expression, if you're comfortable with writing a little code.

Beyond BeautifulSoup

Although `BeautifulSoup` is used throughout this book (and is one of the most popular HTML libraries available for Python), keep in mind that it's not the only option. If BeautifulSoup does not meet your needs, check out these other widely used libraries:

lxml
> This library (*http://lxml.de/*) is used for parsing both HTML and XML documents, and is known for being very low level and heavily based on C. Although it takes a while to learn (a steep learning curve actually means you learn it very fast), it is very fast at parsing most HTML documents.

HTML Parser
> This is Python's built-in parsing library (*http://bit.ly/1Jc5Art*). Because it requires no installation (other than, obviously, having Python installed in the first place), it can be extremely convenient to use.

## CHAPTER 3

Starting to Crawl

So far, the examples in the book have covered single static pages, with somewhat artificial canned examples. In this chapter, we'll start looking at some real-world problems, with scrapers traversing multiple pages and even multiple sites.

Web crawlers are called such because they crawl across the Web. At their core is an element of recursion. They must retrieve page contents for a URL, examine that page for another URL, and retrieve *that* page, ad infinitum.

Beware, however: just because you can crawl the Web doesn't mean that you always should. The scrapers used in previous examples work great in situations where all the data you need is on a single page. With web crawlers, you must be extremely conscientious of how much bandwidth you are using and make every effort to determine if there's a way to make the target server's load easier.

Traversing a Single Domain

Even if you haven't heard of "Six Degrees of Wikipedia," you've almost certainly heard of its namesake, "Six Degrees of Kevin Bacon." In both games, the goal is to link two unlikely subjects (in the first case, Wikipedia articles that link to each other, in the second case, actors appearing in the same film) by a chain containing no more than six total (including the two original subjects).

For example, Eric Idle appeared in *Dudley Do-Right* with Brendan Fraser, who appeared in *The Air I Breathe* with Kevin Bacon.[1] In this case, the chain from Eric Idle to Kevin Bacon is only three subjects long.

---

[1] Thanks to The Oracle of Bacon (*http://oracleofbacon.org*) for satisfying my curiosity about this particular chain.

In this section, we'll begin a project that will become a "Six Degrees of Wikipedia" solution finder. That is, we'll be able to take the Eric Idle page (*http://bit.ly/1GOSY7Z*) and find the fewest number of link clicks that will take us to the Kevin Bacon page (*http://bit.ly/1KwqjU7*).

But What About Wikipedia's Server Load?

According to the Wikimedia Foundation (the parent organization behind Wikipedia), the site's web properties receive approximately 2,500 hits per *second*, with more than 99% of them to the Wikipedia domain (see the "Traffic Volume" section of the "Wikimedia in Figures" page (*http://bit.ly/1cs0toD*)). Because of the sheer volume of traffic, your web scrapers are unlikely to have any noticeable impact on Wikipedia's server load. However, if you run the code samples in this book extensively, or create your own projects that scrape Wikipedia, I encourage you to make a tax-deductible donation to the Wikimedia Foundation (*http://bit.ly/1FNfKLd*)—even a few dollars will offset your server load and help make education resources available for everyone else.

You should already know how to write a Python script that retrieves an arbitrary Wikipedia page and produces a list of links on that page:

```
from urllib.request import urlopen
from bs4 import BeautifulSoup

html = urlopen("http://en.wikipedia.org/wiki/Kevin_Bacon")
bsObj = BeautifulSoup(html)
for link in bsObj.findAll("a"):
    if 'href' in link.attrs:
        print(link.attrs['href'])
```

If you look at the list of links produced, you'll notice that all the articles you'd expect are there: "Apollo 13," "Philadelphia," "Primetime Emmy Award," and so on. However, there are some things that we don't want as well:

```
//wikimediafoundation.org/wiki/Privacy_policy
//en.wikipedia.org/wiki/Wikipedia:Contact_us
```

In fact, Wikipedia is full of sidebar, footer, and header links that appear on every page, along with links to the category pages, talk pages, and other pages that do not contain different articles:

```
/wiki/Category:Articles_with_unsourced_statements_from_April_2014
/wiki/Talk:Kevin_Bacon
```

Recently a friend of mine, while working on a similar Wikipedia-scraping project, mentioned he had written a very large filtering function, with over 100 lines of code, in order to determine whether an internal Wikipedia link was an article page or not. Unfortunately, he had not spent much time up front trying to find patterns between "article links" and "other links," or he might have discovered the trick. If you examine the links that point to article pages (as opposed to other internal pages), they all have three things in common:

- They reside within the div with the id set to bodyContent
- The URLs do not contain semicolons
- The URLs begin with */wiki/*

We can use these rules to revise the code slightly to retrieve only the desired article links:

```
from urllib.request import urlopen
from bs4 import BeautifulSoup
import re

html = urlopen("http://en.wikipedia.org/wiki/Kevin_Bacon")
bsObj = BeautifulSoup(html)
for link in bsObj.find("div", {"id":"bodyContent"}).findAll("a",
                    href=re.compile("^(/wiki/)((?!:).)*$")):
    if 'href' in link.attrs:
        print(link.attrs['href'])
```

If you run this, you should see a list of all article URLs that the Wikipedia article on Kevin Bacon links to.

Of course, having a script that finds all article links in one, hardcoded Wikipedia article, while interesting, is fairly useless in practice. We need to be able to take this code and transform it into something more like the following:

- A single function, getLinks, that takes in a Wikipedia article URL of the form /wiki/<Article_Name> and returns a list of all linked article URLs in the same form.
- A main function that calls getLinks with some starting article, chooses a random article link from the returned list, and calls getLinks again, until we stop the program or until there are no article links found on the new page.

Here is the complete code that accomplishes this:

```
from urllib.request import urlopen
from bs4 import BeautifulSoup
import datetime
import random
import re

random.seed(datetime.datetime.now())
def getLinks(articleUrl):
    html = urlopen("http://en.wikipedia.org"+articleUrl)
    bsObj = BeautifulSoup(html)
    return bsObj.find("div", {"id":"bodyContent"}).findAll("a",
                    href=re.compile("^(/wiki/)((?!:).)*$"))
links = getLinks("/wiki/Kevin_Bacon")
while len(links) > 0:
    newArticle = links[random.randint(0, len(links)-1)].attrs["href"]
    print(newArticle)
    links = getLinks(newArticle)
```

The first thing the program does, after importing the needed libraries, is set the random number generator seed with the current system time. This practically ensures a new and interesting random path through Wikipedia articles every time the program is run.

Pseudorandom Numbers and Random Seeds

In the previous example, I used Python's random number generator to select an article at random on each page in order to continue a random traversal of Wikipedia. However, random numbers should be used with caution.

While computers are great at calculating correct answers, they're terrible at just making things up. For this reason, random numbers can be a challenge. Most random number algorithms strive to produce an evenly distributed and hard-to-predict sequence of numbers, but a "seed" number is needed to give these algorithms something to work with initially. The exact same seed will produce the exact same sequence of "random" numbers every time, so for this reason I've used the system clock as a starter for producing new sequences of random numbers, and, thus, new sequences of random articles. This makes the program a little more exciting to run.

For the curious, the Python pseudorandom number generator is powered by the *Mersenne Twister algorithm*. While it produces random numbers that are difficult to predict and uniformly distributed, it is slightly processor intensive. Random numbers this good don't come cheap!

Next, it defines the `getLinks` function, which takes in an article URL of the form /wiki/..., prepends the Wikipedia domain name, `http://en.wikipedia.org`, and retrieves the BeautifulSoup object for the HTML at that domain. It then extracts a list of article link tags, based on the parameters discussed previously, and returns them.

The main body of the program begins with setting a list of article link tags (the `links` variable) to the list of links in the initial page: *http://bit.ly/1KwqjU7*. It then goes into a loop, finding a random article link tag in the page, extracting the *href* attribute from it, printing the page, and getting a new list of links from the extracted URL.

Of course, there's a bit more to solving a "Six Degrees of Wikipedia" problem than simply building a scraper that goes from page to page. We must also be able to store and analyze the resulting data. For a continuation of the solution to this problem, see Chapter 5.

Handle Your Exceptions!

Although we are omitting most exception handling in the code examples for the sake of brevity in these examples, be aware that there are many potential pitfalls that could arise: What if Wikipedia changed the name of the `bodyContent` tag, for example? (Hint: the code would crash.)

So although these scripts might be fine to run as closely watched examples, autonomous production code requires far more exception handling than we can fit into this book. Look back to Chapter 1 for more information about this.

Crawling an Entire Site

In the previous section, we took a random walk through a website, going from link to link. But what if you need to systematically catalog or search every page on a site? Crawling an entire site, especially a large one, is a memory-intensive process that is best suited to applications where a database to store crawling results is readily available. However, we can explore the behavior of these types of applications without actually running them full-scale. To learn more about running these applications using a database, see Chapter 5.

The Dark and Deep Webs

You've likely heard the terms *deep Web*, *dark Web*, or *hidden Web* being thrown around a lot, especially in the media lately. What do they mean?

The deep Web is simply any part of the Web that's not part of the *surface Web* The surface is part of the Internet that is indexed by search engines. Estimates vary widely, but the deep Web almost certainly makes up about 90% of the Internet. Because Google can't do things like submit forms, find pages that haven't been linked to by a top-level domain, or investigate sites where the *robots.txt* prohibits it, the surface Web stays relatively small.

The dark Web, also known as the Darknet or dark Internet, is another beast entirely. It is run over the existing network infrastructure but uses a Tor client with an application protocol that runs on top of HTTP, providing a secure channel to exchange information. Although it is possible to scrape the Darknet, just like you'd scrape any other website, doing so is outside the scope of this book.

Unlike the dark Web, the deep Web is relatively easy to scrape. In fact, there are many tools in this book that will teach you how to crawl and scrape information from many places that Google bots can't go.

So when might crawling an entire website be useful and when might it actually be harmful? Web scrapers that traverse an entire site are good for many things, including:

Generating a site map

A few years ago, I was faced with a problem: an important client wanted an estimate for a website redesign, but did not want to provide my company with access to the internals of their current content management system, and did not have a publicly available site map. I was able to use a crawler to cover their entire site, gather all internal links, and organize the pages into the actual folder structure they had on their site. This allowed me to quickly find sections of the site I wasn't even aware existed, and accurately count how many page designs would be required, and how much content would need to be migrated.

Gathering data

Another client of mine wanted to gather articles (stories, blog posts, news articles, etc.) in order to create a working prototype of a specialized search platform. Although these website crawls didn't need to be exhaustive, they did need to be fairly expansive (there were only a few sites we were interested in getting data from). I was able to create crawlers that recursively traversed each site and collected only data it found on article pages.

The general approach to an exhaustive site crawl is to start with a top-level page (such as the home page), and search for a list of all internal links on that page. Every one of those links is then crawled, and additional lists of links are found on each one of them, triggering another round of crawling.

Clearly this is a situation that can blow up very quickly. If every page has 10 internal links, and a website is five pages deep (a fairly typical depth for a medium-size website), then the number of pages you need to crawl is 10^5, or 100,000 pages, before you can be sure that you've exhaustively covered the website. Strangely enough, while "5 pages deep and 10 internal links per page" are fairly typical dimensions for a website, there are very few websites with 100,000 or more pages. The reason, of course, is that the vast majority of internal links are duplicates.

In order to avoid crawling the same page twice, it is extremely important that all internal links discovered are formatted consistently, and kept in a running list for easy lookups, while the program is running. Only links that are "new" should be crawled and searched for additional links:

```
from urllib.request import urlopen
from bs4 import BeautifulSoup
import re

pages = set()
def getLinks(pageUrl):
    global pages
    html = urlopen("http://en.wikipedia.org"+pageUrl)
    bsObj = BeautifulSoup(html)
    for link in bsObj.findAll("a", href=re.compile("^(/wiki/)")):
        if 'href' in link.attrs:
            if link.attrs['href'] not in pages:
                #We have encountered a new page
                newPage = link.attrs['href']
                print(newPage)
                pages.add(newPage)
                getLinks(newPage)
getLinks("")
```

In order to get the full effect of how this web-crawling business works, I've relaxed the standards of what constitutes an "internal link we are looking for," from previous examples. Rather than limit the scraper to article pages, it looks for all links that begin with */wiki/* regardless of where they are on the page, and regardless of whether they contain colons. Remember: article pages do not contain colons, but file upload pages, talk pages, and the like do contain colons in the URL).

Initially, `getLinks` is called with an empty URL. This is translated as "the front page of Wikipedia" as soon as the empty URL is prepended with http://en.wikipedia.org inside the function. Then, each link on the first page is iterated through and a check is made to see if it is in the global set of pages (a set of pages that the script has encountered already). If not, it is added to the list, printed to the screen, and the getLinks function is called recursively on it.

A Warning Regarding Recursion

This is a warning rarely seen in software books, but I thought you should be aware: if left running long enough, the preceding program will almost certainly crash.

Python has a default recursion limit (how many times programs can recursively call themselves) of 1,000. Because Wikipedia's network of links is extremely large, this program will eventually hit that recursion limit and stop, unless you put in a recursion counter or something to prevent that from happening.

For "flat" sites that are fewer than 1,000 links deep, this method usually works very well, with some unusual exceptions. For example, I once encountered a website that had a rule for generating internal links to blog posts. The rule was "take the URL for the current page we are on, and append /blog/title_of_blog.php to it."

The problem was that they would append /blog/title_of_blog.php to URLs that were *already* on a page that had /blog/ in the URL. So the site would simply add another /blog/ on. Eventually, my crawler was going to URLs like: /blog/blog/blog/blog.../blog/title_of_blog.php.

Eventually, I had to add a check to make sure that URLs weren't overly ridiculous, containing repeating segments that might indicate an infinite loop. However, if I had left this running unchecked overnight, it could have easily crashed.

Collecting Data Across an Entire Site

Of course, web crawlers would be fairly boring if all they did was hop from one page to the other. In order to make them useful, we need to be able to do something on the page while we're there. Let's look at how to build a scraper that collects the title, the first paragraph of content, and the link to edit the page (if available).

As always, the first step to determine how best to do this is to look at a few pages from the site and determine a pattern. By looking at a handful of Wikipedia pages both articles and non-article pages such as the privacy policy page, the following things should be clear:

- All titles (on all pages, regardless of their status as an article page, an edit history page, or any other page) have titles under h1→span tags, and these are the only h1 tags on the page.

- As mentioned before, all body text lives under the div#bodyContent tag. However, if we want to get more specific and access just the first paragraph of text, we might be better off using div#mw-content-text →p (selecting the first paragraph tag only). This is true for all content pages except file pages (for example: *http://bit.ly/1KwqJtE*), which do not have sections of content text.
- Edit links occur only on article pages. If they occur, they will be found in the li#ca-edit tag, under li#ca-edit → span → a.

By modifying our basic crawling code, we can create a combination crawler/data-gathering (or, at least, data printing) program:

```
from urllib.request import urlopen
from bs4 import BeautifulSoup
import re

pages = set()
def getLinks(pageUrl):
    global pages
    html = urlopen("http://en.wikipedia.org"+pageUrl)
    bsObj = BeautifulSoup(html)
    try:
        print(bsObj.h1.get_text())
        print(bsObj.find(id ="mw-content-text").findAll("p")[0])
        print(bsObj.find(id="ca-edit").find("span").find("a").attrs['href'])
    except AttributeError:
        print("This page is missing something! No worries though!")

    for link in bsObj.findAll("a", href=re.compile("^(/wiki/)")):
        if 'href' in link.attrs:
            if link.attrs['href'] not in pages:
                #We have encountered a new page
                newPage = link.attrs['href']
                print("---------------\n"+newPage)
                pages.add(newPage)
                getLinks(newPage)
getLinks("")
```

The for loop in this program is essentially the same as it was in the original crawling program (with the addition of some printed dashes for clarity, separating the printed content).

Because we can never be entirely sure that all the data is on each page, each print statement is arranged in the order that it is likeliest to appear on the site. That is, the <h1> title tag appears on every page (as far as I can tell, at any rate) so we attempt to get that data first. The text content appears on most pages (except for file pages), so that is the second piece of data retrieved. The "edit" button only appears on pages where both titles and text content already exist, but it does not appear on all of those pages.

Different Patterns for Different Needs

There are obviously some dangers involved with wrapping multiple lines in an exception handler. You cannot tell which line threw the exception, for one thing. Also, if for some reason a page contained an "edit" button but no title, the "edit" button would never be logged. However, it suffices for many instances in which there is an order of likeliness of items appearing on the site, and inadvertently missing a few data points or keeping detailed logs is not a problem.

You might notice that in this and all the previous examples, we haven't been "collecting" data so much as "printing" it. Obviously, data in your terminal is hard to manipulate. We'll look more at storing information and creating databases in Chapter 5.

Crawling Across the Internet

Whenever I give a talk on web scraping, someone inevitably asks: "How do you build Google?" My answer is always twofold: "First, you get many billions of dollars so that you can buy the world's largest data warehouses and place them in hidden locations all around the world. Second, you build a web crawler."

When Google started in 1994, it was just two Stanford graduate students with an old server and a Python web crawler. Now that you know this, you officially have the tools you need to become the next tech multi-billionaire!

In all seriousness, web crawlers are at the heart of what drives many modern web technologies, and you don't necessarily need a large data warehouse to use them. In order to do any cross-domain data analysis, you do need to build crawlers that can interpret and store data across the myriad of different pages on the Internet.

Just like in the previous example, the web crawlers we are going to build will follow links from page to page, building out a map of the Web. But this time, they will not ignore external links; they will follow them. For an extra challenge, we'll see if we can record some kind of information about each page as we move through it. This will be harder than working with a single domain as we did before—different websites have completely different layouts. This means we will have to be very flexible in the kind of information we're looking for and how we're looking for it.

Before you start writing a crawler that simply follows all outbound links willy nilly, you should ask yourself a few questions:

- What data am I trying to gather? Can this be accomplished by scraping just a few predefined websites (almost always the easier option), or does my crawler need to be able to discover new websites I might not know about?
- When my crawler reaches a particular website, will it immediately follow the next outbound link to a new website, or will it stick around for a while and drill down into the current website?
- Are there any conditions under which I would not want to scrape a particular site? Am I interested in non-English content?
- How am I protecting myself against legal action if my web crawler catches the attention of a webmaster on one of the sites it runs across? (Check out Appendix C for more information on this subject.)

A flexible set of Python functions that can be combined to perform a variety of different types of web scraping can be easily written in fewer than 50 lines of code:

```
from urllib.request import urlopen
from bs4 import BeautifulSoup
import re
import datetime
import random

pages = set()
random.seed(datetime.datetime.now())

#Retrieves a list of all Internal links found on a page
def getInternalLinks(bsObj, includeUrl):
    internalLinks = []
    #Finds all links that begin with a "/"
    for link in bsObj.findAll("a", href=re.compile("^(/|.*"+includeUrl+")")):
        if link.attrs['href'] is not None:
            if link.attrs['href'] not in internalLinks:
                internalLinks.append(link.attrs['href'])
    return internalLinks
```

```
#Retrieves a list of all external links found on a page
def getExternalLinks(bsObj, excludeUrl):
    externalLinks = []
    #Finds all links that start with "http" or "www" that do
    #not contain the current URL
    for link in bsObj.findAll("a",
                        href=re.compile("^(http|www)((?!"+excludeUrl+").)*$")):
        if link.attrs['href'] is not None:
            if link.attrs['href'] not in externalLinks:
                externalLinks.append(link.attrs['href'])
    return externalLinks

def splitAddress(address):
    addressParts = address.replace("http://", "").split("/")
    return addressParts

def getRandomExternalLink(startingPage):
    html = urlopen(startingPage)
    bsObj = BeautifulSoup(html)
    externalLinks = getExternalLinks(bsObj, splitAddress(startingPage)[0])
    if len(externalLinks) == 0:
        internalLinks = getInternalLinks(startingPage)
        return getNextExternalLink(internalLinks[random.randint(0,
                                 len(internalLinks)-1)])
    else:
        return externalLinks[random.randint(0, len(externalLinks)-1)]

def followExternalOnly(startingSite):
    externalLink = getRandomExternalLink("http://oreilly.com")
    print("Random external link is: "+externalLink)
    followExternalOnly(externalLink)

followExternalOnly("http://oreilly.com")
```

The preceding program starts at *http://oreilly.com* and randomly hops from external link to external link. Here's an example of the output it produces:

```
Random external link is: http://igniteshow.com/
Random external link is: http://feeds.feedburner.com/oreilly/news
Random external link is: http://hire.jobvite.com/CompanyJobs/Careers.aspx?c=q319
Random external link is: http://makerfaire.com/
```

External links are not always guaranteed to be found on the first page of a website. In order to find external links in this case, a method similar to the one used in the previous crawling example is employed to recursively drill down into a website until it finds an external link.

Figure 3-1 visualizes the operation as a flowchart:

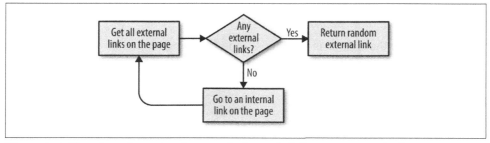

Figure 3-1. Flowchart for script that crawls through different sites on the Internet

Don't Put Example Programs into Production

I keep bringing this up, but it's important for space and readability, the example programs in this book do not always contain the necessary checks and exception handling required for production-ready code.

For example, if an external link is not found anywhere on a site that this crawler encounters (unlikely, but it's bound to happen at some point if you run it for long enough), this program will keep running until it hits Python's recursion limit.

Before running this code for any serious purpose, make sure that you are putting checks in place to handle potential pitfalls.

The nice thing about breaking up tasks into simple functions such as "find all external links on this page" is that the code can later be easily refactored to perform a different crawling task. For example, if our goal is to crawl an entire site for external links, and make a note of each one, we can add the following function:

```
#Collects a list of all external URLs found on the site
allExtLinks = set()
allIntLinks = set()
def getAllExternalLinks(siteUrl):
    html = urlopen(siteUrl)
    bsObj = BeautifulSoup(html)
    internalLinks = getInternalLinks(bsObj,splitAddress(siteUrl)[0])
    externalLinks = getExternalLinks(bsObj,splitAddress(siteUrl)[0])
    for link in externalLinks:
        if link not in allExtLinks:
            allExtLinks.add(link)
            print(link)
    for link in internalLinks:
        if link not in allIntLinks:
            print("About to get link: "+link)
            allIntLinks.add(link)
            getAllExternalLinks(link)
```

```
getAllExternalLinks("http://oreilly.com")
```

This code can be thought of as two loops—one gathering internal links, one gathering external links—working in conjunction with each other. The flowchart looks something like Figure 3-2:

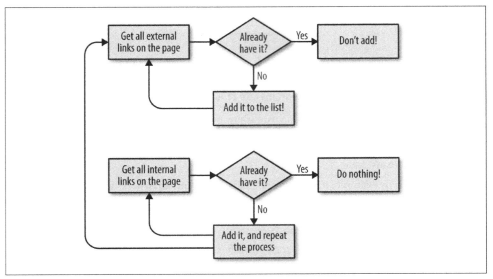

Figure 3-2. Flow diagram for the website crawler that collects all external links

Jotting down or making diagrams of what the code should do before you write the code itself is a fantastic habit to get into, and one that can save you a lot of time and frustration as your crawlers get more complicated.

Handling Redirects

Redirects allow the same web page to be viewable under different domain names. Redirects come in two flavors:

- Server-side redirects, where the URL is changed before the page is loaded
- Client-side redirects, sometimes seen with a "You will be directed in 10 seconds..." type of message, where the page loads before redirecting to the new one.

This section will handle server-side redirects. For more information on client-side redirects, which are performed using JavaScript or HTML, see Chapter 10.

For server-side redirects, you usually don't have to worry. If you're using the urllib library with Python 3.x, it handles redirects automatically! Just be aware that, occasionally, the URL of the page you're crawling might not be exactly the URL that you entered the page on.

Crawling with Scrapy

One of the challenges of writing web crawlers is that you're often performing the same tasks again and again: find all links on a page, evaluate the difference between internal and external links, go to new pages. These basic patterns are useful to know about and to be able to write from scratch, but there are options if you want something else to handle the details for you.

Scrapy is a Python library that handles much of the complexity of finding and evaluating links on a website, crawling domains or lists of domains with ease. Unfortunately, Scrapy has not yet been released for Python 3.x, though it is compatible with Python 2.7.

The good news is that multiple versions of Python (e.g., Python 2.7 and 3.4) usually work well when installed on the same machine. If you want to use Scrapy for a project but also want to use various other Python 3.4 scripts, you shouldn't have a problem doing both.

The Scrapy website offers the tool for download (*http://scrapy.org/download/*) from its website, as well as instructions for installing Scrapy with third-party installation managers such as pip. Keep in mind that you will need to install Scrapy using Python 2.7 (it is not compatible with 2.6 or 3.x) and run all programs using Scrapy with Python 2.7 as well.

Although writing Scrapy crawlers is relatively easy, there is a small amount of setup that needs to be done for each crawler. To create a new Scrapy project in the current directory, run from the command line:

```
$scrapy startproject wikiSpider
```

wikiSpider is the name of our new project. This creates a new directory in the directory the project was created in, with the title wikiSpider. Inside this directory is the following file structure:

- scrapy.cfg
  — wikiSpider
    — __init.py__
    — items.py
    — pipelines.py
    — settings.py

— spiders

— __init.py__

In order to create a crawler, we will add a new file to *wikiSpider/wikiSpider/spiders/articleSpider.py* called *items.py*. In addition, we will define a new item called `Article` inside the *items.py* file.

Your *items.py* file should be edited to look like this (with Scrapy-generated comments left in place, although you can feel free to remove them):

```
# -*- coding: utf-8 -*-
# Define here the models for your scraped items
#
# See documentation in:
# http://doc.scrapy.org/en/latest/topics/items.html

from scrapy import Item, Field

class Article(Item):
    # define the fields for your item here like:
    # name = scrapy.Field()
    title = Field()
```

Each Scrapy `Item` object represents a single page on the website. Obviously, you can define as many fields as you'd like (`url`, `content`, `header image`, etc.), but I'm simply collecting the `title` field from each page, for now.

In your newly created *articleSpider.py* file, write the following:

```
from scrapy.selector import Selector
from scrapy import Spider
from wikiSpider.items import Article


class ArticleSpider(Spider):
    name="article"
    allowed_domains = ["en.wikipedia.org"]
    start_urls = ["http://en.wikipedia.org/wiki/Main_Page",
            "http://en.wikipedia.org/wiki/Python_%28programming_language%29"]

    def parse(self, response):
        item = Article()
        title = response.xpath('//h1/text()')[0].extract()
        print("Title is: "+title)
        item['title'] = title
        return item
```

The name of this object (`ArticleSpider`) is different from the name of the directory (*WikiSpider*), indicating that this class in particular is responsible for spidering only through article pages, under the broader category of WikiSpider. For large sites with many types of content, you might have separate Scrapy items for each type (blog posts, press releases, articles, etc.), each with different fields, but all running under the same Scrapy project.

You can run this `ArticleSpider` from inside the main *WikiSpider* directory by typing:

```
$ scrapy crawl article
```

This calls the scraper by the item name of `article` (not the class or file name, but the name defined on the line: `name="article"` in the `ArticleSpider`).

Along with some debugging information, this should print out the lines:

```
Title is: Main Page
Title is: Python (programming language)
```

The scraper goes to the two pages listed as the `start_urls`, gathers information, and then terminates. Not much of a crawler, but using Scrapy in this way can be useful if you have a list of URLs you need scrape. To turn it into a fully fledged crawler, you need to define a set of rules that Scrapy can use to seek out new URLs on each page it encounters:

```
from scrapy.contrib.spiders import CrawlSpider, Rule
from wikiSpider.items import Article
from scrapy.contrib.linkextractors.sgml import SgmlLinkExtractor

class ArticleSpider(CrawlSpider):
    name="article"
    allowed_domains = ["en.wikipedia.org"]
    start_urls = ["http://en.wikipedia.org/wiki/Python_
                  %28programming_language%29"]
    rules = [Rule(SgmlLinkExtractor(allow=('(/wiki/)((?!:).)*$'),),
                                    callback="parse_item", follow=True)]

    def parse_item(self, response):
        item = Article()
        title = response.xpath('//h1/text()')[0].extract()
        print("Title is: "+title)
        item['title'] = title
        return item
```

This crawler is run from the command line in the same way as the previous one, but it will not terminate (at least not for a very, very long time) until you halt execution using Ctrl+C or by closing the terminal.

Logging with Scrapy

The debug information generated by Scrapy can be useful, but it is often too verbose. You can easily adjust the level of logging by adding a line to the *settings.py* file in your Scrapy project:

```
LOG_LEVEL = 'ERROR'
```

There are five levels of logging in Scrapy, listed in order here:

- CRITICAL
- ERROR
- WARNING
- DEBUG
- INFO

If logging is set to ERROR, only CRITICAL and ERROR logs will be displayed. If logging is set to INFO, all logs will be displayed, and so on.

To output logs to a separate logfile instead of the terminal, simply define a logfile when running from the command line:

```
$ scrapy crawl article -s LOG_FILE=wiki.log
```

This will create a new logfile, if one does not exist, in your current directory and output all logs and print statements to it.

Scrapy uses the Item objects to determine which pieces of information it should save from the pages it visits. This information can be saved by Scrapy in a variety of ways, such as a CSV, JSON, or XML files, using the following commands:

```
$ scrapy crawl article -o articles.csv -t csv
$ scrapy crawl article -o articles.json -t json
$ scrapy crawl article -o articles.xml -t xml
```

Of course, you can use the Item objects yourself and write them to a file or a database in whatever way you want, simply by adding the appropriate code to the parsing function in the crawler.

Scrapy is a powerful tool that handles many problems associated with crawling the Web. It automatically gathers all URLs and compares them against predefined rules; makes sure all URLs are unique; normalizes relative URLs where needed; and recurses to go more deeply into pages.

Although this section hardly scratches the surface of what Scrapy is capable of, I encourage you to check out the Scrapy documentation (*http://bit.ly/1FjCVJS*) or many of the other resources available online. Scrapy is an extremely large and sprawling library with many features. If there's something you'd like to do with Scrapy that has not been mentioned here, there is likely a way (or several) to do it!

## CHAPTER 4

Using APIs

Like many programmers who have worked on large projects, I have my share of horror stories when it comes to working with other people's code. From namespace issues to type issues to misunderstandings of function output, simply trying to get information from point A to method B can be a nightmare.

This is where application programming interfaces come in handy: they provide nice, convenient interfaces between multiple disparate applications. It doesn't matter if the applications are written by different programmers, with different architectures, or even in different languages—APIs are designed to serve as a lingua franca between different pieces of software that need to share information with each other.

Although various APIs exist for a variety of different software applications, in recent times "API" has been commonly understood as meaning "web application API." Typically, a programmer will make a request to an API via HTTP for some type of data, and the API will return this data in the form of XML or JSON. Although most APIs still support XML, JSON is quickly becoming the encoding protocol of choice.

If taking advantage of a ready-to-use program to get information prepackaged in a useful format seems like a bit of a departure from the rest of this book, well, it is and it isn't. Although using APIs isn't generally considered web scraping by most people, both practices use many of the same techniques (sending HTTP requests) and produce similar results (getting information); they often can be very complementary to each other.

For instance, you might want to combine information gleaned from a web scraper with information from a published API in order to make the information more useful to you. In an example later in this chapter, we will look at combining Wikipedia edit histories (which contain IP addresses) with an IP address resolver API in order to get the geographic location of Wikipedia edits around the world.

In this chapter, we'll offer a general overview of APIs and how they work, look at a few popular APIs available today, and look at how you might use an API in your own web scrapers.

How APIs Work

Although APIs are not nearly as ubiquitous as they should be (a large motivation for writing this book, because if you can't find an API, you can still get the data through scraping), you can find APIs for many types of information. Interested in music? There are a few different APIs that can give you songs, artists, albums, and even information about musical styles and related artists. Need sports data? ESPN provides APIs for athlete information, game scores, and more. Google has dozens of APIs in its Developers section (*https://console.developers.google.com*) for language translations, analytics, geolocation, and more.

APIs are extremely easy to use. In fact, you can try out a simple API request just by entering the following in your browser:[1]

```
http://freegeoip.net/json/50.78.253.58
```

This should produce the following response:

```
{"ip":"50.78.253.58","country_code":"US","country_name":"United States,"region_
code":"MA","region_name":"Massachusetts","city":"Chelmsford","zipcode":"01824",
"latitude":42.5879,"longitude":-71.3498,"metro_code":"506","area_code":"978"}
```

So, wait, you navigate to a web address in your browser window and it produces some information (albeit, very well-formatted)? What's the difference between an API and a regular website? Despite the hype around APIs, the answer is often: not much. APIs function via HTTP, the same protocol used to fetch data for websites, download a file, and do almost anything else on the Internet. The only things that makes an API an API is the extremely regulated syntax it uses, and the fact that APIs present their data as JSON or XML, rather than HTML.

Common Conventions

Unlike the subjects of most web scraping, APIs follow an extremely standardized set of rules to produce information, and they produce that information in an extremely standardized way as well. Because of this, it is easy to learn a few simple ground rules that will help you to quickly get up and running with any given API, as long as it's fairly well written.

---

[1] This API resolves IP addresses to geographic locations and is one I'll be using later in the chapter as well. You can learn more about it at *http://freegeoip.net*.

That being said, keep in mind that some APIs do deviate slightly from these rules, so it's important to read an API's documentation the first time you use it, regardless of how familiar you are with APIs in general.

Methods

There are four ways to request information from a web server via HTTP:

- GET
- POST
- PUT
- DELETE

GET is what you use when you visit a website through the address bar in your browser. GET is the method you are using when you make a call to *http://freegeoip.net/json/ 50.78.253.58*. You can think of GET as saying, "Hey, web server, please get me this information."

POST is what you use when you fill out a form, or submit information, presumably to a backend script on the server. Every time you log into a website, you are making a POST request with your username and (hopefully) encrypted password. If you are making a POST request with an API, you are saying, "Please store this information in your database."

PUT is less commonly used when interacting with websites, but is used from time to time in APIs. A PUT request is used to update an object or information. An API might require a POST request to create a new user, for example, but it might need a PUT request if you want to update that user's email address.[2]

DELETE is straightforward; it is used to delete an object. For instance, if I send a DELETE request to *http://myapi.com/user/23*, it will delete the user with the ID 23. DELETE methods are not often encountered in public APIs, which are primarily created to disseminate information rather than allow random users to remove that information from their databases. However, like the PUT method, it's a good one to know about.

Although a handful of other HTTP methods are defined under the specifications for HTTP, these four constitute the entirety of what is used in just about any API you will ever encounter.

---

2 In reality, many APIs use POST requests in lieu of PUT requests when updating information. Whether a new entity is created or an old one is merely updated is often left to how the API request itself is structured. However, it's still good to know the difference, and you will often encounter PUT requests in commonly used APIs.

Authentication

Although some APIs do not use any authentication to operate (meaning anyone can make an API call for free, without registering with the application first), many modern APIs require some type of authentication before they can be used.

Some APIs require authentication in order to charge money per API call, or they might offer their service on some sort of a monthly subscription basis. Others authenticate in order to "rate limit" users (restrict them to a certain number of calls per second, hour, or day), or to restrict the access of certain kinds of information or types of API calls for some users. Other APIs might not place restrictions, but they might want to keep track of which users are making which calls for marketing purposes.

All methods of API authentication generally revolve around the use of a *token* of some sort, which is passed to the web server with each API call made. This token is either provided to the user when the user registers and is a permanent fixture of the user's calls (generally in lower-security applications), or it can frequently change, and is retrieved from the server using a username and password combination.

For example, to make a call to the Echo Nest API in order to retrieve a list of songs by the band Guns N' Roses we would use:

```
http://developer.echonest.com/api/v4/artist/songs?api_key=<your api key here>
%20&name=guns%20n%27%20roses&format=json&start=0&results=100
```

This provides the server with an api_key value of what was provided to me on registration, allowing the server to identify the requester as Ryan Mitchell, and provide the requester with the JSON data.

In addition to passing tokens in the URL of the request itself, tokens might also be passed to the server via a cookie in the request header. We will discuss headers in greater detail later in this chapter as well as in Chapter 12, but by way of brief example, they can be sent using the urllib package from previous chapters:

```
token = "<your api key>"
webRequest = urllib.request.Request("http://myapi.com", headers={"token":token})
html = urlopen(webRequest)
```

Responses

As you saw in the FreeGeoIP example at the beginning of the chapter, an important feature of APIs is that they have well-formatted responses. The most common types of response formatting are *eXtensible Markup Language* (XML) and *JavaScript Object Notation* (JSON).

In recent years, JSON has become vastly more popular than XML for a couple of major reasons. First, JSON files are generally smaller than well-designed XML files. Compare, for example, the XML data:

```
<user><firstname>Ryan</firstname><lastname>Mitchell</lastname><username>Kludgist
</username></user>
```

which clocks in at 98 characters, and the same data in JSON:

```
{"user":{"firstname":"Ryan","lastname":"Mitchell","username":"Kludgist"}}
```

which is only 73 characters, or a whopping 36% smaller than the equivalent XML.

Of course, one could argue that the XML could be formatted like this:

```
<user firstname="ryan" lastname="mitchell" username="Kludgist"></user>
```

but this is considered bad practice because it doesn't support deep nesting of data. Regardless, it still requires 71 characters, about the same length as the equivalent JSON.

Another reason JSON is quickly becoming more popular than XML is simply due to a shift in web technologies. In the past, it was more common for a server-side script such as PHP or .NET to be on the receiving end of an API. Nowadays, it is likely that a framework, such as Angular or Backbone, will be sending and receiving API calls. Server-side technologies are somewhat agnostic as to the form in which their data comes. But JavaScript libraries like Backbone find JSON easier to handle.

Although most APIs still support XML output, we will be using JSON examples in this book. Regardless, it is a good idea to familiarize yourself with both if you haven't already—they are unlikely to go away any time soon.

API Calls

The syntax of an API call can vary wildly from API to API, but there are a few standard practices they often have in common. When retrieving data through a GET request, the URL path describes how you would like to drill down into the data, while the query parameters serve as filters or additional requests tacked onto the search.

For example, in a hypothetical API, you might request the following to retrieve all posts by the user with the ID 1234 during the month of August 2014:

```
http://socialmediasite.com/users/1234/posts?from=08012014&to=08312014
```

Many other APIs use the path in order to specify an API version, the format you would like your data in, and other attributes. For example, the following would return the same data, using API version 4, formatted in JSON:

```
http://socialmediasite.com/api/v4/json/users/1234/posts?from=08012014&to=08312014
```

Other APIs require that you pass the formatting and API version information in as a request parameter, like:

```
http://socialmediasite.com/users/1234/posts?format=json&from=08012014&to=08312014
```

Echo Nest

The Echo Nest is a fantastic example of a company that is built on web scrapers. Although some music-based companies, such as Pandora, depend on human intervention to categorize and annotate music, The Echo Nest relies on automated intelligence and information scraped from blogs and news articles in order to categorize musical artists, songs, and albums.

Even better, this API is freely available for noncommercial use.[3] You cannot use the API without a key, but you can obtain a key by going to The Echo Nest "Create an Account" page (*https://developer.echonest.com/account/register*) and registering with a name, email address, and username.

A Few Examples

The Echo Nest API is built around several basic content types: artists, songs, tracks, and genres. Except for genres, these content types all have unique IDs, which are used to retrieve information about them in various forms, through API calls. For example, if I wanted to retrieve a list of songs performed by Monty Python, I would make the following call to retrieve their ID (remember to replace <your api key> with your own API key):

```
http://developer.echonest.com/api/v4/artist/search?api_key=<your api
    key>&name=monty%20python
```

This produces the following result:

```
{"response": {"status": {"version": "4.2", "code": 0, "message": "Suc
cess"}, "artists": [{"id": "AR5HF791187B9ABAF4", "name": "Monty Pytho
n"}, {"id": "ARWCIDE13925F19A33", "name": "Monty Python's SPAMALOT"},
    {"id": "ARVPRCC12FE0862033", "name": "Monty Python's Graham Chapman"
}]}}
```

I could also use that ID to query for a list of songs:

```
http://developer.echonest.com/api/v4/artist/songs?api_key=<your api key>&id=
    AR5HF791187B9ABAF4&format=json&start=0&results=10
```

Which provides some of Monty Python's hits, along with lesser-known recordings:

---

3 See The Echo Nest Licensing page (*http://developer.echonest.com/licensing.html*) restriction requirements details.

```
{"response": {"status": {"version": "4.2", "code": 0, "message": "Success"},
"start": 0, "total": 476, "songs": [{"id": "SORDAUE12AF72AC547", "title":
"Neville Shunt"}, {"id": "SORBMPW13129A9174D", "title": "Classic (Silbury Hill)
(Part 2)"}, {"id": "SOQXAYQ1316771628E", "title": "Famous Person Quiz (The
Final Rip Off Remix)"}, {"id": "SOUMAYZ133EB4E17E8", "title": "Always Look On
The Bright Side Of Life - Monty Python"}, ...]}}
```

Alternatively, I could make a single call using the name monty%20python in place of the unique ID and retrieve the same information:

```
http://developer.echonest.com/api/v4/artist/songs?api_key=<your api key>2&name=
monty%20python&format=json&start=0&results=10
```

Using that same ID, I can request a list of similar artists:

```
http://developer.echonest.com/api/v4/artist/similar?api_key=<your api key>&id=
AR5HF791187B9ABAF4&format=json&results=10&start=0
```

The results include other comedy artists such as Eric Idle, who was in the Monty Python group:

```
{"response": {"status": {"version": "4.2", "code": 0, "message": "Suc
cess"}, "artists": [{"name": "Life of Brian", "id": "ARNZYOS1272BA7FF
38"}, {"name": "Eric Idle", "id": "ARELDIS1187B9ABC79"}, {"name": "Th
e Simpsons", "id": "ARNR4B91187FB5027C"}, {"name": "Tom Lehrer", "id"
: "ARJMYTZ1187FB54669"}, ...]}}
```

Note that while this list of similar artists contains some genuinely interesting information (e.g., "Tom Lehrer"), the first result is "The Life of Brian," from the film soundtrack that Monty Python released. One of the hazards of using a database culled from many sources with minimal human intervention is that you can get some slightly strange results. This is something to keep in mind when creating your own app using data from third-party APIs.

I've covered just a few examples of how The Echo Nest API can be used. For complete documentation check out Echo Nest API Overview (*http://bit.ly/1HEDq2E*).

The Echo Nest sponsors many hackathons and programming projects focused on the intersection of technology and music. If you need some inspiration, The Echo Nest demo page (*http://bit.ly/1FNgdwU*) is a good place to start.

Twitter

Twitter is notoriously protective of its API and rightfully so. With over 230 million active users and a revenue of over $100 million a *month,* the company is hesitant to let just anyone come along and have any data they want.

Twitter's rate limits (the number of calls it allows each user to make) fall into two categories: 15 calls per 15-minute period, and 180 calls per 15-minute period, depending on the type of call. For instance, you can make up to 12 calls a minute to retrieve basic information about Twitter users, but only one call a minute to retrieve lists of those users' Twitter followers.[4]

Getting Started

In addition to rate limiting, Twitter has a more complicated authorization system than do other APIs such as The Echo Nest, both for obtaining API keys and for using those keys. In order to obtain an API key, you will, of course, need a Twitter account; you can create one relatively painlessly on the signup page (*https://twitter.com/signup*). In addition, you will need to register a new "application" with Twitter on its developer site (*https://apps.twitter.com/app/new*).

After this registration, you will be taken to a page containing your basic application information, including your Consumer Key (Figure 4-1):

Figure 4-1. Twitter's Application Settings page provides basic information about your new application

---

4 For a complete list of rate limits, see *https://dev.twitter.com/rest/public/rate-limits*.

If you click on the "manage keys and access tokens" page, you will be directed to a page containing further information (Figure 4-2):

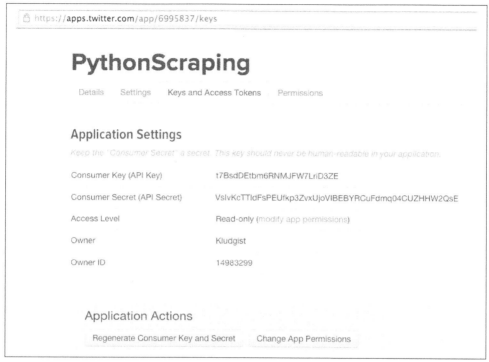

Figure 4-2. You'll need your secret key to use the Twitter API

This page also contains a button to automatically regenerate your keys should your secret key somehow become public (e.g., if you accidentally publish it as an illustration in a technical book).

A Few Examples

Twitter's authentication system, which uses OAuth, is fairly complicated; it's best to wrap it in one of the readily available libraries rather than try to keep track of it yourself. Because of the relative complexity of working with Twitter's API "by hand," this section's samples will focus on using Python code to interact with the API, rather than working with the API itself.

As of this writing, there are many Python 2.x libraries used to interact with Twitter but relatively few Python 3.x libraries available. Fortunately, one of the best Twitter libraries (appropriately called Twitter) is available for Python 3.x. You can download it from the Python Twitter Tools page (*http://bit.ly/1JhNpiu*) and install it in the usual way:

```
$cd twitter-x.xx.x
$python setup.py install
```

 Twitter Credential Permissions

By default, application access tokens are given read-only permission. This is fine for most purposes, unless you want your application to actually make a tweet on your behalf.

To change the permissions of your tokens to read/write, go to the Permissions tab on Twitter's Application Management panel. The tokens will then need to be regenerated for the permission update to take place.

Similarly, you can update the token permissions to be able to access direct messages to your Twitter account if necessary for your application. Be careful, however; you should give tokens only the permissions they absolutely need. In general, it's good practice to generate multiple sets of tokens for multiple applications, rather than reuse too-powerful tokens for applications that don't need all their permissions.

In our first exercise, we search for specific tweets. The following code connects to the Twitter API and prints a JSON list of tweets containing the hashtag #python. Remember to replace the strings in the OAuth line with your actual credentials:

```
from twitter import Twitter

t = Twitter(auth=OAuth(<Access Token>,<Access Token Secret>,
                       <Consumer Key>,<Consumer Secret>))
pythonTweets = t.search.tweets(q = "#python")
print(pythonTweets)
```

Although the output of this script might be overwhelming, keep in mind that you're getting a lot of information per tweet: the date and time the tweet was made, details about any retweets or favorites, and details about the user's account and profile image. Although you might be looking for just a subset of this data, the Twitter API was designed for web developers who want to display the tweets received through the API on their own websites, so there's a lot of extra stuff involved!

You can see an example output of a single tweet when making a status update through the API:

```
from twitter import *

t = Twitter(auth=OAuth("Access Token", "Access Token Secret",
                       "Consumer Key", "Consumer Secret"))
statusUpdate = t.statuses.update(status='Hello, world!')
print(statusUpdate)
```

Here is JSON's description of the tweet:

```
{'created_at': 'Sun Nov 30 07:23:39 +0000 2014', 'place': None, 'in_reply_to_scr
een_name': None, 'id_str': '538956506478428160', 'in_reply_to_user_id: None,'lan
g': 'en', 'in_reply_to_user_id_str': None, 'user': {'profile_sidebar_border_colo
r': '000000', 'profile_background_image_url': 'http://pbs.twimg.com/profile_back
ground_images/497094351076347904/RXn8MUlD.png', 'description':'Software Engine
er@LinkeDrive, Masters student @HarvardEXT, @OlinCollege graduate, writer @OReil
lyMedia. Really tall. Has pink hair. Female, despite the name.','time_zone': 'Ea
stern Time (US & Canada)', 'location': 'Boston, MA', 'lang': 'en', 'url': 'http:
//t.co/FM6dHXloIw', 'profile_location': None, 'name': 'Ryan Mitchell', 'screen_n
ame': 'Kludgist', 'protected': False, 'default_profile_image': False, 'id_str':
'14983299', 'favourites_count': 140, 'contributors_enabled': False, 'profile_use
_background_image': True, 'profile_background_image_url_https': 'https://pbs.twi
mg.com/profile_background_images/497094351076347904/RXn8MUlD.png', 'profile_side
bar_fill_color': '889654', 'profile_link_color': '0021B3', 'default_profile': Fa
lse, 'statuses_count': 3344, 'profile_background_color': 'FFFFFF', 'profile_imag
e_url': 'http://pbs.twimg.com/profile_images/496692905335984128/XJh_d5f5_normal.
jpeg', 'profile_background_tile': True, 'id': 14983299, 'friends_count': 409, 'p
rofile_image_url_https': 'https://pbs.twimg.com/profile_images/49669290533598412
8/XJh_d5f5_normal.jpeg', 'following': False, 'created_at': 'Mon Jun 02 18:35:1
8 +0000 2008', 'is_translator': False, 'geo_enabled': True, 'is_translation_enabl
ed': False, 'follow_request_sent': False, 'followers_count': 2085, 'utc_offset'
: -18000, 'verified': False, 'profile_text_color': '383838', 'notifications': F
alse, 'entities': {'description': {'urls': []}, 'url': {'urls': [{'indices': [
0, 22], 'url': 'http://t.co/FM6dHXloIw', 'expanded_url': 'http://ryanemitchell.
com', 'display_url': 'ryanemitchell.com'}]}}, 'listed_count': 22, 'profile_banne
r_url': 'https://pbs.twimg.com/profile_banners/14983299/1412961553'}, 'retweeted
': False, 'in_reply_to_status_id_str': None, 'source': '<a href="http://ryanemit
chell.com" rel="nofollow">PythonScraping</a>', 'favorite_count': 0, 'text': 'Hell
o,world!', 'truncated': False, 'id': 538956506478428160, 'retweet_count': 0, 'fa
vorited': False, 'in_reply_to_status_id': None, 'geo': None, 'entities': {'user_m
entions': [], 'hashtags': [], 'urls': [], 'symbols': []}, 'coordinates': None, '
contributors': None}
```

Yes, this is the result of sending a single tweet. Sometimes I think Twitter limits access to its API because of the bandwidth required to respond to every request!

For any request that retrieves a list of tweets, you can limit the number of tweets received by specifying a count:

```
pythonStatuses = t.statuses.user_timeline(screen_name="montypython", count=5)
print(pythonStatuses)
```

In this case, we are asking for the last five tweets that were posted to @montypython's timeline (this includes any retweets they might have made).

Although these three examples (searching for tweets, retrieving the tweets of a specific user, and posting your own tweets) cover a great deal of what most people do with the Twitter API, the capabilities of the Twitter Python library are far more numerous. You can search and manipulate Twitter lists, follow and unfollow users, look up profile information for users, and more. The complete documentation can be found on GitHub (*http://bit.ly/1FnfobM*).

Google APIs

Google has one of the most comprehensive, easy-to-use collections of APIs on the Web today. Whenever you're dealing with some sort of basic subject, such as language translation, geolocation, calendars, or even genomics, Google has an API for it. Google also has APIs for many of its popular apps, such as Gmail, YouTube, and Blogger.

There are two main reference pages for browsing Google APIs. The first is the Products page (*https://developers.google.com/products/*), which serves as an organized repository of its APIs, software development kits, and other projects that might be of interest to software developers. The other is the APIs console (*http://bit.ly/1a1mwMP*), which provides a convenient interface to turn API services on and off, view rate limits and usage at a glance, and even spin up a Google-powered cloud computing instance if you feel like it.

Most of Google's APIs are free although some, such as its search API, require a paid license. Google is fairly liberal with its collection of free APIs allowing from 250 requests per day to 20,000,000 requests per day with a basic account. There is also the option to raise the rate limits on some of the APIs by verifying your identity with a credit card (the card is not charged). For example, the Google Places API has a basic rate limit of 1,000 requests per 24-hour period, but this can be raised to 150,000 requests by verifying your identity. For more information, see the Usage Limits and Billing page (*http://bit.ly/1BA2WUJ*).

Getting Started

If you have a Google account, you can view the list of available APIs and create an API key using the Google Developers Console (*http://bit.ly/1AGHsu7*). If you don't have a Google account, signing up is easy to do via the Create Your Google Account page (*https://accounts.google.com/SignUp*).

Once you've logged in or created your account, you can view your account credentials, including API keys, on the API console page (*http://bit.ly/1I2v0VB*); click "Credentials" in the left menu (Figure 4-3):

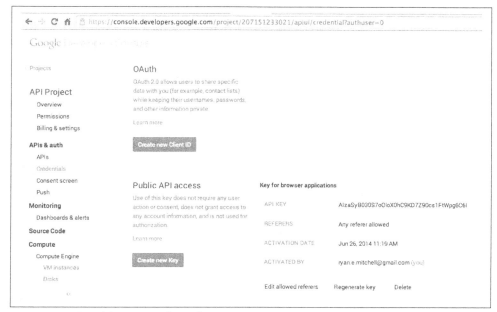

Figure 4-3. Google's API Credentials page

On the Credentials page, you can click the "Create new Key" button to create an API key, with the option to limit the referring IP address or URL that can use it. To create an API key that can be used from any URL or IP address, simply leave the "Accept Request From These Server IP Addresses" box blank when prompted. Keep in mind, however, that it is important to keep your key secret if you do not limit the originating IP address—any calls made using your API key will count against your rate limit, even if they are unauthorized.

You can create multiple API keys as well. For example, you might have a separate API key for each project, or for each web domain that you own. However, Google's API rate limits are per account, not per key, so although this might be a handy way to manage your API permissions, it will not work to get around rate limiting!

A Few Examples

Google's most popular (and in my opinion most interesting) APIs can be found in its collection of Maps APIs. You might be familiar with this feature through the embeddable Google Maps found on many websites. However, the Maps APIs go far beyond embedding maps—you can resolve street addresses to latitude/longitude coordinates, get the elevation of any point on Earth, create a variety of location-based visualizations, and get time zone information for an arbitrary location, among other bits of information.

When trying these examples out on your own, remember to activate each needed API from Google's API console before sending a request. Google uses these API activations for its metrics ("how many users does this API have?"), so you're required to explicitly activate the API before using.

Using Google's Geocode API, you can make a simple GET request from your browser to resolve any street address (in this case, the Boston Museum of Science) to a latitude and longitude:

```
https://maps.googleapis.com/maps/api/geocode/json?address=1+Science+Park+Boston
+MA+02114&key=<your API key>
```

```
"results" : [ { "address_components" : [ { "long_name" : "Museum Of Science Drive
way", "short_name" : "Museum Of Science Driveway", "types" : [ "route" ] }, { "l
ong_name" : "Boston", "short_name" : "Boston", "types" : [ "locality", "politica
l" ] }, { "long_name" : "Massachusetts", "short_name" : "MA", "types" : [ "admin
istrative_area_level_1", "political" ] }, { "long_name" : "United States", "shor
t_name" : "US", "types" : [ "country", "political" ] }, { "long_name" : "0211
4", "short_name" : "02114", "types" : [ "postal_code" ] } ], "formatted_address"
: "Museum Of Science Driveway, Boston, MA 02114, USA", "geometry" : { "bounds" :
{ "northeast" : { "lat" : 42.368454, "lng" : -71.06961339999999 }, "southwest" :
{ "lat" : 42.3672568, "lng" : -71.0719624 }, "location" : { "lat" : 42.3677994
, "lng" : -71.0708078 }, "location_type" : "GEOMETRIC_CENTER", "viewport" : { "n
ortheast" : { "lat" : 42.3692043802915, "lng" : -71.06943891970849 }, "southwest
" : { "lat" : 42.3665064197085, "lng" : -71.0721368802915 } } }, "types" : [ "ro
ute" ] } ], "status" : "OK" }
```

Note that the address we send the API doesn't have to be especially well formatted. Google being Google, the Geocode API is excellent at taking addresses that are missing postal codes or state information (or even misspelled addresses), and giving you back its best guess at what the correct address is. For instance, the deplorably spelled request argument 1+Skience+Park+Bostton+MA (without even a postal code) returns the same result.

I have used the Geocode API on several occasions, not only to format user-entered addresses on a website, but to crawl the Web looking for things that look like addresses, and using the API to reformat them into something easier to store and search.

To get the time zone information for our newly found latitude and longitude, you can use the Time zone API:

```
https://maps.googleapis.com/maps/api/timezone/json?location=42.3677994,-71.0708
078&timestamp=1412649030&key=<your API key>
```

Which provides the response:

```
{ "dstOffset" : 3600, "rawOffset" : -18000, "status" : "OK", "timeZon
eId" : "America/New_York", "timeZoneName" : "Eastern Daylight Time" }
```

A Unix timestamp is required to make a request to the Time Zone API. This allows Google to provide you with a time zone appropriately adjusted for daylight saving time. Even in areas where the time zone is not affected by the time of year (such as Phoenix, which does not use daylight saving time), the timestamp is still required in an API request.

To round out this all-too-brief tour of the Google Maps API collection, you can also fetch the elevation for this latitude and longitude:

```
https://maps.googleapis.com/maps/api/elevation/json?locations=42.3677994,-71.070
8078&key=<your API key>
```

This returns the elevation in meters above sea level, along with the "resolution," which indicates the distance in meters of the farthest data point this elevation was interpolated from. A smaller value for resolution indicates a higher degree of accuracy in the given elevation:

```
{ "results" : [ { "elevation" : 5.127755641937256, "location" : { "la
t" : 42.3677994, "lng" : -71.0708078 }, "resolution" : 9.543951988220
215 } ], "status" : "OK" }
```

Parsing JSON

In this chapter, we've looked at various types of APIs and how they function, and we've looked at some sample JSON responses from these APIs. Now let's look at how we can parse and use this information.

At the beginning of the chapter I used the example of the *freegeoip.net* IP, which resolves IP addresses to physical addresses:

```
http://freegeoip.net/json/50.78.253.58
```

I can take the output of this request and use Python's JSON parsing functions to decode it:

```
import json
from urllib.request import urlopen

def getCountry(ipAddress):
    response = urlopen("http://freegeoip.net/json/"+ipAddress).read()
                      .decode('utf-8')
    responseJson = json.loads(response)
    return responseJson.get("country_code")

print(getCountry("50.78.253.58"))
```

This prints out the country code for the IP address: *50.78.253.58*.

The JSON parsing library used is part of Python's core library. Just type in `import json` at the top, and you're all set! Unlike many languages that might parse JSON into a special JSON object or JSON node, Python uses a more flexible approach and turns JSON objects into dictionaries, JSON arrays into lists, JSON strings into strings, and so forth. In this way, it makes it extremely easy to access and manipulate values stored in JSON.

The following gives a quick demonstration of how Python's JSON library handles the different values that might be encountered in a JSON string:

```
import json

jsonString = '{"arrayOfNums":[{"number":0},{"number":1},{"number":2}],
               "arrayOfFruits":{"fruit":"apple"},{"fruit":"banana"},
                               {"fruit":"pear"}]}'
jsonObj = json.loads(jsonString)

print(jsonObj.get("arrayOfNums"))
print(jsonObj.get("arrayOfNums")[1])
print(jsonObj.get("arrayOfNums")[1].get("number")+
      jsonObj.get("arrayOfNums")[2].get("number"))
print(jsonObj.get("arrayOfFruits")[2].get("fruit"))
```

The output of which is:

```
[{'number': 0}, {'number': 1}, {'number': 2}]
{'number': 1}
3
pear
```

Line 1 is a list of dictionary objects, line 2 is a dictionary object, line 3 is an integer (the sum of the integers accessed in the dictionaries), and line 4 is a string.

Bringing It All Back Home

Although the *raison d'être* of many modern web applications is to take existing data and format it in a more appealing way, I would argue that this isn't very interesting thing to do in most instances. If you're using an API as your only data source, the best you can do is merely copy someone else's database that already exists, and which is, essentially, already published. What can be far more interesting is to take two or more data sources and combine them in a novel way, or use an API as a tool to look at scraped data from a new perspective.

Let's look at one example of how data from APIs can be used in conjunction with web scraping: to see which parts of the world contribute the most to Wikipedia.

If you've spent much time on Wikipedia, you've likely come across an article's revision history page, which displays a list of recent edits. If users are logged into Wikipedia when they make the edit, their username is displayed. If they are not logged in, their IP address is recorded, as shown in Figure 4-4.

Python: Revision history

View logs for this page

Browse history

From year (and earlier): 2014   From month (and earlier): all   Tag filter: Go

For any version listed below, click on its date to view it. For more help, see Help:Page history and Help:Edit summary.
External tools: Revision history statistics ⚙ · Revision history search ⚙ · Edits by user ⚙ · Number of watchers ⚙ · Page view statistics ⚙

(cur) = difference from current version, (prev) = difference from preceding version, **m** = minor edit, → = section edit, ← = automatic edit summary
(newest l oldest) View (newer 50 l older 50) (20 l 50 l 100 l 250 l 500)

Compare selected revisions

- (cur l prev) ⊙ 00:42, 29 August 2014 Discospinster (talk l contribs) **m** . . (1,715 bytes) (-21) . . *(Reverted edits by 121.97.110.145 (talk) to last revision by Bgwhite (HG))* (undo)
- (cur l prev)⊙ 00:41, 29 August 2014 121.97.110.145 (talk) . . (1,736 bytes) (+21) . . *(→in computing)* (undo)
- (cur l prev) ○ 05:53, 10 June 2014 Bgwhite (talk l contribs) . . (1,715 bytes) (+45) . . *(Reverted to revision 608857990 by Bgwhite: No content between TOC and first headline per WP:TOC and WP:LEAD. This is an accessibility issue for users of screen readers. . (TW))* (undo)
- (cur l prev) ○ 23:01, 9 June 2014 Nvmbs (talk l contribs) . . (1,670 bytes) (-62) . . *(rephrase for link in the front)* (undo)
- (cur l prev) ○ 17:26, 9 June 2014 Bjennelle (talk l contribs) . . (1,732 bytes) (+17) . . *(Link to the python snake when it's mentioned.)* (undo)

Figure 4-4. The IP address of an anonymous editor on the revision history page for Wikipedia's Python entry

The IP address outlined on the history page is *121.97.110.145*. By using the *freegeoip.net* API, as of this writing (IP address can occasionally shift geographically) that IP address is from Quezon, Phillipines.

This information isn't all that interesting on its own, but what if we could gather many, many, points of geographic data about Wikipedia edits and where they occur? A few years ago I did just that and used Google's Geochart library (*http://bit.ly/1ADw9Dd*) to create an interesting chart (*http://bit.ly/1cs2CAK*) that shows where edits on the English-language Wikipedia, along with the Wikipedias written in other languages, originate from (Figure 4-5).

Figure 4-5. Visualization of Wikipedia edits created using Google's Geochart library

Creating a basic script that crawls Wikipedia, looks for revision history pages, and then looks for IP addresses on those revision history pages isn't difficult. Using modified code from Chapter 3, the following script does just that:

```
from urllib.request import urlopen
from bs4 import BeautifulSoup
import datetime
import random
import re

random.seed(datetime.datetime.now())
def getLinks(articleUrl):
    html = urlopen("http://en.wikipedia.org"+articleUrl)
    bsObj = BeautifulSoup(html)
    return bsObj.find("div", {"id":"bodyContent"}).findAll("a",
                      href=re.compile("^(/wiki/)((?!:).)*$"))

def getHistoryIPs(pageUrl):
    #Format of revision history pages is:
    #http://en.wikipedia.org/w/index.php?title=Title_in_URL&action=history
    pageUrl = pageUrl.replace("/wiki/", "")
    historyUrl = "http://en.wikipedia.org/w/index.php?title="
                 +pageUrl+"&action=history"
    print("history url is: "+historyUrl)
    html = urlopen(historyUrl)
    bsObj = BeautifulSoup(html)
    #finds only the links with class "mw-anonuserlink" which has IP addresses
    #instead of usernames
    ipAddresses = bsObj.findAll("a", {"class":"mw-anonuserlink"})
    addressList = set()
    for ipAddress in ipAddresses:
        addressList.add(ipAddress.get_text())
    return addressList

links = getLinks("/wiki/Python_(programming_language)")

while(len(links) > 0):
    for link in links:
        print("-------------------")
        historyIPs = getHistoryIPs(link.attrs["href"])
        for historyIP in historyIPs:
            print(historyIP)

    newLink = links[random.randint(0, len(links)-1)].attrs["href"]
    links = getLinks(newLink)
```

This program uses two main functions: getLinks (which was also used in Chapter 3), and the new getHistoryIPs, which searches for the contents of all links with the class `mw-anonuserlink` (indicating an anonymous user with an IP address, rather than a username) and returns it as a set.

Let's Talk About Sets

Up until this point in the book, I've relied almost exclusively on two Python data structures to store multiple pieces of data: lists and dictionaries. With both of these options, why use a set?

Python sets are unordered, meaning you shouldn't reference a specific position in the set and expect to get the value you're looking for. The order in which you add items to the set is not necessarily the order in which you'll get them back. One nice property of sets that I'm taking advantage of in the code sample is that they won't hold multiples of the same item. If you add a string to a set when that string already exists, it will not be duplicated. In this way, I can quickly get a list of only the unique IP addresses on the revision history page, disregarding multiple edits by the same user.

A couple of things to keep in mind when deciding between sets and lists in code that needs to scale: although lists are slightly faster to iterate over, sets are slightly faster for doing lookups (determining whether an object exists in the set or not).

This code also uses a somewhat arbitrary (yet effective for the purposes of this example) search pattern to look for articles from which to retrieve revision histories. It starts by retrieving the histories of all Wikipedia articles linked to by the starting page (in this case, the article on the Python programming language). Afterward, it selects a new starting page randomly, and retrieves all revision history pages of articles linked to by that page. It will continue until it hits a page with no links.

Now that we have code that retrieves IP addresses as a string, we can combine this with the `getCountry` function from the previous section in order to resolve these IP addresses to countries. I modified `getCountry` slightly, in order to account for invalid or malformed IP addresses that will result in a "404 Not Found" error (as of this writing, *freegeoip.net* does not resolve IPv6, for instance, which might trigger such an error):

```python
def getCountry(ipAddress):
    try:
        response = urlopen("http://freegeoip.net/json/"
                           +ipAddress).read().decode('utf-8')
    except HTTPError:
        return None
    responseJson = json.loads(response)
    return responseJson.get("country_code")

links = getLinks("/wiki/Python_(programming_language)")
```

```
while(len(links) > 0):
    for link in links:
        print("------------------")
        historyIPs = getHistoryIPs(link.attrs["href"])
        for historyIP in historyIPs:
            country = getCountry(historyIP)
            if country is not None:
                print(historyIP+" is from "+country)

    newLink = links[random.randint(0, len(links)-1)].attrs["href"]
    links = getLinks(newLink)
```

The complete executable code can be found at *http://www.pythonscraping.com/code/6-3.txt*. Here's a sample output:

```
------------------
history url is: http://en.wikipedia.org/w/index.php?title=Programming_
paradigm&action=history
68.183.108.13 is from US
86.155.0.186 is from GB
188.55.200.254 is from SA
108.221.18.208 is from US
141.117.232.168 is from CA
76.105.209.39 is from US
182.184.123.106 is from PK
212.219.47.52 is from GB
72.27.184.57 is from JM
49.147.183.43 is from PH
209.197.41.132 is from US
174.66.150.151 is from US
```

More About APIs

In this chapter, we've looked at a few ways that modern APIs are commonly used to access data on the Web, in particular uses of APIs that you might find useful in web scraping. However, I'm afraid that this does not do justice to the broad scope that "software sharing data with disparate software" entails.

Because this book is about web scraping and is not intended as a general guide on data collection, I can only point you in the direction of some excellent resources for further research on the subject, if you need it.

Leonard Richardson, Mike Amundsen, and Sam Ruby's *RESTful Web APIs* provides a strong overview of the theory and practice of using APIs on the Web. In addition, Mike Amundsen has a fascinating video series, *Designing APIs for the Web* (*http://oreil.ly/1GOXNhE*), that teaches you how to create your own APIs, a useful thing to know if you decide to make your scraped data available to the public in a convenient format.

Web scraping and web APIs might seem like very different subjects at first glance. However, I hope that this chapter has shown that they are complementary skills on the same continuum of data collection. In some sense, using a web API can even be thought of as a subset of the subject of web scraping. After all, you are ultimately writing a script that collects data from a remote web server, and parsing it into a usable format, as you would do with any web scraper.

## CHAPTER 5

Storing Data

Although printing out to the terminal is a lot of fun, it's not incredibly useful when it comes to data aggregation and analysis. In order to make the majority of web scrapers remotely useful, you need to be able to save the information that they scrape.

In this chapter, we will look at three main methods of data management that are sufficient for almost any imaginable application. Do you need to power the backend of a website or create your own API? You'll probably want your scrapers to write to a database. Need a fast and easy way to collect some documents off the Internet and put them on your hard drive? You'll probably want to create a file stream for that. Need occasional alerts, or aggregated data once a day? Send yourself an email!

Above and beyond web scraping, the ability to store and interact with large amounts of data is incredibly important for just about any modern programming application. In fact, the information in this chapter is necessary for implementing many of the examples in later sections of the book. I highly recommend that you at least skim it if you're unfamiliar with automated data storage.

Media Files

There are two main ways to store media files: by reference, and by downloading the file itself. You can store a file by reference simply by storing the URL that the file is located at. This has several advantages:

- Scrapers run much faster, and require much less bandwidth, when they don't have to download files.
- You save space on your own machine by storing only the URLs.
- It is easier to write code that only stores URLs and doesn't need to deal with additional file downloads.

- You can lessen the load on the host server by avoiding large file downloads.

Here are the disadvantages:

- Embedding these URLs in your own website or application is known as *hotlinking* and doing it is a very quick way to get you in hot water on the Internet.
- You do not want to use someone else's server cycles to host media for your own applications.
- The file hosted at any particular URL is subject to change. This might lead to embarrassing effects if, say, you're embedding a hotlinked image on a public blog. If you're storing the URLs with the intent to store the file later, for further research, it might eventually go missing or be changed to something completely irrelevant at a later date.
- Real web browsers do not just request a page's HTML and move on—they download all of the assets required by the page as well. Downloading files can help make your scraper look like an actual human is browsing the site, which can be an advantage.

If you're debating over whether to store a file or simply a URL to a file, you should ask yourself whether you're likely to actually view or read that file more than once or twice, or if this database of files is just going to be sitting around gathering electronic dust for most of its life. If the answer is the latter, it's probably best to simply store the URL. If it's the former, read on!

In Python 3.x, `urllib.request.urlretrieve` can be used to download files from any remote URL:

```
from urllib.request import urlretrieve
from urllib.request import urlopen
from bs4 import BeautifulSoup

html = urlopen("http://www.pythonscraping.com")
bsObj = BeautifulSoup(html)
imageLocation = bsObj.find("a", {"id": "logo"}).find("img")["src"]
urlretrieve (imageLocation, "logo.jpg")
```

This downloads the logo from *http://pythonscraping.com* and stores it as *logo.jpg* in the same directory that the script is running from.

This works well if you only need to download a single file and know what to call it and what the file extension is. But most scrapers don't download a single file and call it a day. The following will download all internal files, linked to by any tag's `src` attribute, from the home page of *http://pythonscraping.com*:

```
import os
from urllib.request import urlretrieve
from urllib.request import urlopen
from bs4 import BeautifulSoup
```

```
downloadDirectory = "downloaded"
baseUrl = "http://pythonscraping.com"

def getAbsoluteURL(baseUrl, source):
    if source.startswith("http://www."):
        url = "http://"+source[11:]
    elif source.startswith("http://"):
        url = source
    elif source.startswith("www."):
        url = source[4:]
        url = "http://"+source
    else:
        url = baseUrl+"/"+source
    if baseUrl not in url:
        return None
    return url

def getDownloadPath(baseUrl, absoluteUrl, downloadDirectory):
    path = absoluteUrl.replace("www.", "")
    path = path.replace(baseUrl, "")
    path = downloadDirectory+path
    directory = os.path.dirname(path)

    if not os.path.exists(directory):
        os.makedirs(directory)

    return path

html = urlopen("http://www.pythonscraping.com")
bsObj = BeautifulSoup(html)
downloadList = bsObj.findAll(src=True)

for download in downloadList:
    fileUrl = getAbsoluteURL(baseUrl, download["src"])
    if fileUrl is not None:
        print(fileUrl)

urlretrieve(fileUrl, getDownloadPath(baseUrl, fileUrl, downloadDirectory))
```

Run with Caution

You know all those warnings you hear about downloading unknown files off the Internet? This script downloads everything it comes across to your computer's hard drive. This includes random bash scripts, *.exe* files, and other potential malware.

Think you're safe because you'd never actually execute anything sent to your downloads folder? Especially if you run this program as an administrator, you're asking for trouble. What happens if you run across a file on a website that sends itself to *../../../../usr/bin/python*? The next time you run a Python script from the command line, you could actually be deploying malware on your machine!

This program is written for illustrative purposes only; it should not be randomly deployed without more extensive filename checking, and it should only be run in an account with limited permissions. As always, backing up your files, not storing sensitive information on your hard drive, and a little common sense go a long way.

This script uses a lambda function (introduced in Chapter 2) to select all tags on the front page that have the src attribute, then cleans and normalizes the URLs to get an absolute path for each download (making sure to discard external links). Then, each file is downloaded to its own path in the local folder *downloaded* on your own machine.

Notice that Python's os module is used briefly to retrieve the target directory for each download and create missing directories along the path if needed. The os module acts as an interface between Python and the operating system, allowing it to manipulate file paths, create directories, get information about running processes and environment variables, and many other useful things.

Storing Data to CSV

CSV, or *comma-separated values*, is one of the most popular file formats in which to store spreadsheet data. It is supported by Microsoft Excel and many other applications because of its simplicity. The following is an example of a perfectly valid CSV file:

```
fruit,cost
apple,1.00
banana,0.30
pear,1.25
```

As with Python, whitespace is important here: Each row is separated by a newline character, while columns within the row are separated by commas (hence the "comma-separated"). Other forms of CSV files (sometimes called "character-separated value" files) use tabs or other characters to separate rows, but these file formats are less common and less widely supported.

If you're looking to download CSV files directly off the Web and store them locally, without any parsing or modification, you don't need this section. Simply download them like you would any other file and save them with the CSV file format using the methods described in the previous section.

Modifying a CSV file, or even creating one entirely from scratch, is extremely easy with Python's csv library:

```
import csv

csvFile = open("../files/test.csv", 'wt')
try:
    writer = csv.writer(csvFile)
    writer.writerow(('number', 'number plus 2', 'number times 2'))
    for i in range(10):
        writer.writerow( (i, i+2, i*2))
finally:
    csvFile.close()
```

A precautionary reminder: file creation in Python is fairly bullet-proof. If *../files/ test.csv* does not already exist, Python will create the directory and the file automatically. If it already exists, Python will overwrite *test.csv* with the new data.

After running, you should see a CSV file:

```
number,number plus 2,number times 2
0,2,0
1,3,2
2,4,4
...
```

One common web-scraping task is to retrieve an HTML table and write it as a CSV file. Wikipedia's Comparison of Text Editors (*http://bit.ly/1BA6h6d*) provides a fairly complex HTML table, complete with color coding, links, sorting, and other HTML garbage that needs to be discarded before it can be written to CSV. Using BeautifulSoup and the get_text() function copiously, you can do that in fewer than 20 lines:

```
import csv
from urllib.request import urlopen
from bs4 import BeautifulSoup

html = urlopen("http://en.wikipedia.org/wiki/Comparison_of_text_editors")
bsObj = BeautifulSoup(html)
#The main comparison table is currently the first table on the page
table = bsObj.findAll("table",{"class":"wikitable"})[0]
rows = table.findAll("tr")
```

```
csvFile = open("../files/editors.csv", 'wt')
writer = csv.writer(csvFile)
try:
    for row in rows:
        csvRow = []
        for cell in row.findAll(['td', 'th']):
            csvRow.append(cell.get_text())
            writer.writerow(csvRow)
finally:
    csvFile.close()
```

Before You Implement This in Real Life

This script is great to integrate into scrapers if you encounter many HTML tables that need to be converted to CSV files, or many HTML tables that need to be collected into a single CSV file. However, if you just need to do it once, there's a better tool for that: copying and pasting. Selecting and copying all of the content of an HTML table and pasting it into Excel will get you the CSV file you're looking for without running a script!

The result should be a well-formatted CSV file saved locally, under *../files/editors.csv* —perfect for sending and sharing with folks who haven't quite gotten the hang of MySQL yet!

MySQL

MySQL (officially pronounced "My es-kew-el," although many say, "My Sequel") is the most popular open source relational database management system today. Somewhat unusually for an open source project with large competitors, its popularity has historically been neck and neck with the two other major closed source database systems: Microsoft's SQL Server and Oracle's DBMS.

Its popularity is not without cause. For most applications, it's very hard to go wrong with MySQL. It's a very scaleable, robust, and full-featured DBMS, used by top websites: YouTube,[1] Twitter,[2] and Facebook,[3] among many others.

---

[1] Joab Jackson, "YouTube Scales MySQL with Go Code," PCWorld, December 15, 2012 (*http://bit.ly/1LWVmc8*).

[2] Jeremy Cole and Davi Arnaut, "MySQL at Twitter," The Twitter Engineering Blog, April 9, 2012 (*http://bit.ly/1KHDKns*).

[3] "MySQL and Database Engineering: Mark Callaghan," March 4, 2012 (*http://on.fb.me/1RFMqvw*).

Because of its ubiquity, price ("free" is a pretty great price), and out-of-box usability, it makes a fantastic database for web-scraping projects, and we will use it throughout the remainder of this book.

"Relational" Database?

"Relational data" is data that has relations. Glad we cleared that up!

Just kidding! When computer scientists talk about relational data, they're referring to data that doesn't exist in a vacuum—it has properties that relate it to other pieces of data. For example, "User A goes to school at Institution B," where User A can be found in the "users" table in the database and Institution B can be found in the "institutions" table in the database.

Later in this chapter, we'll take a look at modeling different types of relations and how to store data in MySQL (or any other relational database) effectively.

Installing MySQL

If you're new to MySQL, installing a database might sound a little intimidating (if you're an old hat at it, feel free to skip this section). In reality, it's as simple as installing just about any other kind of software. At its core, MySQL is powered by a set of data files, stored on your server or local machine, that contain all the information stored in your database. The MySQL software layer on top of that provides a convenient way of interacting with the data, via a command-line interface. For example, the following command will dig through the data files and return a list of all users in your database whose first name is "Ryan":

```
SELECT * FROM users WHERE firstname = "Ryan"
```

If you're on Linux, installing MySQL is as easy as:

```
$sudo apt-get install mysql-server
```

Just keep an eye on the installation process, approve the memory requirements, and enter a new password for your new root user when prompted.

For Mac OS X and Windows, things are a little trickier. If you haven't already, you'll need to create an Oracle account before downloading the package.

If you're on Mac OS X, you'll need to first get the installation package (*http://bit.ly/1Jc8lZO*).

Select the *.dmg* package, and log in with or create your Oracle account to download the file. After opening, you should be guided through a fairly straightforward installation wizard (Figure 5-1):

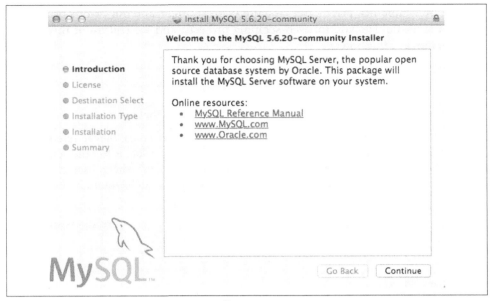

Figure 5-1. The Mac OS X MySQL installer

The default installation steps should suffice, and for the purposes of this book, I will assume you have a default MySQL installation.

If downloading and running an installer seems a little tedious, you can always install the package manager, Homebrew (*http://brew.sh/*). With Homebrew installed, you can also install MySQL by running:

```
$brew install mysql
```

Homebrew is a great open source project with very good Python package integration. In fact, most of the third-party Python modules used in this book can be installed very easily with Homebrew. If you don't have it already, I highly recommend checking it out!

Once MySQL is installed on Mac OS X, you can start the MySQL server as follows:

```
$cd /usr/local/mysql
$sudo ./bin/mysqld_safe
```

On Windows, installing and running MySQL is slightly more complicated, but the good news is that there's a convenient installer (*http://bit.ly/1FVKDP9*) that simplifies the process. Once downloaded, it will guide you through the steps you'll need to take (see Figure 5-2):

Figure 5-2. The MySQL Windows Installer

You should be able to install MySQL using the default selections, with one exception: on the Setup Type page, I recommend you choose "Server Only" to avoid installing a lot of additional Microsoft software and libraries.

From there, you should be able to use the default installation settings and follow the prompts to start your MySQL server.

Some Basic Commands

Once your MySQL server is running, you have many options for interacting with the database. There are plenty of software tools that act as an intermediary so that you don't have to deal with MySQL commands (or at least deal with them less often). Tools like phpMyAdmin and MySQL Workbench can make it easy to quickly view, sort, and insert data. However, it's still important to know your way around the command line.

Except for variable names, MySQL is case insensitive; for example, SELECT is the same as sElEcT. However, by convention, all MySQL keywords are in all caps when you are writing a MySQL statement. Conversely, most developers prefer to name their tables and databases in lowercase, although this standard is often ignored.

When you first log into MySQL, there are no databases to add data to. You can create one:

```
>CREATE DATABASE scraping;
```

Because every MySQL instance can have multiple databases, before we can start interacting with a database we need to specify to MySQL which database we want to use:

```
>USE scraping;
```

From this point on (at least until we close the MySQL connection or switch to another database), all commands entered will be run against the new "scraping" database.

That all seems pretty straightforward. It must be similarly easy to create a table in the database, right? Let's try to create a table to store a collection of scraped web pages:

```
>CREATE TABLE pages;
```

This results in the error:

```
ERROR 1113 (42000): A table must have at least 1 column
```

Unlike a database, which can exist without any tables, a table in MySQL cannot exist without columns. In order to define columns in MySQL, you must enter them in a comma-delimited list, within parentheses, after the CREATE TABLE <tablename> statement:

```
>CREATE TABLE pages (id BIGINT(7) NOT NULL AUTO_INCREMENT, title VARCHAR(200),
content VARCHAR(10000), created TIMESTAMP DEFAULT CURRENT_TIMESTAMP, PRIMARY KEY
(id));
```

Each column definition has three parts:

- The name (id, title, created, etc.)
- The variable type (BIGINT(7), VARCHAR, TIMESTAMP)
- Optionally, any additional attributes (NOT NULL AUTO_INCREMENT)

At the end of the list of columns, you must define a table's "key." MySQL uses keys to organize the content in the table for fast lookups. Later in this chapter, I'll describe how to use these keys to your advantage for speedier databases, but for now, using a table's id column as the key is generally the best way to go.

After the query executes, you can see what the structure of the table looks like at any time by using DESCRIBE:

```
> DESCRIBE pages;
+---------+----------------+------+-----+-------------------+----------------+
| Field   | Type           | Null | Key | Default           | Extra          |
+---------+----------------+------+-----+-------------------+----------------+
| id      | bigint(7)      | NO   | PRI | NULL              | auto_increment |
| title   | varchar(200)   | YES  |     | NULL              |                |
| content | varchar(10000) | YES  |     | NULL              |                |
| created | timestamp      | NO   |     | CURRENT_TIMESTAMP |                |
+---------+----------------+------+-----+-------------------+----------------+
4 rows in set (0.01 sec)
```

Of course, this is still an empty table. You can insert some test data into the pages table, by using the following line:

```
> INSERT INTO pages (title, content) VALUES ("Test page title", "This is some te
st page content. It can be up to 10,000 characters long.");
```

Notice that although the table has four columns (id, title, content, created), you need to define only two of them (title and content) in order to insert a row. That's because the id column is autoincremented (MySQL automatically adds a 1 each time a new row is inserted) and generally can take care of itself. In addition, the timestamp column is set to contain the current time as a default.

Of course, we *can* override these defaults:

```
INSERT INTO pages (id, title, content, created) VALUES (3, "Test page title", "
This is some test page content. It can be up to 10,000 characters long.", "2014-
09-21 10:25:32");
```

As long as the integer you provide for the id column doesn't already exist in the database, this override will work perfectly fine. However, it is generally bad practice to do this; it's best to let MySQL handle the id and timestamp columns unless there is a compelling reason to do it differently.

Now that we have some data in the table, you can use a wide variety of methods to select this data. Here are a few examples of SELECT statements:

```
>SELECT * FROM pages WHERE id = 2;
```

This statement tells MySQL, "Select all from pages where id equals 2." The asterisk (*) acts as a wildcard, returning all of the rows where the clause (where id equals 2) is true. It returns the second row in the table, or an empty result if there is no row with an id of 2. For example, the following case-insensitive query returns all the rows where the title field contains "test" (the % symbol acts as a wildcard in MySQL strings):

```
>SELECT * FROM pages WHERE title LIKE "%test%";
```

But what if you have a table with many columns, and you only want a particular piece of data returned? Rather than selecting all, you can do something like this:

```
>SELECT id, title FROM pages WHERE content LIKE "%page content%";
```

This returns just the `id` and `title` where the content contains the phrase "page content."

`DELETE` statements have much the same syntax as `SELECT` statements:

```
>DELETE FROM pages WHERE id = 1;
```

For this reason it is a good idea, especially when working on important databases that can't be easily restored, to write any `DELETE` statements as a `SELECT` statement first (in this case, `SELECT * FROM pages WHERE id = 1`), test to make sure only the rows you want to delete are returned, and then replace `SELECT *` with `DELETE`. Many programmers have horror stories of miscoding the clause on a `DELETE` statement, or worse, leaving it off entirely when they were in a hurry, and ruining customer data. Don't let it happen to you!

Similar precautions should be taken with `UPDATE` statements:

```
>UPDATE pages SET title="A new title", content="Some new content" WHERE id=2;
```

For the purposes of this book, we will be working only with simple MySQL statements, doing basic selecting, inserting, and updating. If you're interested in learning more commands and techniques with this powerful database tool, I recommend Paul DuBois's *MySQL Cookbook*.

Integrating with Python

Unfortunately, Python support for MySQL is not built in. However, there are a good number of open source libraries you can use, both with Python 2.x and Python 3.x, that allow you to interact with a MySQL database. One of the most popular of these is PyMySQL (*http://www.pymysql.org/*).

As of this writing, the current version of PyMySQL is 0.6.2, and you can download and install this version with the following commands:

```
$ curl -L https://github.com/PyMySQL/PyMySQL/tarball/pymysql-0.6.2 | tar xz
$ cd PyMySQL-PyMySQL-f953785/
$ python setup.py install
```

Remember to check for the latest version of PyMySQL on the website and update the version number in the first line of this command, as needed.

After installation, you should have access to the PyMySQL package automatically, and while your local MySQL server is running, you should be able to execute the following script successfully (remember to add the root password for your database):

```
import pymysql
conn = pymysql.connect(host='127.0.0.1', unix_socket='/tmp/mysql.sock',
                       user='root', passwd=None, db='mysql')
cur = conn.cursor()
cur.execute("USE scraping")
```

```
cur.execute("SELECT * FROM pages WHERE id=1")
print(cur.fetchone())
cur.close()
conn.close()
```

There are two new types of objects at work in this example: the Connection object (conn), and the Cursor object (cur).

The connection/cursor model is commonly used in database programming, although some users might find it tricky to differentiate the two at first. The connection is responsible for, well, connecting to the database of course, but also sending the database information, handling rollbacks (when a query or set of queries needs to be aborted and the database needs to be returned to its previous state), and creating new cursor objects.

A connection can have many cursors. A cursor keeps track of certain *state* information, such as which database it is using. If you have multiple databases and need to write information across all of them, you might have multiple cursors to handle this. A cursor also contains the results of the latest query it has executed. By calling functions on the cursor, such as cur.fetchone(), you can access this information.

It is important that both the cursor and the connection are closed after you are done using them. Not doing this might result in *connection leaks*, a buildup of unclosed connections that are no longer being used but the software isn't able to close because it's under the impression that you might still use them. This is the sort of thing that brings databases down all the time, so remember to close your connections!

The most common thing you'll probably want to do, starting out, is to be able to store your scraping results in a database. Let's take a look at how this could be done, using a previous example: the Wikipedia scraper.

Dealing with Unicode text can be tough when web scraping. By default, MySQL does not handle Unicode. Fortunately, you can turn on this feature (just keep in mind that doing so will increase the size of your database). Because we're bound to run into a variety of colorful characters on Wikipedia, now is a good time to tell your database to expect some Unicode:

```
ALTER DATABASE scraping CHARACTER SET = utf8mb4 COLLATE = utf8mb4_unicode_ci;
ALTER TABLE pages CONVERT TO CHARACTER SET utf8mb4 COLLATE utf8mb4_unicode_ci;
ALTER TABLE pages CHANGE title title VARCHAR(200) CHARACTER SET utf8mb4 COLLATE
utf8mb4_unicode_ci;
ALTER TABLE pages CHANGE content content VARCHAR(10000) CHARACTER SET utf8mb4 CO
LLATE utf8mb4_unicode_ci;
```

These four lines change the following: the default character set for the database, for the table, and for both of the two columns, from utf8mb4 (still technically Unicode, but with notoriously terrible support for most Unicode characters) to utf8mb4_uni code_ci.

You'll know that you're successful if you try inserting a few umlauts or Mandarin characters into the `title` or `content` field in the database and it succeeds with no errors.

Now that the database is prepared to accept a wide variety of all that Wikipedia can throw at it, you can run the following:

```
from urllib.request import urlopen
from bs4 import BeautifulSoup
import datetime
import random
import pymysql

conn = pymysql.connect(host='127.0.0.1', unix_socket='/tmp/mysql.sock',
                       user='root', passwd=None, db='mysql', charset='utf8')
cur = conn.cursor()
cur.execute("USE scraping")

random.seed(datetime.datetime.now())

def store(title, content):
    cur.execute("INSERT INTO pages (title, content) VALUES (\"%s\",
                \"%s\")", (title, content))
    cur.connection.commit()

def getLinks(articleUrl):
    html = urlopen("http://en.wikipedia.org"+articleUrl)
    bsObj = BeautifulSoup(html)
    title = bsObj.find("h1").find("span").get_text()
    content = bsObj.find("div", {"id":"mw-content-text"}).find("p").get_text()
    store(title, content)
    return bsObj.find("div", {"id":"bodyContent"}).findAll("a",
                      href=re.compile("^(/wiki/)((?!:).)*$"))

links = getLinks("/wiki/Kevin_Bacon")
try:
    while len(links) > 0:
        newArticle = links[random.randint(0, len(links)-1)].attrs["href"]
        print(newArticle)
        links = getLinks(newArticle)
finally:
    cur.close()
    conn.close()
```

There are a few things to note here: first, `"charset='utf8'"` is added to the database connection string. This tells the connection that it should send all information to the database as UTF-8 (and, of course, the database should already be configured to handle this).

Second, note the addition of a `store` function. This takes in two string variables, `title` and `content`, and adds them to an `INSERT` statement that is executed by the cursor and then committed by the cursor's connection. This is an excellent example of the separation of the cursor and the connection; while the cursor has some stored information about the database and its own context, it needs to operate through the connection in order to send information back to the database and insert some information.

Last, you'll see that a `finally` statement was added to the program's main loop, at the bottom of the code. This will ensure that, regardless of how the program is interrupted or the exceptions that might be thrown during its execution (and, of course, because the Web is messy, you should always assume exceptions will be thrown), the cursor and the connection will both be closed immediately before the program ends. It is a good idea to include a `try...finally` statement whenever you are scraping the Web and have an open database connection.

Although PyMySQL is not a huge package, there are a fair number of useful functions that this book simply can't accommodate. Check out this documentation *http://bit.ly/1KHzoga*.

Database Techniques and Good Practice

There are people who spend their entire careers studying, tuning, and inventing databases. I am not one of them, and this is not that kind of book. However, as with many subjects in computer science, there are a few tricks you can learn quickly to at least make your databases sufficient, and sufficiently speedy, for most applications.

First, with very few exceptions, always add `id` columns to your tables. All tables in MySQL must have at least one primary key (the key column that MySQL sorts on), so that MySQL knows how to order it, and it can often be difficult to choose these keys intelligently. The debate over whether to use an artificially created `id` column for this key or some unique attribute such as `username` has raged among data scientists and software engineers for years, although I tend to lean on the side of creating `id` columns. The reasons for doing it one way or the other are complicated but for nonenterprise systems, you should always be using an `id` column as an autoincremented primary key.

Second, use intelligent indexing. A dictionary (like the book, not the Python object) is a list of words indexed alphabetically. This allows quick lookups whenever you need a word, as long as you know how it's spelled. You could also imagine a dictionary that was organized alphabetically by the word's definition. This wouldn't be nearly as useful unless you were playing some strange game of *Jeopardy!* where a definition was presented and you needed to come up with the word. But in the world of database lookups, these sorts of situations happen. For example, you might have a field in your database that you will often be querying against:

```
>SELECT * FROM dictionary WHERE definition="A small furry animal that says meow";
+------+------+------------------------------------+
| id   | word | definition                         |
+------+------+------------------------------------+
| 200  | cat  | A small furry animal that says meow |
+------+------+------------------------------------+
1 row in set (0.00 sec)
```

You might very well want to add an additional key to this table (in addition to the key presumably already in place on the id) in order to make lookups on the definition column faster. Unfortunately, adding additional indexing requires more space for the new index, as well as some additional processing time when inserting new rows. To make this a little easier, you can tell MySQL to index only the first few characters in the column value. This command creates an index on the first 16 characters in the definition field:

```
CREATE INDEX definition ON dictionary (id, definition(16));
```

This index will make your lookups much faster when searching for words by their full definition, and also not add too much in the way of extra space and upfront processing time.

On the subject of query time versus database size (one of the fundamental balancing acts in database engineering), one of the common mistakes made, especially with web scraping where you often have large amounts of natural text data, is to store lots of repeating data. For example, say you want to measure the frequency of certain phrases that crop up across websites. These phrases might be found from a given list, or automatically generated via some text-analysis algorithm. You might be tempted to store the data as something like this:

```
+--------+--------------+------+-----+---------+----------------+
| Field  | Type         | Null | Key | Default | Extra          |
+--------+--------------+------+-----+---------+----------------+
| id     | int(11)      | NO   | PRI | NULL    | auto_increment |
| url    | varchar(200) | YES  |     | NULL    |                |
| phrase | varchar(200) | YES  |     | NULL    |                |
+--------+--------------+------+-----+---------+----------------+
```

This adds a row to the database each time you find a phrase on a site and records the URL it was found at. However, by splitting the data up into three separate tables, you can shrink your dataset enormously:

```
>DESCRIBE phrases
+--------+--------------+------+-----+---------+----------------+
| Field  | Type         | Null | Key | Default | Extra          |
+--------+--------------+------+-----+---------+----------------+
| id     | int(11)      | NO   | PRI | NULL    | auto_increment |
| phrase | varchar(200) | YES  |     | NULL    |                |
+--------+--------------+------+-----+---------+----------------+

>DESCRIBE urls
+-------+--------------+------+-----+---------+----------------+
| Field | Type         | Null | Key | Default | Extra          |
+-------+--------------+------+-----+---------+----------------+
| id    | int(11)      | NO   | PRI | NULL    | auto_increment |
| url   | varchar(200) | YES  |     | NULL    |                |
+-------+--------------+------+-----+---------+----------------+

>DESCRIBE foundInstances
+-------------+---------+------+-----+---------+----------------+
| Field       | Type    | Null | Key | Default | Extra          |
+-------------+---------+------+-----+---------+----------------+
| id          | int(11) | NO   | PRI | NULL    | auto_increment |
| urlId       | int(11) | YES  |     | NULL    |                |
| phraseId    | int(11) | YES  |     | NULL    |                |
| occurrences | int(11) | YES  |     | NULL    |                |
+-------------+---------+------+-----+---------+----------------+
```

Although the table definitions are larger, you can see that the majority of the columns are just integer id fields. These take up far less space. In addition, the full text of each URL and phrase is stored exactly once.

Unless you install some third-party package or keep meticulous logs, it can be impossible to tell when a piece of data was added, updated, or removed from your database. Depending on the available space for your data, the frequency of changes, and the importance of determining when those changes happened, you might want to consider keeping several timestamps in place: "created," "updated," and "deleted."

"Six Degrees" in MySQL

In Chapter 3, I introduced the "Six Degrees of Wikipedia" problem, in which the goal is to find the connection between any two Wikipedia articles through a series of links (i.e., find a way to get from one Wikipedia article to the next just by clicking on links from one page to the next).

In order to solve this problem, it is necessary to not only build bots that can crawl the site (which we have already done), but store the information in an architecturally sound way to make data analysis easy later on.

Autoincremented id columns, timestamps, and multiple tables: they all come into play here. In order to figure out how to best store this information, you need to think abstractly. A link is simply something that connects Page A to Page B. It could just as easily connect Page B to Page A, but this would be a separate link. We can uniquely identify a link by saying, "There exists a link on page A, which connects to page B. That is, INSERT INTO links (fromPageId, toPageId) VALUES (A, B); (where "A" and "B" are the unique IDs for the two pages).

A two-table system designed to store pages and links, along with creation dates and unique IDs, can be constructed as follows:

```
CREATE TABLE `wikipedia`.`pages` (
  `id` INT NOT NULL AUTO_INCREMENT,
  `url` VARCHAR(255) NOT NULL,
  `created` TIMESTAMP NOT NULL DEFAULT CURRENT_TIMESTAMP,
  PRIMARY KEY (`id`));

CREATE TABLE `wikipedia`.`links` (
  `id` INT NOT NULL AUTO_INCREMENT,
  `fromPageId` INT NULL,
  `toPageId` INT NULL,
  `created` TIMESTAMP NOT NULL DEFAULT CURRENT_TIMESTAMP,
  PRIMARY KEY (`id`));
```

Notice that, unlike with previous crawlers that print the title of the page, I'm not even storing the title of the page in the pages table. Why is that? Well, recording the title of the page requires that you actually visit the page to retrieve it. If we want to build an efficient web crawler to fill out these tables, we want to be able to store the page, as well as links to it, even if we haven't necessarily visited the page yet.

Of course, although this doesn't hold true for all sites, the nice thing about Wikipedia links and page titles is that one can be turned into the other through simple manipulation. For example, *http://en.wikipedia.org/wiki/Monty_Python* indicates that the title of the page is "Monty Python."

The following will store all pages on Wikipedia that have a "Bacon number" (the number of links between it and the page for Kevin Bacon, inclusive) of 6 or less: from urllib.request import urlopen.

```
from bs4 import BeautifulSoup
import re
import pymysql

conn = pymysql.connect(host='127.0.0.1', unix_socket='/tmp/mysql.sock', user=
                       'root', passwd=None, db='mysql', charset='utf8')
cur = conn.cursor()
cur.execute("USE wikipedia")

def insertPageIfNotExists(url):
    cur.execute("SELECT * FROM pages WHERE url = %s", (url))
    if cur.rowcount == 0:
        cur.execute("INSERT INTO pages (url) VALUES (%s)", (url))
```

```
            conn.commit()
            return cur.lastrowid
        else:
            return cur.fetchone()[0]

    def insertLink(fromPageId, toPageId):
        cur.execute("SELECT * FROM links WHERE fromPageId = %s AND toPageId = %s",
                        (int(fromPageId), int(toPageId)))
        if cur.rowcount == 0:
            cur.execute("INSERT INTO links (fromPageId, toPageId) VALUES (%s, %s)",
                        (int(fromPageId), int(toPageId)))
            conn.commit()

    pages = set()
    def getLinks(pageUrl, recursionLevel):
        global pages
        if recursionLevel > 4:
            return;
        pageId = insertPageIfNotExists(pageUrl)
        html = urlopen("http://en.wikipedia.org"+pageUrl)
        bsObj = BeautifulSoup(html)
        for link in bsObj.findAll("a",
                                href=re.compile("^(/wiki/)((?!:).)*$")):
                                insertLink(pageId,
                                        insertPageIfNotExists(link.attrs['href']))
            if link.attrs['href'] not in pages:
                #We have encountered a new page, add it and search it for links
                newPage = link.attrs['href']
                pages.add(newPage)
                getLinks(newPage, recursionLevel+1)
    getLinks("/wiki/Kevin_Bacon", 0)
    cur.close()
    conn.close()
```

Recursion is always a tricky thing to implement in code that is designed to run for a long time. In this case, a recursionLevel variable is passed to the getLinks function, which tracks how many times that function has been recursed on (each time it is called, recursionLevel is incremented). When recursionLevel reaches 5, the function automatically returns without searching further. This limit ensures that a stack overflow never occurs.

Keep in mind that this program would likely take days to complete. Although I have indeed run it, my database contains a mere fraction of the pages with a Kevin Bacon number of 6 or less, for the sake of Wikipedia's servers. However, this is sufficient for our analysis of finding paths between linked Wikipedia articles.

For the continuation of this problem and the final solution, see Chapter 8 on solving directed graph problems .

Email

Just like web pages are sent over HTTP, email is sent over SMTP (Simple Mail Transfer Protocol). And, just like you use a web server client to handle sending out web pages over HTTP, servers use various email clients, such as Sendmail, Postfix, or Mailman, to send and receive email.

Although sending email with Python is relatively easy to do, it does require that you have access to a server running SMTP. Setting up an SMTP client on your server or local machine is tricky, and outside the scope of this book, but there are many excellent resources to help with this task, particularly if you are running Linux or Mac OS X.

In the following code examples, I will assume that you are running an SMTP client locally. (To modify this code for a remote SMTP client, just change localhost to your remote server's address.)

Sending an email with Python requires just nine lines of code:

```
import smtplib
from email.mime.text import MIMEText

msg = MIMEText("The body of the email is here")

msg['Subject'] = "An Email Alert"
msg['From'] = "ryan@pythonscraping.com"
msg['To'] = "webmaster@pythonscraping.com"

s = smtplib.SMTP('localhost')
s.send_message(msg)
s.quit()
```

Python contains two important packages for sending emails: *smtplib* and *email*.

Python's email module contains useful formatting functions for creating email "packets" to send. The MIMEText object, used here, creates an empty email formatted for transfer with the low-level MIME (Multipurpose Internet Mail Extensions) protocol, across which the higher-level SMTP connections are made. The MIMEText object, msg, contains to/from email addresses, as well as a body and a header, which Python uses to create a properly formatted email.

The smtplib package contains information for handling the connection to the server. Just like a connection to a MySQL server, this connection must be torn down every time it is created, to avoid creating too many connections.

This basic email function can be extended and made more useful by enclosing it in a function:

```
import smtplib
from email.mime.text import MIMEText
```

```
from bs4 import BeautifulSoup
from urllib.request import urlopen
import time

def sendMail(subject, body):
    msg = MIMEText(body)
    msg['Subject'] = subject
    msg['From'] = "christmas_alerts@pythonscraping.com"
    msg['To'] = "ryan@pythonscraping.com"

s = smtplib.SMTP('localhost')
s.send_message(msg)
s.quit()

bsObj = BeautifulSoup(urlopen("https://isitchristmas.com/"))
while(bsObj.find("a", {"id":"answer"}).attrs['title'] == "NO"):
    print("It is not Christmas yet.")
    time.sleep(3600)
bsObj = BeautifulSoup(urlopen("https://isitchristmas.com/"))
sendMail("It's Christmas!",
        "According to http://itischristmas.com, it is Christmas!")
```

This particular script checks the website *https://isitchristmas.com* (the main feature of which is a giant "YES" or "NO," depending on the day of the year) once an hour. If it sees anything other than a "NO," it will send you an email alerting you that it's Christmas.

Although this particular program might not seem much more useful than a calendar hanging on your wall, it can be slightly tweaked to do a variety of extremely useful things. It can email you alerts in response to site outages, test failures, or even the appearance of an out-of-stock product you're waiting for on Amazon—none of which your wall calendar can do.

Reading Documents

It is tempting to think of the Internet primarily as a collection of text-based websites interspersed with newfangled web 2.0 multimedia content that can mostly be ignored for the purposes of web scraping. However, this ignores what the Internet most fundamentally is: a content-agnostic vehicle for transmitting files.

Although the Internet has been around in some form or another since the late 1960s, HTML didn't debut until 1992. Until then, the Internet consisted mostly of email and file transmission; the concept of web pages as we know them today didn't really exist. In other words, the Internet is not a collection of HTML files. It is a collection of information, with HTML files often being used as a frame to showcase it. Without being able to read a variety of document types, including text, PDF, images, video, email, and more, we are missing out on a huge part of the available data.

This chapter covers dealing with documents, whether you're downloading them to a local folder or reading them and extracting data. We'll also take a look at dealing with various types of text encoding, which can make it possible to even read foreign-language HTML pages.

Document Encoding

A document's encoding tells applications—whether they are your computer's operating system or your own Python code—how to read it. This encoding can usually be deduced from its file extension, although this file extension is not mandated by its encoding. I could, for example, save *myImage.jpg* as *myImage.txt* with no problems—at least until my text editor tried to open it. Fortunately, this situation is rare, and a document's file extension is usually all you need to know in order to read it correctly.

On a fundamental level, all documents are encoded in 0s and 1s. On top of that, there are encoding algorithms that define things such as "how many bits per character" or "how many bits represent the color for each pixel" (in the case of image files). On top of that, you might have a layer of compression, or some space-reducing algorithm, as is the case with PNG files.

Although dealing with non-HTML files might seem intimidating at first, rest assured that with the right library, Python will be properly equipped to deal with any format of information you want to throw at it. The only difference between a text file, a video file, and an image file is how their 0s and 1s are interpreted. In this chapter, I'll cover several commonly encountered types of files: text, PDFs, PNGs, and GIFs.

Text

It is somewhat unusual to have files stored as plain text online, but it is popular among bare-bones or "old-school" sites to have large repositories of text files. For example, the Internet Engineering Task Force (IETF) stores all of its published documents as HTML, PDF, and text files (see *http://bit.ly/1RCAj2f* as an example). Most browsers will display these text files just fine and you should be able to scrape them with no problem.

For most basic text documents, such as the practice file located at http://www.python-scraping.com/pages/warandpeace/chapter1.txt, you can use the following method:

```
from urllib.request import urlopen
textPage = urlopen(
            "http://www.pythonscraping.com/pages/warandpeace/chapter1.txt")
print(textPage.read())
```

Normally, when we retrieve a page using urlopen, we turn it into a BeautifulSoup object in order to parse the HTML. In this case, we can read the page directly. Turning it into a BeautifulSoup object, while perfectly possible, would be counterproductive—there's no HTML to parse, so the library would be useless. Once the text file is read in as a string, you merely have to analyze it like you would any other string read into Python. The disadvantage here, of course, is that you don't have the ability to use HTML tags as context clues, pointing you in the direction of the text you actually need, versus the text you don't want. This can present a challenge when you're trying to extract certain information from text files.

Text Encoding and the Global Internet

Remember earlier when I said a file extension was all you needed to read a file correctly? Well, strangely enough, that rule doesn't apply to the most basic of all documents: the *.txt* file.

Nine times out of 10, reading in text using the previously described methods will work just fine. However, dealing with text on the Internet can be a tricky business.

Next we'll cover the basics of English and foreign-language encoding, from ASCII to Unicode to ISO, and how to deal with them.

A brief overview of encoding types

In the early 1990s, a nonprofit named The Unicode Consortium attempted to bring about a universal text encoder by establishing encodings for every character that needs to be used in any text document, in any language. The goal was to include everything from the Latin alphabet this book is written in, to Cyrillic (кириллица), Chinese pictograms (象形), math and logic symbols ($\Sigma, \geq$), and even emoticons and "miscellaneous" symbols, such as the biohazard sign (☣) and peace symbol (☮).

The resulting encoder, as you might already know, was dubbed UTF-8, which stands for, confusingly, "*Universal Character Set - Transformation Format 8 bit*". It is a common misconception that UTF-8 stores all characters in 8 bits. However, the "8 bit" refers to the smallest size that a character requires to be displayed, not the maximum size. (If every character in UTF-8 were really stored in 8 bits, this would allow only 2^8, or 256 possible characters. Clearly not enough room for everything from a Chinese pictogram to a peace symbol.)

In reality, each character in UTF-8 starts with an indicator that says "only one byte is used to encode this character" or "the next two bytes encodes a single character," with up to four bytes being possible. Because these four bytes also contain the information about how many bytes are being used to encode the character, the full 32 bits (32 = 4 bytes x 8 bits per byte) are not used; rather, up to 21 bits of information can be used, for a total of 2,097,152 possible characters, of which, 1,114,112 are currently used.

Although Unicode was a godsend for many applications, some habits are hard to break, and ASCII is still a popular choice for many users.

ASCII, a text-encoding standard used since the 1960s, uses 7 bits to encode each of its characters, for a total of 2^7, or 128 characters. This is enough for the Latin alphabet (both uppercase and lowercase), punctuation, and, essentially all of the characters found on the average English speaker's keyboard.

In 1960, of course, the difference between storing a text file with 7 bits per character and 8 bits per character was significant because storage was so expensive. Computer scientists of the day fought over whether an extra bit should be added for the convenience of having a nice round number versus the practicality of files requiring less storage space. In the end, 7 bits won. However, in modern computing, each 7-bit sequence is padded with an extra "0" at the beginning,[1] leaving us with the worst of both worlds—14% larger files, and the lack of flexibility of only 128 characters.

---

1 This "padding" bit will come back to haunt us with the ISO standards, a little later.

When UTF-8 was designed, the creators decided to use this "padding bit" in ASCII documents to their advantage by declaring all bytes starting with a "0" to indicate that only one byte is used in the character, and making the two encoding schemes for ASCII and UTF-8 identical. Therefore, the following characters are valid in both UTF-8 and ASCII:

```
01000001 - A
01000010 - B
01000011 - C
```

And the following characters are valid only in UTF-8, and will be rendered as "nonprintable" if the document is interpreted as an ASCII document:

```
11000011 10000000 - À
11000011 10011111 - ß
11000011 10100111 - ç
```

In addition to UTF-8, there are other UTF standards such as UTF-16, UTF-24, and UTF-32, although documents encoded in these formats are rarely encountered except in unusual circumstances, which are outside the scope of this book.

The problem with all Unicode standards, of course, is that any document written in a single foreign language is much larger than it has to be. Although your language might only require 100 or so characters to be used, you will need at least 16 bits for each character rather than just 8 bits, as is the case for the English-specific ASCII. This makes foreign-language text documents about twice the size of English-language text documents, at least for foreign languages that don't use the Latin character set.

ISO solves this problem by creating specific encodings for each language. Like Unicode, it has the same encodings that ASCII does, but uses the "padding" 0 bit at the beginning of every character to allow it to create special characters for all of the languages that require them. This works best for European languages that also rely heavily on the Latin alphabet (which remain in positions 0-127 in the encoding), but require some additional special characters. This allows ISO-8859-1 (designed for the Latin alphabet) to have symbols such as fractions (e.g., ½) or the copyright sign (©).

Other ISO character sets, such as ISO-8859-9 (Turkish), ISO-8859-2 (German, among other languages), and ISO-8859-15 (French, among other languages) can also be found with some regularity.

Although the popularity of ISO-encoded documents has been declining in recent years, about 9% of websites on the Internet are still encoded with some flavor of ISO,[2] making it essential to know about and check for encodings before scraping a site.

---

[2] According to *http://w3techs.com/technologies/history_overview/character_encoding*, which uses web crawlers to gather these sorts of statistics.

Encodings in action

In the previous section, we've used the default settings for urlopen to read in .txt documents you might encounter on the Internet. This works great for most English text. However, the second you encounter Russian, Arabic, or even a word like résumé, you might run into problems.

Take the following code, for example:

```
from urllib.request import urlopen
textPage = urlopen(
            "http://www.pythonscraping.com/pages/warandpeace/chapter1-ru.txt")
print(textPage.read())
```

This reads in the first chapter of the original *War and Peace* (written in Russian and French) and prints it to the screen. This screen text reads, in part:

```
b"\xd0\xa7\xd0\x90\xd0\xa1\xd0\xa2\xd0\xac \xd0\x9f\xd0\x95\xd0\xa0\xd0\x92\xd0\
x90\xd0\xaf\n\nI\n\n\xe2\x80\x94 Eh bien, mon prince.
```

In addition, visiting this page in most browsers results in gibberish (see Figure 6-1).

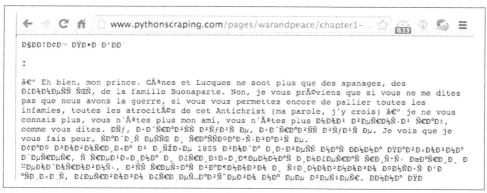

Figure 6-1. French and Cyrillic text encoded in ISO-8859-1, the default text document encoding in many browsers

Even for native Russian speakers, that might be a bit difficult to make sense of. The problem is that Python is attempting to read the document as an ASCII document, whereas the browser is attempting to read it as an ISO-8859-1 encoded document. Neither one, of course, realizes it's a UTF-8 document.

We can explicitly define the string to be UTF-8, which correctly formats the output into Cyrillic characters:

```
from urllib.request import urlopen
textPage = urlopen(
            "http://www.pythonscraping.com/pages/warandpeace/chapter1-ru.txt")
print(str(textPage.read(), 'utf-8'))
```

Using this concept in `BeautifulSoup` and Python 3.x looks like this:

```
html = urlopen("http://en.wikipedia.org/wiki/Python_(programming_language)")
bsObj = BeautifulSoup(html)
content = bsObj.find("div", {"id":"mw-content-text"}).get_text()
content = bytes(content, "UTF-8")
content = content.decode("UTF-8")
```

You might be tempted to use UTF-8 encoding for every web scraper you write. After all, UTF-8 will also handle ASCII characters smoothly. However, it's important to remember the 9% of websites out there that use some version of ISO encoding. Unfortunately, in the case of text documents, it's impossible to concretely determine what encoding a document has. There are some libraries that can examine the document and make a best guess (using a little logic to realize that "Ñ€Ð°ÑÑÐ°Ð·Ñ" is probably not a word), but many times it's wrong.

Fortunately, in the case of HTML pages, the encoding is usually contained in a tag found in the `<head>` section of the site. Most sites, particularly English-language sites, have the tag:

```
<meta charset="utf-8" />
```

Whereas the European Computer Manufacturers Association's website (*http://www.ecma-international.org/*) has this tag:[3]

```
<META HTTP-EQUIV="Content-Type" CONTENT="text/html; charset=iso-8859-1">
```

If you plan on doing a lot of web scraping, particularly of international sites, it might be wise to look for this meta tag and use the encoding it recommends when reading the contents of the page.

CSV

When web scraping you are likely to encounter either a CSV file or a coworker who likes data formatted in this way. Fortunately, Python has a fantastic library (*http://bit.ly/1ADxgCW*) for both reading and writing CSV files. Although this library is capable of handling many variations of CSV, I will focus primarily on the standard format. If you have a special case you need to handle, consult the documentation!

Reading CSV Files

Python's csv library is geared primarily toward working with local files, on the assumption that the CSV data you need is stored on your machine. Unfortunately,

---

3 Ecma was one of the original contributors to the ISO standard, so it's no surprise its website is encoded with a flavor of ISO.

---

this isn't always the case, especially when you're web scraping. There are several ways to work around this:

- Download the file locally by hand and point Python at the local file location
- Write a Python script to download the file, read it, and (optionally) delete it after retrieval
- Retrieve the file as a string from the Web, and wrap the string in a StringIO object so that it behaves like a file

Although the first two options are workable, taking up hard drive space with files when you could very easily keep them in memory is bad practice. It's much better to read the file in as a string and wrap it in an object that allows Python to treat it like a file, without ever actually saving the file. The following script retrieves a CSV file from the Internet (in this case, a list of Monty Python albums at *http://bit.ly/ 1QjuMv8*) and prints it, row by row, to the terminal:

```
from urllib.request import urlopen
from io import StringIO
import csv

data = urlopen("http://pythonscraping.com/files/MontyPythonAlbums.csv")
            .read().decode('ascii', 'ignore')
dataFile = StringIO(data)
csvReader = csv.reader(dataFile)

for row in csvReader:
print(row)
```

The output is too long to print in full but should look something like:

```
['Name', 'Year']
["Monty Python's Flying Circus", '1970']
['Another Monty Python Record', '1971']
["Monty Python's Previous Record", '1972']
...
```

As you can see from the code sample, the reader object returned by csv.reader is iterable, and composed of Python list objects. Because of this, each row in the csvReader object is accessible in the following way:

```
for row in csvReader:
    print("The album \""+row[0]+"\" was released in "+str(row[1]))
```

Which gives the output:

```
The album "Name" was released in Year
The album "Monty Python's Flying Circus" was released in 1970
The album "Another Monty Python Record" was released in 1971
The album "Monty Python's Previous Record" was released in 1972
...
```

Notice the first line: The album 'Name' was released in Year. Although this might be an easy-to-ignore result when writing example code, you don't want this getting into your data in the real world. A lesser programmer might simply skip the first row in the csvReader object, or write in some special case to handle it. Fortunately, there's an alternative to the csv.reader function that takes care of all of this for you automatically. Enter DictReader:

```
from urllib.request import urlopen
from io import StringIO
import csv

data = urlopen("http://pythonscraping.com/files/MontyPythonAlbums.csv")
            .read().decode('ascii', 'ignore')
dataFile = StringIO(data)
dictReader = csv.DictReader(dataFile)

print(dictReader.fieldnames)

for row in dictReader:
    print(row)
```

csv.DictReader returns the values of each row in the CSV file as dictionary objects rather than list objects, with fieldnames stored in the variable dictReader.field names and as keys in each Dictionary object:

```
['Name', 'Year']
{'Name': "Monty Python's Flying Circus", 'Year': '1970'}
{'Name': 'Another Monty Python Record', 'Year': '1971'}
{'Name': "Monty Python's Previous Record", 'Year': '1972'}
```

The downside, of course, is that it takes slightly longer to create, process, and print these DictReaders as opposed to csvReaders, but the convenience and usability is often worth the additional overhead.

PDF

As a Linux user, I know the pain of being sent a *.docx* file that my non-Microsoft software mangles and struggling trying to find the codecs to interpret some new Apple media format. In some ways, Adobe was revolutionary in creating its Portable Document Format in 1993. PDFs allowed users on different platforms to view image and text documents in exactly the same way, regardless of the platform they were viewing it on.

Although storing PDFs on the Web is somewhat passé (why store content in a static, slow-loading format when you could write it up as HTML?), PDFs remain ubiquitous, particularly when dealing with official forms and filings.

In 2009, a Briton named Nick Innes made the news when he requested public student test result information from the Buckinghamshire City Council, which was available under the United Kindom's version of the Freedom of Information Act. After some repeated requests and denials, he finally received the information he was looking for —in the form of 184 PDF documents.

Although Innes persisted and eventually received a more properly formatted database, had he been an expert web scraper he likely could have saved himself a lot of time in the courts and used the PDF documents directly, with one of Python's many PDF parsing modules.

Unfortunately, many of the PDF parsing libraries built for Python 2.x were not upgraded with the launch of Python 3.x. However, because the PDF is a relatively simple and open source document format, there are many decent Python libraries, even in Python 3.x, that can read them.

PDFMiner3K is one such relatively easy-to-use library. It is very flexible, allowing for command-line usage or integration into existing code. It can also handle a variety of language encodings—again, something that often comes in handy on the Web.

You can download this Python module (*http://bit.ly/1FNj3Cb*) and install it by unzipping the folder and running:

```
$python setup.py install
```

The documentation is located at */pdfminer3k-1.3.0/docs/index.html* within the extracted folder, although the current documentation tends to be geared more toward the command-line interface than integration with Python code.

Here is a basic implementation that allows you to read arbitrary PDFs to a string, given a local file object:

```python
from pdfminer.pdfinterp import PDFResourceManager, process_pdf
from pdfminer.converter import TextConverter
from pdfminer.layout import LAParams
from io import StringIO
from io import open

def readPDF(pdfFile):
    rsrcmgr = PDFResourceManager()
    retstr = StringIO()
    laparams = LAParams()
    device = TextConverter(rsrcmgr, retstr, laparams=laparams)

    process_pdf(rsrcmgr, device, pdfFile)
    device.close()

    content = retstr.getvalue()
    retstr.close()
    return content
```

```
pdfFile = urlopen("http://pythonscraping.com/pages/warandpeace/chapter1.pdf");
outputString = readPDF(pdfFile)
print(outputString)
pdfFile.close()
```

The nice thing about this function is that if you're working with files locally, you can simply substitute a regular Python file object for the one returned by urlopen, and use the line:

```
pdfFile = open("../pages/warandpeace/chapter1.pdf", 'rb')
```

The output might not be perfect, especially for PDFs with images, oddly formatted text, or text arranged in tables or charts. However, for most text-only PDFs the output should be no different than if the PDF were a text file.

Microsoft Word and .docx

At the risk of offending my friends at Microsoft: I do not like Microsoft Word. Not because it's necessarily a bad piece of software, but because of the way its users misuse it. It has a particular talent for turning what should be simple text documents or PDFs into large, slow, difficult-to-open beasts that often lose all formatting from machine to machine, and are, for whatever reason, editable when the content is often meant to be static. Word files were never meant for frequent transmission. Nevertheless, they are ubiquitous on certain sites, containing important documents, information, and even charts and multimedia; in short, everything that can and should be created with HTML.

Before about 2008, Microsoft Office products used the proprietary *.doc* file format. This binary-file format was difficult to read and poorly supported by other word processors. In an effort to get with the times and adopt a standard that was used by many other pieces of software, Microsoft decided to use the Open Office XML-based standard, which made the files compatible with open source and other software.

Unfortunately, Python's support for this file format, used by Google Docs, Open Office, and Microsoft Office, still isn't great. There is the python-docx library (*http://bit.ly/1HYruOw*), but this only gives users the ability to create documents and read only basic file data such as the size and title of the file, not the actual contents. To read the contents of a Microsoft Office file, we'll need to roll our own solution.

The first step is to read the XML from the file:

```
from zipfile import ZipFile
from urllib.request import urlopen
from io import BytesIO

wordFile = urlopen("http://pythonscraping.com/pages/AWordDocument.docx").read()
wordFile = BytesIO(wordFile)
```

```
document = ZipFile(wordFile)
xml_content = document.read('word/document.xml')
print(xml_content.decode('utf-8'))
```

This reads a remote Word document as a binary file object (BytesIO is analogous to StringIO, used earlier in this chapter), unzips it using Python's core zipfile library (all *.docx* files are zipped to save space), and then reads the unzipped file, which is XML.

The Word document at *http://bit.ly/1Jc8Zql* is shown in Figure 6-2.

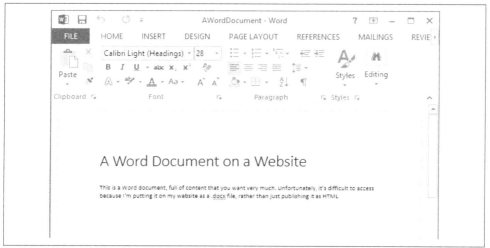

Figure 6-2. This is a Word document that's full of content you might want very much but it's difficult to access because I'm putting it on my website as a .docx file instead of publishing it as HTML

The output of the Python script reading my simple Word document is the following:

```
<!--?xml version="1.0" encoding="UTF-8" standalone="yes"?-->
<w:document mc:ignorable="w14 w15 wp14" xmlns:m="http://schemas.openx
mlformats.org/officeDocument/2006/math" xmlns:mc="http://schemas.open
xmlformats.org/markup-compatibility/2006" xmlns:o="urn:schemas-micros
oft-com:office:office" xmlns:r="http://schemas.openxmlformats.org/off
iceDocument/2006/relationships" xmlns:v="urn:schemas-microsoft-com:vm
l" xmlns:w="http://schemas.openxmlformats.org/wordprocessingml/2006/m
ain" xmlns:w10="urn:schemas-microsoft-com:office:word" xmlns:w14="htt
p://schemas.microsoft.com/office/word/2010/wordml" xmlns:w15="http://
schemas.microsoft.com/office/word/2012/wordml" xmlns:wne="http://sche
mas.microsoft.com/office/word/2006/wordml" xmlns:wp="http://schemas.o
penxmlformats.org/drawingml/2006/wordprocessingDrawing" xmlns:wp14="h
ttp://schemas.microsoft.com/office/word/2010/wordprocessingDrawing" x
mlns:wpc="http://schemas.microsoft.com/office/word/2010/wordprocessin
gCanvas" xmlns:wpg="http://schemas.microsoft.com/office/word/2010/wor
dprocessingGroup" xmlns:wpi="http://schemas.microsoft.com/office/word
```

```
/2010/wordprocessingInk" xmlns:wps="http://schemas.microsoft.com/offi
ce/word/2010/wordprocessingShape"><w:body><w:p w:rsidp="00764658" w:r
sidr="00764658" w:rsidrdefault="00764658"><w:ppr><w:pstyle w:val="Tit
le"></w:pstyle></w:ppr><w:r><w:t>A Word Document on a Website</w:t></
w:r><w:bookmarkstart w:id="0" w:name="_GoBack"></w:bookmarkstart><w:b
ookmarkend w:id="0"></w:bookmarkend></w:p><w:p w:rsidp="00764658" w:r
sidr="00764658" w:rsidrdefault="00764658"></w:p><w:p w:rsidp="0076465
8" w:rsidr="00764658" w:rsidrdefault="00764658" w:rsidrpr="00764658">
<w: r> <w:t>This is a Word document, full of content that you want ve
ry much. Unfortunately, it's difficult to access because I'm putting
it on my website as a .</w:t></w:r><w:prooferr w:type="spellStart"></
w:prooferr><w:r><w:t>docx</w:t></w:r><w:prooferr w:type="spellEnd"></
w:prooferr> <w:r> <w:t xml:space="preserve"> file, rather than just p
ublishing it as HTML</w:t> </w:r> </w:p> <w:sectpr w:rsidr="00764658"
 w:rsidrpr="00764658"> <w:pgszw:h="15840" w:w="12240"></w:pgsz><w:pgm
ar w:bottom="1440" w:footer="720" w:gutter="0" w:header="720" w:left=
"1440" w:right="1440" w:top="1440"></w:pgmar> <w:cols w:space="720"><
/w:cols&g; <w:docgrid w:linepitch="360"></w:docgrid> </w:sectpr> </w:
body> </w:document>
```

There's clearly a lot of information here but it's buried. Fortunately, all of the text in the document, including the title at the top, is contained in <w:t> tags, which makes it easy to grab:

```python
from zipfile import ZipFile
from urllib.request import urlopen
from io import BytesIO
from bs4 import BeautifulSoup

wordFile = urlopen("http://pythonscraping.com/pages/AWordDocument.docx").read()
wordFile = BytesIO(wordFile)
document = ZipFile(wordFile)
xml_content = document.read('word/document.xml')

wordObj = BeautifulSoup(xml_content.decode('utf-8'))
textStrings = wordObj.findAll("w:t")
for textElem in textStrings:
    print(textElem.text)
```

The output isn't perfect but it's getting there, and printing each <w:t> tag on a new line makes it easy to see how Word is splitting up the text:

```
A Word Document on a Website
This is a Word document, full of content that you want very much. Unfortunately,
it's difficult to access because I'm putting it on my website as a . docx
    file, rather than just publishing it as HTML
```

Notice that the word "docx" is on its own line. In the original XML, it is surrounded with the tag <w:proofErr w:type="spellStart"/>. This is Word's way of highlighting "docx" with the red squiggly underline, indicating that it believes there's a spelling error in the name of its own file format.

The title of the document is preceded by the style descriptor tag `<w:pstyle w:val="Title">`. Although this doesn't make it extremely easy for us to identify titles (or other styled text) as such, using BeautifulSoup's navigation features can be useful:

```
textStrings = wordObj.findAll("w:t")
for textElem in textStrings:
    closeTag = ""
    try:
        style = textElem.parent.previousSibling.find("w:pstyle")
        if style is not None and style["w:val"] == "Title":
        print("<h1>")
        closeTag = "</h1>"
    except AttributeError:
    #No tags to print
    pass
    print(textElem.text)
    print(closeTag)
```

This function can be easily expanded to print tags around a variety of different text styles or label them in some other way.

Advanced Scraping

You've laid some web-scraping groundwork; now comes the fun part. Up until this point our web scrapers have been relatively dumb. They're unable to retrieve information unless it's immediately presented to them in a nice format by the server. They take all information at face value and simply store it without any analysis. They get tripped up by forms, website interaction, and even JavaScript. In short, they're no good for retrieving information unless that information really wants to be retrieved.

This part of the book will help you analyze raw data to get the story beneath the data —the story that websites often hide beneath layers of JavaScript, login forms, and antiscraping measures.

You'll learn how to use web scrapers to test your sites, automate processes, and access the Internet on a large scale. By the end of this section, you should have the tools to gather and manipulate nearly any type of data, in any form, across any part of the Internet.

Cleaning Your Dirty Data

So far in this book we've ignored the problem of badly formatted data by using generally well-formatted data sources, dropping data entirely if it deviated from what we were expecting. But often, in web scraping, you can't be too picky about where you get your data from.

Due to errant punctuation, inconsistent capitalization, line breaks, and misspellings, dirty data can be a big problem on the Web. In this chapter, I'll cover a few tools and techniques to help you prevent the problem at the source by changing the way you write code, and clean the data once it's in the database.

Cleaning in Code

Just as you write code to handle overt exceptions, you should practice defensive coding to handle the unexpected.

In linguistics, an *n-gram* is a sequence of *n* words used in text or speech. When doing natural-language analysis, it can often be handy to break up a piece of text by looking for commonly used n-grams, or recurring sets of words that are often used together.

In this section, we will focus on obtaining properly formatted n-grams rather than using them to do any analysis. Later, in Chapter 8, you can see 2-grams and 3-grams in action to do text summarization and analysis.

The following will return a list of 2-grams found in the Wikipedia article on the Python programming language:

```
from urllib.request import urlopen
from bs4 import BeautifulSoup

def ngrams(input, n):
  input = input.split(' ')
```

```
    output = []
    for i in range(len(input)-n+1):
      output.append(input[i:i+n])
    return output

html = urlopen("http://en.wikipedia.org/wiki/Python_(programming_language)")
bsObj = BeautifulSoup(html)
content = bsObj.find("div", {"id":"mw-content-text"}).get_text()
ngrams = ngrams(content, 2)
print(ngrams)
print("2-grams count is: "+str(len(ngrams)))
```

The ngrams function takes in an input string, splits it into a sequence of words (assuming all words are separated by spaces), and adds the n-gram (in this case, a 2-gram) that each word starts into an array.

This returns some genuinely interesting and useful 2-grams from the text:

```
['of', 'free'], ['free', 'and'], ['and', 'open-source'], ['open-source', 'softwa
re']
```

but also a lot of junk:

```
['software\nOutline\nSPDX\n\n\n\n\n\n\n\nOperating', 'system\nfamilies\n\n\n\n
AROS\nBSD\nDarwin\neCos\nFreeDOS\nGNU\nHaiku\nInferno\nLinux\nMach\nMINIX\nOpenS
olaris\nPlan'], ['system\nfamilies\n\n\n\nAROS\nBSD\nDarwin\neCos\nFreeDOS\nGNU\
nHaiku\nInferno\nLinux\nMach\nMINIX\nOpenSolaris\nPlan', '9\nReactOS\nTUD:OS\n\n
\n\n\n\n\n\nDevelopment\n\n\n\nBasic'], ['9\nReactOS\nTUD:OS\n\n\n\n\n\n\n\n\n
Development\n\n\n\nBasic', 'For']
```

In addition, because there is a 2-gram created for each and every word encountered (except for the last one), there are 7,411 2-grams in the article at the time of this writing. Not a very manageable dataset!

Using some regular expressions to remove escape characters (such as \n) and filtering to remove any Unicode characters, we can clean up the output somewhat:

```
def ngrams(input, n):
    content = re.sub('\n+', " ", content)
    content = re.sub(' +', " ", content)
    content = bytes(content, "UTF-8")
    content = content.decode("ascii", "ignore")
    print(content)
    input = input.split(' ')
    output = []
    for i in range(len(input)-n+1):
        output.append(input[i:i+n])
    return output
```

This first replaces all instances of the newline character (or multiple newline characters) with a space, then replaces all instances of multiple spaces in a row with a single space, ensuring that all words have one space between them. Then, escape characters are eliminated by encoding the content with UTF-8.

These steps greatly improve the output of the function, but there are still some issues:

```
['Pythoneers.[43][44]', 'Syntax'], ['7', '/'], ['/', '3'], ['3', '=='], ['==', '
2']
```

At this point, the decisions that need to be made in order to process this data become more interesting. There are a few more rules we can add to get closer to ideal data:

- Single character "words" should be discarded, unless that character is "i" or "a"
- Wikipedia citation marks (numbers enclosed in brackets) should be discarded
- Punctuation marks should be discarded (note: this rule is somewhat of a simplification and will be explored in greater detail in Chapter 9, but is fine for the purpose of this example)

Now that the list of "cleaning tasks" is getting longer, it's best to move these out and put them in a separate function, cleanInput:

```python
from urllib.request import urlopen
from bs4 import BeautifulSoup
import re
import string

def cleanInput(input):
    input = re.sub('\n+', " ", input)
    input = re.sub('\[[0-9]*\]', "", input)
    input = re.sub(' +', " ", input)
    input = bytes(input, "UTF-8")
    input = input.decode("ascii", "ignore")
    cleanInput = []
    input = input.split(' ')
    for item in input:
        item = item.strip(string.punctuation)
        if len(item) > 1 or (item.lower() == 'a' or item.lower() == 'i'):
            cleanInput.append(item)
    return cleanInput

def ngrams(input, n):
    input = cleanInput(input)
    output = []
    for i in range(len(input)-n+1):
        output.append(input[i:i+n])
    return output
```

Note the use of import string and string.punctuation to get a list of all punctuation characters in Python. You can view the output of string.punctuation from a Python terminal:

```
>>> import string
>>> print(string.punctuation)
!"#$%&'()*+,-./:;<=>?@[\]^_`{|}~
```

By using `item.strip(string.punctuation)` inside a loop iterating through all words in the content, any punctuation characters on either side of the word will be stripped, although hyphenated words (where the punctuation character is bounded by letters on either side) will remain untouched.

The output of this effort results in much cleaner 2-grams:

```
['Linux', 'Foundation'], ['Foundation', 'Mozilla'], ['Mozilla', 'Foundation'], [
'Foundation', 'Open'], ['Open', 'Knowledge'], ['Knowledge', 'Foundation'], ['Fou
ndation', 'Open'], ['Open', 'Source']
```

Data Normalization

Everyone has encountered a poorly designed web form: "Enter your phone number. Your phone number must be in the form 'xxx-xxx-xxxx.'"

As a good programmer, you will likely think to yourself, "Why don't they just strip out the non-numeric characters I put in there and do it themselves?" Data normalization is the process of ensuring that strings that are linguistically or logically equivalent to each other, such as the phone numbers "(555) 123-4567" and "555.123.4567," are displayed, or at least compared, as equivalent.

Using the n-gram code from the previous section, we can add on some data normalization features.

One obvious problem with this code is that it contains many duplicate 2-grams. Every 2-gram it encounters gets added to the list, with no record of its frequency. Not only is it interesting to record the frequency of these 2-grams, rather than just their existence, but it can be useful in charting the effects of changes to the cleaning and data normalization algorithms. If data is normalized successfully, the total number of unique n-grams will be reduced, while the total count of n-grams found (i.e., the number of unique or non-unique items identified as a n-gram) will not be reduced. In other words, there will be fewer "buckets" for the same number of n-grams.

Unfortunately for the purposes of this exercise, Python dictionaries are unsorted. "Sorting a dictionary" doesn't make any sense, unless you are copying the values in the dictionary to some other content type and sorting that. An easy solution to this problem is the `OrderedDict`, from Python's collections library:

```
from collections import OrderedDict

...

ngrams = ngrams(content, 2)
ngrams = OrderedDict(sorted(ngrams.items(), key=lambda t: t[1], reverse=True))
print(ngrams)
```

Here I'm taking advantage of Python's `sorted` function (*https://docs.python.org/3/howto/sorting.html*) in order to put the items into a new `OrderedDict` object, sorted by the value. The results:

```
("['Software', 'Foundation']", 40), ("['Python', 'Software']", 38), ("['of', 'th
e']", 35), ("['Foundation', 'Retrieved']", 34), ("['of', 'Python']", 28), ("['in
', 'the']", 21), ("['van', 'Rossum']", 18)
```

As of this writing, there are 7,696 total 2-grams and 6,005 unique 2-grams, with the most popular 2-gram being "Software Foundation," followed by "Python Software." However, analysis of the results shows that "Python Software" actually appears in the form of "Python software" an additional two times. Similarly, both "van Rossum" and "Van Rossum" make an appearance in the list separately.

Adding the line:

```
input = input.upper()
```

to the `cleanInput` function keeps the total number of 2-grams found steady at 7,696, while decreasing the number of unique 2-grams to 5,882.

Beyond this, it's usually good to stop and consider how much computing power you want to expend normalizing data. There are a number of situations in which different spellings of words are equivalent, but in order to resolve this equivalency you need to run a check on every single word to see if it matches any of your preprogrammed equivalencies.

For example, "Python 1st" and "Python first" both appear in the list of 2-grams. However, to make a blanket rule that says "All 'first,' 'second,' 'third,' etc. will be resolved to 1st, 2nd, 3rd, etc. (or vice versa)" would result in an additional 10 or so checks per word.

Similarly, the inconsistent use of hyphens ("co-ordinated" versus "coordinated"), misspellings, and other natural language incongruities will affect the groupings of *n*-grams, and might muddy the results of the output if the incongruities are common enough.

One solution, in the case of hyphenated words, might be to remove hyphens entirely and treat the word as a single string, which would require only a single operation. However, this would also mean that hyphenated phrases (an all-too-common occurrence) will be treated as a single word. Going the other route and treating hyphens as spaces might be a better option. Just be prepared for the occasional "co ordinated" and "ordinated attack" to slip in!

Cleaning After the Fact

There is only so much you can, or want to do, in code. In addition, you might be dealing with a dataset that you didn't create, or a dataset that would be a challenge to even know how to clean without seeing it first.

A knee-jerk reaction that many programmers have in this sort of situation is "write a script," which can be an excellent solution. However, there are also third-party tools, such as OpenRefine, that are capable of not only cleaning data quickly and easily, but allow your data to be easily seen and used by nonprogrammers.

OpenRefine

OpenRefine (*http://openrefine.org/*) is an open source project started by a company called Metaweb in 2009. Google acquired Metaweb in 2010, changing the name of the project from Freebase Gridworks to Google Refine. In 2012, Google dropped support for Refine and changed the name again, to OpenRefine, where anyone is welcome to contribute to the development of the project.

Installation

OpenRefine is unusual in that although its interface is run in a browser, it is technically a desktop application that must be downloaded and installed. You can download the application for Linux, Windows, and Mac OS X from its website (*http://bit.ly/1HEIGmS*).

 If you're a Mac user and run into any trouble opening the file, go to System Preferences → Security & Privacy → General → and check "Anywhere" under "Allow apps downloaded from." Unfortunately, during the transition from a Google project to an open source project, OpenRefine appears to have lost its legitimacy in the eyes of Apple.

In order to use OpenRefine, you'll need to save your data as a CSV (file refer back to "Storing Data to CSV" in Chapter 5 if you need a refresher on how to do this). Alternatively, if you have your data stored in a database, you might be able to export it to a CSV file.

Using OpenRefine

In the following examples, we'll use data scraped from Wikipedia's "Comparison of Text Editors" table (*http://bit.ly/1BA6h6d*); see Figure 7-1. Although this table is relatively well formatted, it contains many edits by people over a long time, so it has a few minor formatting inconsistencies. In addition, because its data is meant to be read by humans rather than machines, some of the formatting choices (e.g., using "Free" rather than "$0.00") is inappropriate for programming inputs.

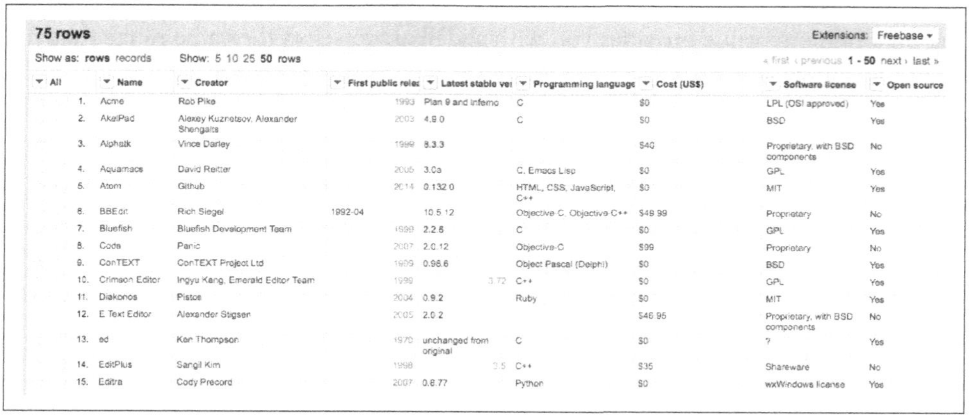

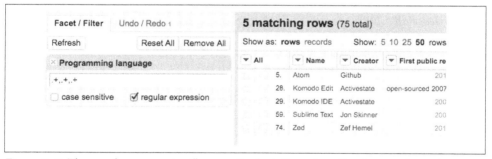

Figure 7-1. Data from Wikipedia's "comparison of text editors" as shown in the main OpenRefine screen

The first thing to note about OpenRefine is that each column label has an arrow next to it. This arrow provides a menu of tools that can be used with that column for filtering, sorting, transforming, or removing data.

Filtering. Data filtering can be performed using two methods: filters and facets. Filters are good for using regular expressions to filter the data; for example, "Only show me data that contains four or more comma-seperated programming languages in the Programming language column," seen in Figure 7-2.

Figure 7-2. The regular expression ".+,.+,.+" selects for values that have at least three comma-separated items

Filters can be combined, edited, and added easily by manipulating the blocks in the righthand column. They also can be combined with facets.

Facets are great for including or excluding data based on the entire contents of the column. (e.g., "Show all rows that use the GPL or MIT license, and were first released after 2005," seen in Figure 7-3). They have built-in filtering tools. For instance, filtering on a numeric value provides you with slide bars to select the value range that you want to include.

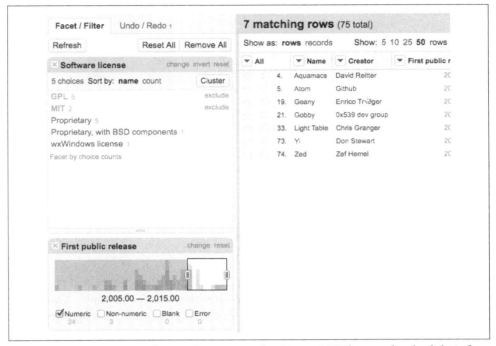

Figure 7-3. This displays all text editors using the GPL or MIT license that had their first public release after 2005

However you filter your data, it can be exported at any point to one of several types of formats that OpenRefine supports. This includes CSV, HTML (an HTML table), Excel, and several other formats.

Cleaning.   Data filtering can be done successfully only if the data is relatively clean to start with. For instance, in the facet example in the previous section, a text editor that had a release date of "01-01-2006" would not have been selected in the "First public release" facet, which was looking for a value of "2006" and ignoring values that didn't look like that.

Data transformation is performed in OpenRefine using the OpenRefine Expression Language, called GREL (the "G" is left over from OpenRefine's previous name, Google Refine). This language is used to create short lambda functions that transform the values in the cells based on simple rules. For example:

```
if(value.length() != 4, "invalid", value)
```

When this function is applied to the "First stable release" column, it preserves the values of the cells where the date is in a "YYYY" format, and marks all other columns as "invalid."

Arbitrary GREL statements can be applied by clicking the down arrow next to any column's label and going to edit cells → transform.

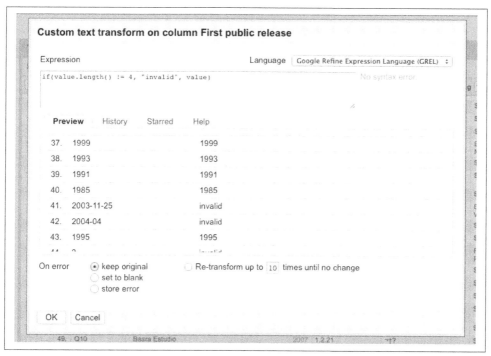

Figure 7-4. Inserting a GREL statement into a project (a preview display is shown below the statement)

However, marking all less than ideal values as invalid, while making them easy to spot, doesn't do us much good. We'd rather try to salvage information from the badly formatted values if possible. This can be done using GREL's `match` function:

```
value.match(".*([0-9]{4}).*").get(0)
```

This attempts to match the string value against the regular expression given. If the regular expression matches the string, an array is returned. Any substrings that match the "capture group" in the regular expression (demarcated by the parentheses in the expression, in this example, "[0-9]{4}") are returned as array values.

This code, in effect, finds all instances of four decimals in a row and returns the first one. This is usually sufficient to extract years from text or badly formatted dates. It also has the benefit of returning "null" for nonexistent dates. (GREL does not throw a null pointer exception when performing operations on a null variable)

Many other data transformations are possible with cell editing and GREL. A complete guide to the language can be found on OpenRefine's GitHub page (*http://bit.ly/1FnfobM*).

Reading and Writing Natural Languages

So far the data we have worked with generally has been in the form of numbers or countable values. In most cases, we've simply stored the data without conducting any analysis after the fact. In this chapter, we'll attempt to tackle the tricky subject of the English language.[1]

How does Google know what you're looking for when you type "cute kitten" into its Image Search? Because of the text that surrounds the cute kitten images. How does YouTube know to bring up a certain Monty Python sketch when you type "dead parrot" into its search bar? Because of the title and description text that accompanies each uploaded video.

In fact, even typing in terms such as "deceased bird monty python" immediately brings up the same "Dead Parrot" sketch, even though the page itself contains no mention of the words "deceased" or "bird." Google knows that a "hot dog" is a food and that a "boiling puppy" is an entirely different thing. How? It's all statistics!

Although you might not think that text analysis has anything to do with your project, understanding the concepts behind it can be extremely useful for all sorts of machine learning, as well as the more general ability to model real-world problems in probabilistic and algorithmic terms.

---

[1] Although many of the techniques described in this chapter can be applied to all or most languages, it's okay for now to focus on natural language processing in English only. Tools such as Python's Natural Language Toolkit, for example, focus on English. Fifty-six percent of the Internet is still in English (with German following at a mere 6%, according to *http://w3techs.com/technologies/overview/content_language/all*). But who knows? English's hold on the majority of the Internet will almost certainly change in the future, and further updates may be necessary in the next few years.

For instance, the Shazam music service can identify audio as containing a certain song recording, even if that audio contains ambient noise or distortion. Google is working on automatically captioning images based on nothing but the image itself.[2] By comparing known images of, say, hot dogs to other images of hot dogs, the search engine can gradually learn what a hot dog looks like and observe these patterns in additional images it is shown.

Summarizing Data

In Chapter 7, we looked at breaking up text content into n-grams, or sets of phrases that are *n*-words in length. At a very basic level, this can be used to determine which sets of words and phrases tend to be most commonly used in a section of text. In addition, it can be used to create natural-sounding data summaries by going back to the original text and extracting sentences around some of these most popular phrases.

One piece of sample text we'll be using to do this is the inauguration speech of the ninth president of the United States, William Henry Harrison. Harrison's presidency sets two records in the history of the office: one for the longest inauguration speech, and another for the shortest time in office, 32 days.

We'll use the full text of this speech (*http://bit.ly/1FNjvQS*) as the source for many of the code samples in this chapter.

Slightly modifying the n-gram used to find code in Chapter 7, we can produce code that looks for sets of 2-grams and sorts them using Python's sorting function in the "operator" module:

```
from urllib.request import urlopen
from bs4 import BeautifulSoup
import re
import string
import operator

def cleanInput(input):
    input = re.sub('\n+', " ", input).lower()
    input = re.sub('\[[0-9]*\]', "", input)
    input = re.sub(' +', " ", input)
    input = bytes(input, "UTF-8")
    input = input.decode("ascii", "ignore")
    cleanInput = []
    input = input.split(' ')
    for item in input:
```

---

2 See "A Picture Is Worth a Thousand (Coherent) Words: Building a Natural Description of Images," November 17, 2014 (*http://bit.ly/1HEJ8kX*).

```
        item = item.strip(string.punctuation)
        if len(item) > 1 or (item.lower() == 'a' or item.lower() == 'i'):
            cleanInput.append(item)
    return cleanInput

def ngrams(input, n):
    input = cleanInput(input)
    output = {}
    for i in range(len(input)-n+1):
        ngramTemp = " ".join(input[i:i+n])
        if ngramTemp not in output:
            output[ngramTemp] = 0
        output[ngramTemp] += 1
    return output

content = str(
    urlopen("http://pythonscraping.com/files/inaugurationSpeech.txt").read(),
            'utf-8')
ngrams = ngrams(content, 2)
sortedNGrams = sorted(ngrams.items(), key = operator.itemgetter(1), reverse=True)
print(sortedNGrams)
```

The output produces, in part:

```
[('of the', 213), ('in the', 65), ('to the', 61), ('by the', 41), ('t
he constitution', 34), ('of our', 29), ('to be', 26), ('from the', 24
), ('the people', 24), ('and the', 23), ('it is', 23), ('that the', 2
3), ('of a', 22), ('of their', 19)
```

Of these 2-grams, "the constitution" seems like a reasonably popular subject in the speech, but "of the," "in the," and "to the" don't seem especially noteworthy. How can you automatically get rid of unwanted words in an accurate way?

Fortunately, there are people out there who carefully study the differences between "interesting" words and "uninteresting" words, and their work can help us do just that. Mark Davies, a linguistics professor at Brigham Young University, maintains the Corpus of Contemporary American English (*http://corpus.byu.edu/coca/*), a collection of over 450 million words from the last decade or so of popular American publications.

The list of 5,000 most frequently found words is available for free, and fortunately, this is far more than enough to act as a basic filter to weed out the most common 2-grams. Just the first 100 words vastly improves the results, with the addition of an isCommon function:

```
def isCommon(ngram):
    commonWords = ["the", "be", "and", "of", "a", "in", "to", "have", "it",
        "i", "that", "for", "you", "he", "with", "on", "do", "say", "this",
        "they", "is", "an", "at", "but","we", "his", "from", "that", "not",
        "by", "she", "or", "as", "what", "go", "their","can", "who", "get",
        "if", "would", "her", "all", "my", "make", "about", "know", "will",
```

```
                "as", "up", "one", "time", "has", "been", "there", "year", "so",
                "think", "when", "which", "them", "some", "me", "people", "take",
                "out", "into", "just", "see", "him", "your", "come", "could", "now",
                "than", "like", "other", "how", "then", "its", "our", "two", "more",
                "these", "want", "way", "look", "first", "also", "new", "because",
                "day", "more", "use", "no", "man", "find", "here", "thing", "give",
                "many", "well"]
    for word in ngram:
        if word in commonWords:
            return True
    return False
```

This produces the following 2-grams that were found more than twice in the text body:

```
('united states', 10), ('executive department', 4), ('general governm
ent', 4), ('called upon', 3), ('government should', 3), ('whole count
ry', 3), ('mr jefferson', 3), ('chief magistrate', 3), ('same causes'
, 3), ('legislative body', 3)
```

Appropriately enough, the first two items in the list are "United States" and "executive department," which we would expect for a presidential inauguration speech.

It's important to note that we are using a list of common words from relatively modern times to filter the results, which might not be appropriate given that the text was written in 1841. However, because we're using only the first 100 or so words on the list—which we can assume are more stable over time than, say, the last 100 words —and we appear to be getting satisfactory results, we can likely save ourselves the effort of tracking down or creating a list of the most common words from 1841 (although such an effort might be interesting).

Now that some key topics have been extracted from the text, how does this help us write text summaries? One way is to search for the first sentence that contains each "popular" n-gram, the theory being that the first instance will yield a satisfactory overview of the body of the content. The first five most popular 2-grams yield these bullet points:

- The Constitution of the United States is the instrument containing this grant of power to the several departments composing the government.

- Such a one was afforded by the executive department constituted by the Constitution.

- The general government has seized upon none of the reserved rights of the states.

- Called from a retirement which I had supposed was to continue for the residue of my life to fill the chief executive office of this great and free nation, I appear before you, fellow-citizens, to take the oaths which the constitution prescribes as a necessary qualification for the performance of its duties; and in obedience to a custom coeval with our government and what I believe to be your expectations I proceed to present to you a summary of the principles which will govern me in the discharge of the duties which I shall be called upon to perform.

- The presses in the necessary employment of the government should never be used to clear the guilty or to varnish crime.

Sure, it might not be published in CliffsNotes any time soon, but considering that the original document was 217 sentences in length, and the fourth sentence ("Called from a retirement...") condenses the main subject down fairly well, it's not too bad for a first pass.

Markov Models

You might have heard of Markov text generators. They've become popular for entertainment purposes, as in the Twitov app (*http://twitov.extrafuture.com/*), as well as their use for generating real-sounding spam emails to fool detection systems.

All of these text generators are based on the Markov model, which is often used to analyze large sets of random events, where one discrete event is followed by another discrete event with a certain probability.

For example, we might build a Markov model of a weather system as illustrated in Figure 8-1.

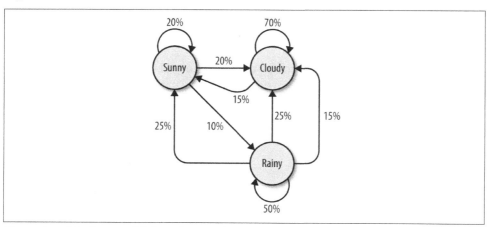

Figure 8-1. Markov model describing a theoretical weather system

In this model, each sunny day has a 70% chance of the following day also being sunny, with a 20% chance of the following day being cloudy with a mere 10% chance of rain. If the day is rainy, there is a 50% chance of rain the following day, a 25% chance of sun, and a 25% chance of clouds.

Note:

- All percentages leading away from any one node must add up to exactly 100%. No matter how complicated the system, there must always be a 100% chance that it can lead somewhere else in the next step.
- Although there are only three possibilities for the weather at any given time, you can use this model to generate an infinite list of weather states.
- Only the state of the current node you are on influences where you will go to next. If you're on the "sunny" node, it doesn't matter if the preceding 100 days were sunny or rainy—the chances of sun the next day are exactly the same: 70%.
- It might be more difficult to reach some nodes than others. The math behind this is reasonably complicated, but it should be fairly easy to see that "rainy" (with less than "100%" worth of arrows pointing toward it) is a much less likely state to reach in this system, at any given point in time, than "sunny" or "cloudy."

Obviously, this is a very simple system, and Markov models can grow arbitrarily large in size. In fact, Google's page rank algorithm is based partly on a Markov model, with websites represented as nodes and inbound/outbound links represented as connections between nodes. The "likelihood" of landing on a particular node represents the relative popularity of the site. That is, if our weather system represented an extremely small Internet, "rainy" would have a low page rank, while "cloudy" would have a high page rank.

With all of this in mind, let's bring it back down to a more concrete example: analyzing and writing text.

Again using the inauguration speech of William Henry Harrison analyzed in the previous example, we can write the following code that generates arbitrarily long Markov chains (with the chain length set to 100) based on the structure of its text:

```python
from urllib.request import urlopen
from random import randint

def wordListSum(wordList):
    sum = 0
    for word, value in wordList.items():
        sum += value
    return sum

def retrieveRandomWord(wordList):

    randIndex = randint(1, wordListSum(wordList))
    for word, value in wordList.items():
        randIndex -= value
        if randIndex <= 0:
            return word

def buildWordDict(text):
```

```
#Remove newlines and quotes
text = text.replace("\n", " ");
text = text.replace("\"", "");

#Make sure punctuation marks are treated as their own "words,"
#so that they will be included in the Markov chain
punctuation = [',','.',';',':']
for symbol in punctuation:
    text = text.replace(symbol, " "+symbol+" ");

words = text.split(" ")
#Filter out empty words
words = [word for word in words if word != ""]

wordDict = {}
for i in range(1, len(words)):
    if words[i-1] not in wordDict:
            #Create a new dictionary for this word
        wordDict[words[i-1]] = {}
    if words[i] not in wordDict[words[i-1]]:
        wordDict[words[i-1]][words[i]] = 0
    wordDict[words[i-1]][words[i]] = wordDict[words[i-1]][words[
                                                        i]] + 1

    return wordDict

text = str(urlopen("http://pythonscraping.com/files/inaugurationSpeech.txt")
        .read(), 'utf-8')
wordDict = buildWordDict(text)

#Generate a Markov chain of length 100
length = 100
chain = ""
currentWord = "I"
for i in range(0, length):
    chain += currentWord+" "
    currentWord = retrieveRandomWord(wordDict[currentWord])

print(chain)
```

The output of this code changes every time it is run, but here's an example of the uncannily nonsensical text it will generate:

```
I sincerely believe in Chief Magistrate to make all necessary sacrifices and
oppression of the remedies which we may have occurred to me in the arrangement
and disbursement of the democratic claims them , consolatory to have been best
political power in fervently commending every other addition of legislation , by
the interests which violate that the Government would compare our aboriginal
neighbors the people to its accomplishment . The latter also susceptible of the
Constitution not much mischief , disputes have left to betray . The maxim which
may sometimes be an impartial and to prevent the adoption or
```

So what's going on in the code?

The function `buildWordDict` takes in the string of text, which was retrieved from the Internet. It then does some cleaning and formatting, removing quotes, and putting spaces around other punctuation so it is effectively treated as a separate word. After this, it builds a two-dimensional dictionary—a "dictionary of dictionaries—that has the following form:

```
{word_a : {word_b : 2, word_c : 1, word_d : 1},
 word_e : {word_b : 5, word_d : 2},...}
```

In this example dictionary, "word_a" was found four times, two instances of which were followed by "word_b," one instance followed by "word_c," and one instance followed by "word_d." "Word_e" was followed seven times, five times by "word_b" and twice by "word_d."

If we were to draw a node model of this result, the node representing "word_a" would have a 50% arrow pointing toward "word_b" (which followed it two out of four times), a 25% arrow pointing toward "word_c," and a 25% arrow pointing toward "word_d."

Once this dictionary is built up, it can be used as a lookup table to see where to go next, no matter which word in the text you happen to be on.[3] Using the sample dictionary of dictionaries, we might currently be on "word_e," which means that we'll pass the dictionary `{word_b : 5, word_d: 2}` to the `retrieveRandomWord` function. This function in turn retrieves a random word from the dictionary, weighted by the number of times it occurs.

By starting with a random starting word (in this case, the ubiquitous "I"), we can traverse through the Markov chain easily, generating as many words as we like.

Six Degrees of Wikipedia: Conclusion

In Chapter 3, we created a scraper that collects links from one Wikipedia article to the next, starting with the article on Kevin Bacon, and stores them in a database. Why are we bringing it up again? Because it turns out the problem of choosing a path of links that starts on one page and ends up on the target page (i.e., finding a string of pages between *http://bit.ly/1d7SU7h* and *http://bit.ly/1GOSY7Z*) is the same as finding a Markov chain where both the first word and last word are defined. These sorts of problems are *directed graph* problems, where A → B does not necessarily mean that B → A. The word "football" might often be followed by the word "player," but you'll find that the word "player" is much less often followed by the word "football."

---

3 The exception is the last word in the text because nothing follows the last word. In our example text, the last word is a period (.), which is convenient because it has 215 other occurrences in the text and so does not represent a dead end. However, in real-world implementations of the Markov generator, the last word of the text might be something you need to account for.

Although Kevin Bacon's Wikipedia article links to the article on his home city, Philadelphia, the article on Philadelphia does not reciprocate by linking back to him.

In contrast, the original Six Degrees of Kevin Bacon game is an *undirected graph* problem. If Kevin Bacon starred in *Flatliners* with Julia Roberts, then Julia Roberts necessarily starred in *Flatliners* with Kevin Bacon, so the relationship goes both ways (it has no "direction"). Undirected graph problems tend to be less common in computer science than directed graph problems, and both are computationally difficult to solve.

Although much work has been done on these sorts of problems and multitudes of variations on them, one of the best and most common ways to find shortest paths in a directed graph—and thus find paths between the Wikipedia article on Kevin Bacon and all other Wikipedia articles—is through a *breadth-first search*.

A breadth-first search is performed by first searching all links that link directly to the starting page. If those links do not contain the target page (the page you are searching for), then a second level of links—pages that are linked by a page that is linked by the starting page—is searched. This process continues until either the depth limit (6 in this case) is reached or the target page is found.

A complete solution to the breadth-first search, using a table of links as described in Chapter 5, is as follows:

```
from urllib.request import urlopen
from bs4 import BeautifulSoup
import pymysql

conn = pymysql.connect(host='127.0.0.1', unix_socket='/tmp/mysql.sock',
                       user='root', passwd=None, db='mysql', charset='utf8')
cur = conn.cursor()
cur.execute("USE wikipedia")

class SolutionFound(RuntimeError):
    def __init__(self, message):
        self.message = message

def getLinks(fromPageId):
    cur.execute("SELECT toPageId FROM links WHERE fromPageId = %s", (fromPageId))
    if cur.rowcount == 0:
        return None
    else:
        return [x[0] for x in cur.fetchall()]

def constructDict(currentPageId):
    links = getLinks(currentPageId)
    if links:
        return dict(zip(links, [{}]*len(links)))
    return {}
```

```
#The link tree may either be empty or contain multiple links
def searchDepth(targetPageId, currentPageId, linkTree, depth):
    if depth == 0:
        #Stop recursing and return, regardless
        return linkTree
    if not linkTree:
        linkTree = constructDict(currentPageId)
        if not linkTree:
            #No links found. Cannot continue at this node
            return {}
    if targetPageId in linkTree.keys():
        print("TARGET "+str(targetPageId)+" FOUND!")
        raise SolutionFound("PAGE: "+str(currentPageId))

    for branchKey, branchValue in linkTree.items():
        try:
            #Recurse here to continue building the tree
            linkTree[branchKey] = searchDepth(targetPageId, branchKey,
                                              branchValue, depth-1)
        except SolutionFound as e:
            print(e.message)
            raise SolutionFound("PAGE: "+str(currentPageId))
    return linkTree

try:
    searchDepth(134951, 1, {}, 4)
    print("No solution found")
except SolutionFound as e:
    print(e.message)
```

The functions getLinks and constructDict are helper functions that retrieve links from the database given a page, and format those links into a dictionary. The main function, searchDepth, works recursively to simultaneously construct and search a tree of links, working one level at a time. It operates on the following rules:

- If the given recursion limit has been reached (i.e., if it has called itself too many times), return without doing any work.
- If the dictionary of links it has been given is empty, populate it with links for the current page. If the current page has no links, return.
- If the current page contains a link to the page we are searching for, throw an exception that alerts copies of itself on up the stack that the solution has been found. Each stack then prints the current page it is on, and throws the exception again, resulting in a perfect list of pages leading to the solution being printed on the screen.
- If the solution is not found, call itself while subtracting one from the depth count in order to search the next level of links.

The output for searching for a link between the page on Kevin Bacon (page ID 1, in my database) and the page on Eric Idle (page ID 78520 in my database) is:

```
TARGET 134951 FOUND!
PAGE: 156224
PAGE: 155545
PAGE: 3
PAGE: 1
```

This translates into the relationship of links: Kevin Bacon → San Diego Comic Con International → Brian Froud → Terry Jones → Eric Idle

In addition to solving "6 degree" problems and modeling which words tend to follow which other words in sentences, directed and undirected graphs can be used to model a variety of different situations encountered in web scraping. Which websites link to which other websites? Which research papers cite which other research papers? Which products tend to be shown with which other products on a retail site? What is the strength of this link? Is the link reciprocal?

Recognizing these fundamental types of relationships can be extremely helpful for making models, visualizations, and predictions based on scraped data.

Natural Language Toolkit

So far, this chapter has focused primarily on the statistical analysis of words in bodies of text. Which words are most popular? Which words are unusual? Which words are likely to come after which other words? How are they grouped together? What we are missing is understanding, to the extent that we can, what the words represent.

The Natural Language Toolkit (NLTK) is a suite of Python libraries designed to identify and tag parts of speech found in natural English text. Its development began in 2000, and over the past 15 years dozens of developers around the world have contributed to the project. Although the functionality it provides is tremendous (entire books are devoted to NLTK), this section will focus on just a few of its uses.

Installation and Setup

The NLTK module can be installed the same as other Python modules, either by downloading the package through the NLTK website directly or by using any number of third-party installers with the keyword "nltk." For complete installation instructions, you see the NLTK website (*http://www.nltk.org/install.html*).

After installing the module it's a good idea to download its preset text repositories so you can try out some of the features more easily. Type this on the Python command line:

```
>>> import nltk
>>> nltk.download()
```

This opens the NLTK Downloader (Figure 8-2).

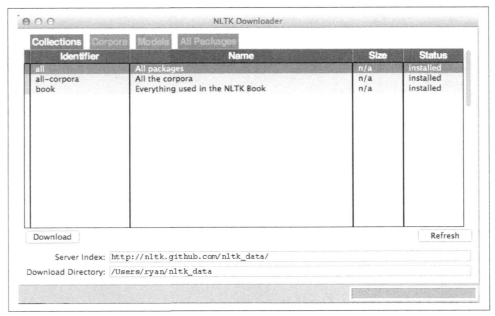

Figure 8-2. The NLTK Downloader lets you browse and download optional packages and text libraries associated with the NLTK module

I recommend installing all of the available packages. Because everything is text based the downloads are very small; you never know what you'll end up using, and you can easily uninstall packages at any time.

Statistical Analysis with NLTK

NLTK is great for generating statistical information about word counts, word frequency, and word diversity in sections of text. If all you need is a relatively straightforward calculation (e.g., the number of unique words used in a section of text), importing NLTK might be overkill—it's a very large module. However, if you need to do relatively extensive analysis of a text, you have a number of functions at your fingertips that will give you just about any metric you want.

Analysis with NLTK always starts with the Text object. Text objects can be created from simple Python strings in the following way:

```
from nltk import word_tokenize
from nltk import Text

tokens = word_tokenize("Here is some not very interesting text")
text = Text(tokens)
```

The input for the word_tokenize function can be any Python text string. If you don't have any long strings handy but still want to play around with the features, NLTK has quite a few books already built into the library, which can accessed using the import function:

```
from nltk.book import *
```

This loads the nine books:

```
*** Introductory Examples for the NLTK Book ***
Loading text1, ..., text9 and sent1, ..., sent9
Type the name of the text or sentence to view it.
Type: 'texts()' or 'sents()' to list the materials.
text1: Moby Dick by Herman Melville 1851
text2: Sense and Sensibility by Jane Austen 1811
text3: The Book of Genesis
text4: Inaugural Address Corpus
text5: Chat Corpus
text6: Monty Python and the Holy Grail
text7: Wall Street Journal
text8: Personals Corpus
text9: The Man Who Was Thursday by G . K . Chesterton 1908
```

We will be working with text6, "Monty Python and the Holy Grail" (the screenplay for the 1975 movie) in all of the following examples.

Text objects can be manipulated much like normal Python arrays, as if they were an array containing words of the text. Using this property, you can count the number of unique words in a text and compare it against the total number of words:

```
>>> len(text6)/len(words)
7.833333333333333
```

The preceding shows that each word in the script was used about eight times on average. You can also put the text into a frequency distribution object to see what some of the most common words are and the frequencies for various words:

```
>>> from nltk import FreqDist
>>> fdist = FreqDist(text6)
>>> fdist.most_common(10)
[(':', 1197), ('.', 816), ('!', 801), (',', 731), ("'", 421), ('[', 3
19), (']', 312), ('the', 299), ('I', 255), ('ARTHUR', 225)]
>>> fdist["Grail"]
34
```

Because this is a screenplay, some artifacts of how it is written can pop up. For instance, "ARTHUR" in all caps crops up frequently because it appears before each of King Arthur's lines in the script. In addition, a colon (:) appears before every single line, acting as a separator between the name of the character and the character's line. Using this fact, we can see that there are 1,197 lines in the movie!

What we have called 2-grams in previous chapters NLTK refers to as bigrams (from time to time you might also hear 3-grams referred to as "trigrams," but I personally prefer n-gram rather than bigram or trigram). You can create, search, and list 2-grams extremely easily:

```
>>> from nltk import bigrams
>>> bigrams = bigrams(text6)
>>> bigramsDist = FreqDist(bigrams)
>>> bigramDist[("Sir", "Robin")]
18
```

To search for the 2-grams "Sir Robin" we need to break it up into an array ("Sir", "Robin"), to match the way the 2-grams are represented in the frequency distribution. There is also a `trigrams` module that works in the exact same way. For the general case, you can also import the `ngrams` module:

```
>>> from nltk import ngrams
>>> fourgrams = ngrams(text6, 4)
>>> fourgramsDist = FreqDist(fourgrams)
>>> fourgramsDist[("father", "smelt", "of", "elderberries")]
1
```

Here, the `ngrams` function is called to break up a text object into n-grams of any size, governed by the second parameter. In this case, I'm breaking the text into 4-grams. Then, I can demonstrate that the phrase "father smelt of elderberries" occurs in the screenplay exactly once.

Frequency distributions, text objects, and n-grams also can be iterated through and operated on in a loop. The following prints out all 4-grams that begin with the word "coconut," for instance:

```
from nltk.book import *
from nltk import ngrams
fourgrams = ngrams(text6, 4)
for fourgram in fourgrams:
    if fourgram[0] == "coconut":
        print(fourgram)
```

The NLTK library has a vast array of tools and objects designed to organize, count, sort, and measure large swaths of text. Although we've barely scratched the surface of their uses, most of these tools are very well designed and operate rather intuitively for someone familiar with Python.

Lexicographical Analysis with NLTK

So far, we've compared and categorized all the words we've encountered based only on the value they represent by themselves. There is no differentiation between homonyms or the context in which the words are used.

Although some people might be tempted to dismiss homonyms as rarely problematic, you might be surprised at how frequently they crop up. Most native English speakers probably don't even register that a word is a homonym, much less consider that it might possibly be confused for another word in a different context.

"He was objective in achieving his objective of writing an objective philosophy, primarily using verbs in the objective case" is easy for humans to parse but might make a web scraper think the same word is being used four times and cause it to simply discard all the information about the meaning behind each word.

In addition to sussing out parts of speech, being able to distinguish a word being used in one way versus another might be useful. For example, you might want to look for company names made up of common English words, or analyze someone's opinions about a company "ACME Products is good" and "ACME Products is not bad" can have the same meaning, even if one sentence uses "good" and the other uses "bad".

Penn Treebank's Tags

NLTK uses by default a popular system of tagging parts of speech developed by the University of Pennsylvania's Penn Treebank Project (*http://bit.ly/1a1mXqf*). Although some of the tags make sense (e.g., CC is a coordinating conjunction), others can be confusing (e.g., RP is a particle). Use the following as a reference for the tags referred to in this section:

CC	Coordinating conjunction
CD	Cardinal number
DT	Determiner
EX	Existential "there"
FW	Foreign word
IN	Preposition, subordinating conjunction
JJ	Adjective
JJR	Adjective, comparative
JJS	Adjective, superlative
LS	List item marker
MD	Modal
NN	Noun, singular or mass
NNS	Noun, plural
NNP	Proper noun, singular

NNPS	Proper noun, plural
PDT	Predeterminer
POS	Possessive ending
PRP	Personal pronoun
PRP$	Possessive pronoun
RB	Adverb
RBR	Adverb, comparative
RBS	Adverb, superlative
RP	Particle
SYM	Symbol
TO	"to"
UH	Interjection
VB	Verb, base form
VBD	Verb, past tense
VBG	Verb, gerund or present participle
VBN	Verb, past participle
VBP	Verb, non-third person singular present
VBZ	Verb, third person singular present
WDT	wh-determiner
WP	Wh-pronoun
WP$	Possessive wh-pronoun
WRB	Wh-adverb

In addition to measuring language, NLTK can assist in finding meaning in the words based on context and its own very large dictionaries. At a basic level, NLTK can identify parts of speech:

```
>>> from nltk.book import *
>>> from nltk import word_tokenize
>>> text = word_tokenize("Strange women lying in ponds distributing swords is no
basis for a system of government.  Supreme executive power derives from a mandate
from the masses, not from some farcical aquatic ceremony.")
>>> from nltk import pos_tag
>>> pos_tag(text)
[('Strange', 'NNP'), ('women', 'NNS'), ('lying', 'VBG'), ('in', 'IN')
, ('ponds', 'NNS'), ('distributing', 'VBG'), ('swords', 'NNS'), ('is'
```

```
, 'VBZ'), ('no', 'DT'), ('basis', 'NN'), ('for', 'IN'), ('a', 'DT'),
('system', 'NN'), ('of', 'IN'), ('government', 'NN'), ('.', '.'), ('S
upreme', 'NNP'), ('executive', 'NN'), ('power', 'NN'), ('derives', 'N
NS'), ('from', 'IN'), ('a', 'DT'), ('mandate', 'NN'), ('from', 'IN'),
 ('the', 'DT'), ('masses', 'NNS'), (',', ','), ('not', 'RB'), ('from'
, 'IN'), ('some', 'DT'), ('farcical', 'JJ'), ('aquatic', 'JJ'), ('cer
emony', 'NN'), ('.', '.')]
```

Each word is separated into a *tuple* containing the word and a tag identifying the part of speech (see the preceding Penn Treebank Tags sidebar for more information about these tags). Although this might seem like a very straightforward lookup the complexity needed to perform the task correctly becomes apparent with the following example:

```
>>> text = word_tokenize("The dust was thick so he had to dust")
>>> pos_tag(text)
[('The', 'DT'), ('dust', 'NN'), ('was', 'VBD'), ('thick', 'JJ'), ('so
', 'RB'), ('he', 'PRP'), ('had', 'VBD'), ('to', 'TO'), ('dust', 'VB')
]
```

Notice that the word "dust" is used twice in the sentence: once as a noun, and again as a verb. NLTK identifies both usages correctly, based on their context in the sentence. NLTK identifies parts of speech using a *context-free grammar* defined by the English language. Context-free grammars are, essentially, sets of rules that define which things are allowed to follow which other things in ordered lists. In this case, they define which parts of speech are allowed to follow which other parts of speech. Whenever an ambiguous word such as "dust" is encountered, the rules of the context-free grammar is consulted and an appropriate part of speech that follows the rules is selected.

Machine Learning and Machine Training

You can have NLTK generate brand-new context-free grammars when training it, for example, on a foreign language. If you tag large sections of text by hand in the language using the appropriate Penn Treebank Tags, you can feed them back into NLTK and train it to properly tag other text it might encounter. This type of training is a necessary component of any machine-learning activity that we will revisit in Chapter 11, when training scrapers to recognize CAPTCHA characters.

So, what's the point of knowing whether a word is a verb or a noun in a given context? It might be neat in a computer science research lab, but how does it help with web scraping?

A very common problem in web scraping deals with search. You might be scraping text off a site and want to be able to search it for instances of the word "google," but only when it's being used as a verb, not a proper noun. Or you might be looking only for instances of the company Google and don't want to rely on people's correct use of capitalization in order to find those instances. Here, the `pos_tag` function can be extremely useful:

```
from nltk import word_tokenize, sent_tokenize, pos_tag
sentences = sent_tokenize("Google is one of the best companies in the world.
I constantly google myself to see what I'm up to.")
nouns = ['NN', 'NNS', 'NNP', 'NNPS']

for sentence in sentences:
    if "google" in sentence.lower():
        taggedWords = pos_tag(word_tokenize(sentence))
        for word in taggedWords:
            if word[0].lower() == "google" and word[1] in nouns:
                print(sentence)
```

This prints only sentences that contain the word "google" (or "Google") as some sort of a noun, not a verb. Of course, you could be more specific and demand that only instances of Google tagged with "NNP" (a proper noun) are printed, but even NLTK makes mistakes at times, and it can be good to leave yourself a little wiggle room, depending on the application.

Much of the ambiguity of natural language can be resolved using NLTK's `pos_tag` function. By searching text not just for instances of your target word or phrase but instances of your target word or phrase *plus* its tag, you can greatly increase the accuracy and effectiveness of your scraper's searches.

Additional Resources

Processing, analyzing, and understanding natural language by machine is one of the most difficult tasks in computer science, and countless volumes and research papers have been written on the subject. I hope that the coverage here will inspire you to think beyond conventional web scraping, or at least give some initial direction about where to begin when undertaking a project that requires natural language analysis.

There are many excellent resources on introductory language processing and Python's Natural Language Toolkit. In particular, Steven Bird, Ewan Klein, and Edward Loper's book *Natural Language Processing with Python* presents both a comprehensive and introductory approach to the topic.

In addition, James Pustejovsky and Amber Stubbs' *Natural Language Annotations for Machine Learning* provides a slightly more advanced theoretical guide. You'll need a knowledge of Python to implement the lessons; the topics covered work perfectly with Python's Natural Language Toolkit.

Crawling Through Forms and Logins

One of the first questions that comes up when you start to move beyond the basics of web scraping is: "How do I access information behind a login screen?" The Web is increasingly moving toward interaction, social media, and user-generated content. Forms and logins are an integral part of these types of sites and almost impossible to avoid. Fortunately, they are also relatively easy to deal with.

Up until this point, most of our interactions with web servers in our example scrapers has consisted of using HTTP GET to request information. In this chapter, we'll focus on the POST method which pushes information to a web server for storage and analysis.

Forms basically give users a way to submit a POST request that the web server can understand and use. Just like link tags on a website help users format GET requests, HTML forms help them format POST requests. Of course, with a little bit of coding, it is possible to simply create these requests ourselves and submit them with a scraper.

Python Requests Library

Although it's possible to navigate web forms using only the Python core libraries, sometimes a little syntactic sugar makes life a lot sweeter. When you start to do more than a basic GET request with urllib it can help to look outside the Python core libraries.

The Requests library (*http://www.python-requests.org*) is excellent at handling complicated HTTP requests, cookies, headers, and much more.

Here's what Requests creator Kenneth Reitz has to say about Python's core tools:

Python's standard `urllib2` module provides most of the HTTP capabilities you need, but the API is thoroughly broken. It was built for a different time—and a different web. It requires an enormous amount of work (even method overrides) to perform the simplest of tasks.

Things shouldn't be this way. Not in Python.

As with any Python library, the Requests library can be installed with any third-party Python library manager, such as pip, or by downloading and installing the source file (*http://bit.ly/1HYtkPr*).

Submitting a Basic Form

Most web forms consist of a few HTML fields, a submit button, and an "action" page, where the actual form processing is done. The HTML fields usually consist of text but might also contain a file upload or some other non-text content.

Most popular websites block access to their login forms in their *robots.txt* file (Appendix C discusses the legality of scraping such forms), so to play it safe I've constructed a series of different types of forms and logins at *pythonscraping.com* that you can run your web scrapers against. The most basic of these forms is located at *http://bit.ly/1AGKPRU*.

The entirety of the form is:

```
<form method="post" action="processing.php">
First name: <input type="text" name="firstname"><br>
Last name: <input type="text" name="lastname"><br>
<input type="submit" value="Submit">
</form>
```

A couple of things to notice here: first, the name of the two input fields are `firstname` and `lastname`. This is important. The names of these fields determine the names of the variable parameters that will be `POST`ed to the server when the form is submitted. If you want to mimic the action that the form will take when `POST`ing your own data, you need to make sure that your variable names match up.

The second thing to note is that the action of the form is actually at *processing.php* (the absolute path is *http://bit.ly/1d7TPVk*). Any `post` requests to the form should be made on *this* page, not on the page that the form itself resides. Remember: the purpose of HTML forms is only to help website visitors format proper requests to send to the page that does the real action. Unless you are doing research to format the request itself, you don't need to bother much with the page that the form can be found on.

Submitting a form with the Requests library can be done in four lines, including the import and the instruction to print the content (yes, it's that easy):

```
import requests

params = {'firstname': 'Ryan', 'lastname': 'Mitchell'}
r = requests.post("http://pythonscraping.com/files/processing.php", data=params)
print(r.text)
```

After the form is submitted, the script should return with the page's content:

```
Hello there, Ryan Mitchell!
```

This script can be applied to many simple forms encountered on the Internet. The form to sign up for the O'Reilly Media newsletter, for example, looks like this:

```
<form action="http://post.oreilly.com/client/o/oreilly/forms/
              quicksignup.cgi" id="example_form2" method="POST">
    <input name="client_token" type="hidden" value="oreilly" />
    <input name="subscribe" type="hidden" value="optin" />
    <input name="success_url" type="hidden" value="http://oreilly.com/store/
           newsletter-thankyou.html" />
    <input name="error_url" type="hidden" value="http://oreilly.com/store/
           newsletter-signup-error.html" />
    <input name="topic_or_dod" type="hidden" value="1" />
    <input name="source" type="hidden" value="orm-home-t1-dotd" />
    <fieldset>
        <input class="email_address long" maxlength="200" name=
                   "email_addr" size="25" type="text" value=
                   "Enter your email here" />
        <button alt="Join" class="skinny" name="submit" onclick=
                    "return addClickTracking('orm','ebook','rightrail','dod'
                                              );" value="submit">Join</button>
    </fieldset>
</form>
```

Although it can look daunting at first, remember that in most cases (we'll cover the exceptions later), you're only looking for two things:

- The name of the field (or fields) you want to submit with data (in this case, the name is email_address)
- The action attribute of the form itself; that is, the page that the form actually posts to (in this case, *http://post.oreilly.com/client/o/oreilly/forms/quicksignup.cgi*)

Just add in the required information and run it:

```
import requests
params = {'email_addr': 'ryan.e.mitchell@gmail.com'}
r = requests.post("http://post.oreilly.com/client/o/oreilly/forms/
                   quicksignup.cgi", data=params)
print(r.text)
```

In this case, the website returned is simply another form to fill out, before you can actually make it onto O'Reilly's mailing list, but the same concept could be applied to that form as well. However, I would request that you use your powers for good, and not spam the publisher with invalid signups, if you want to try this at home.

Radio Buttons, Checkboxes, and Other Inputs

Obviously, not all web forms are a collection of text fields followed by a submit button. Standard HTML contains a wide variety of possible form input fields: radio buttons, checkboxes, and select boxes, to name a few. In HTML5, there's the addition of sliders (range input fields), email, dates, and more. With custom JavaScript fields the possibilities are endless, with colorpickers, calendars, and whatever else the developers come up with next.

Regardless of the seeming complexity of any sort of form field, there are only two things you need to worry about: the name of the element and its value. The element's name can be easily determined by looking at the source code and finding the name attribute. The value can sometimes be trickier, as it might be populated by JavaScript immediately before form submission. Colorpickers, as an example of a fairly exotic form field, will likely have a value of something like #F03030.

If you're unsure of the format of an input field's value, there are a number of tools you can use to track the GET and POST requests your browser is sending to and from sites. The best and perhaps most obvious way to track GET requests, as mentioned before, is to simply look at the URL of a site. If the URL is something like:

```
http://domainname.com?thing1=foo&thing2=bar
```

You know that this corresponds to a form of this type:

```
<form method="GET" action="someProcessor.php">
<input type="someCrazyInputType" name="thing1" value="foo" />
<input type="anotherCrazyInputType" name="thing2" value="bar" />
<input type="submit" value="Submit" />
</form>
```

Which corresponds to the Python parameter object:

```
{'thing1':'foo', 'thing2':'bar'}
```

You can see this in Figure 9-1.

If you're stuck with a complicated-looking POST form, and you want to see exactly which parameters your browser is sending to the server, the easiest way is to use your browser's inspector or developer tool to view them.

Figure 9-1. The Form Data section, highlighted in a box, shows the POST parameters "thing1" and "thing2" with their values "foo" and "bar"

The Chrome developer tool can be accessed via the menu by going to View → Developer → Developer Tools. It provides a list of all queries that your browser produces while interacting with the current website and can be a good way to view the composition of these queries in detail.

Submitting Files and Images

Although file uploads are common on the Internet, file uploads are not something often used in web scraping. It is possible, however, that you might want to write a test for your own site that involves a file upload. At any rate, it's a useful thing to know how to do.

There is a practice file upload form at *http://pythonscraping/files/form2.html*. The form on the page has the following markup:

```
<form action="processing2.php" method="post" enctype="multipart/form-data">
   Submit a jpg, png, or gif: <input type="file" name="image"><br>
   <input type="submit" value="Upload File">
</form>
```

Except for the `<input>` tag having the type attribute `file`, it looks essentially the same as the text-based forms used in the previous examples. Fortunately, the way the forms are used by the Python Requests library is also very similar:

```
import requests

files = {'uploadFile': open('../files/Python-logo.png', 'rb')}
r = requests.post("http://pythonscraping.com/pages/processing2.php",
                    files=files)
print(r.text)
```

Note that in lieu of a simple string, the value submitted to the form field (with the name uploadFile) is now a Python File object, as returned by the open function. In this example, I am submitting an image file, stored on my local machine, at the path *../files/Python-logo.png*, relative to where the Python script is being run from.

Yes, it's really that easy!

Handling Logins and Cookies

So far, we've mostly discussed forms that allow you submit information to a site or let you to view needed information on the page immediately after the form. How is this different from a login form, which lets you exist in a permanent "logged in" state throughout your visit to the site?

Most modern websites use cookies to keep track of who is logged in and who is not. Once a site authenticates your login credentials a it stores in your browser a cookie, which usually contains a server-generated token, timeout, and tracking information. The site then uses this cookie as a sort of proof of authentication, which is shown to each page you visit during your time on the site. Before the widespread use of cookies in the mid-90s, keeping users securely authenticated and tracking them was a huge problem for websites.

Although cookies are a great solution for web developers, they can be problematic for web scrapers. You can submit a login form all day long, but if you don't keep track of the cookie the form sends back to you afterward, the next page you visit will act as though you've never logged in at all.

I've created a simple login form at *http://bit.ly/1KwvSSG* (the username can be anything, but the password must be "password").

This form is processed at *http://bit.ly/1d7U2I1*, and contains a link to the "main site" page, *http://bit.ly/1JcansT*.

If you attempt to access the welcome page or the profile page without logging in first, you'll get an error message and instructions to log in first before continuing. On the profile page, a check is done on your browser's cookies to see whether its cookie was set on the login page.

Keeping track of cookies is easy with theRequests library:

```
import requests

params = {'username': 'Ryan', 'password': 'password'}
r = requests.post("http://pythonscraping.com/pages/cookies/welcome.php", params)
print("Cookie is set to:")
print(r.cookies.get_dict())
print("-----------")
print("Going to profile page...")
r = requests.get("http://pythonscraping.com/pages/cookies/profile.php",
                 cookies=r.cookies)
print(r.text)
```

Here I am sending the login parameters to the welcome page, which acts as the processor for the login form. I retrieve the cookies from the results of the last request, print the result for verification, and then send them to the profile page by setting the cookies argument.

This works well for simple situations, but what if you're dealing with a more complicated site that frequently modifies cookies without warning, or if you'd rather not even think about the cookies to begin with? The Requests session function works perfectly in this case:

```
import requests

session = requests.Session()

params = {'username': 'username', 'password': 'password'}
s = session.post("http://pythonscraping.com/pages/cookies/welcome.php", params)
print("Cookie is set to:")
print(s.cookies.get_dict())
print("-----------")
print("Going to profile page...")
s = session.get("http://pythonscraping.com/pages/cookies/profile.php")
print(s.text)
```

In this case, the session object (retrieved by calling requests.Session()) keeps track of session information, such as cookies, headers, and even information about protocols you might be running on top of HTTP, such as HTTPAdapters.

Requests is a fantastic library, second perhaps only to Selenium (which we'll cover in Chapter 10) in the completeness of what it handles without programmers having to think about it or write the code themselves. Although it might be tempting to sit back and let the library do all the work, it's extremely important to always be aware of what the cookies look like and what they are controlling when writing web scrapers. It could save many hours of painful debugging or figuring out why a website is behaving strangely!

HTTP Basic Access Authentication

Before the advent of cookies, one popular way to handle logins was with HTTP *basic access authentication*. You still see it from time to time, especially on high-security or corporate sites, and with some APIs. I've created a page at *http://pythonscraping.com/pages/auth/login.php* that has this type of authentication (Figure 9-2).

Figure 9-2. The user must provide a username and password to get to the page protected by basic access authentication

As usual with these examples, you can log in with any username, but the password must be "password."

The Requests package contains an `auth` module specifically designed to handle HTTP authentication:

```
import requests
from requests.auth import AuthBase
from requests.auth import HTTPBasicAuth

auth = HTTPBasicAuth('ryan', 'password')
r = requests.post(url="http://pythonscraping.com/pages/auth/login.php", auth=
                  auth)
print(r.text)
```

Although this appears to be a normal `POST` request, an `HTTPBasicAuth` object is passed as the `auth` argument in the request. The resulting text will be the page protected by the username and password (or an Access Denied page, if the request failed).

Other Form Problems

Web forms are a hot point of entry for malicious bots. You don't want bots creating user accounts, taking up valuable server processing time, or submitting spam comments on a blog. For this reason, there are often a number of security features that are incorporated into HTML forms on modern websites that might not be immediately apparent.

For help with CAPTCHAs, check out Chapter 11, which covers image processing and text recognition in Python.

If you encounter a mysterious error, or the server is rejecting your form submission for an unknown reason, check out Chapter 12, which covers honey pots, hidden fields, and other security measures that websites take to protect their forms.

Scraping JavaScript

Client-side scripting languages are languages that are run in the browser itself, rather than on a web server. The success of a client-side language depends on your browser's ability to interpret and execute the language correctly. (This is why it's so easy to disable JavaScript in your browser.)

Partly due to the difficulty of getting every browser manufacturer to agree on a standard, there are far fewer client-side languages than there are server-side languages. This is a good thing when it comes to web scraping: the fewer languages there are to deal with the better.

For the most part, there are only two languages you'll frequently encounter online: ActionScript (which is used by Flash applications) and JavaScript. ActionScript is used far less frequently today than it was 10 years ago, and is often used to stream multimedia files, as a platform for online games, or to display "intro" pages for websites that haven't gotten the hint that no one wants to watch an intro page. At any rate, because there isn't much demand for scraping Flash pages, I will instead focus on the client-side language that's ubiquitous in modern web pages: JavaScript.

JavaScript is, by far, the most common and most well-supported client-side scripting language on the Web today. It can be used to collect information for user tracking, submit forms without reloading the page, embed multimedia, and even power entire online games. Even deceptively simple-looking pages can often contain multiple pieces of JavaScript. You can find it embedded between <script> tags in the page's source code:

```
<script>
    alert("This creates a pop-up using JavaScript");
</script>
```

A Brief Introduction to JavaScript

Having at least some idea of what is going on in the code you are scraping can be immensely helpful. With that in mind it's a good idea to familiarize yourself with JavaScript.

JavaScript is a weakly typed language, with a syntax that is often compared to C++ and Java. Although certain elements of the syntax, such as operators, loops, and arrays, might be similar, the weak typing and script-like nature of the language can make it a difficult beast to deal with for some programmers.

For example, the following recursively calculates values in the Fibonacci sequence, and prints them out to the browser's developer console:

```
<script>
function fibonacci(a, b){
    var nextNum = a + b;
    console.log(nextNum+" is in the Fibonacci sequence");
    if(nextNum < 100){
        fibonacci(b, nextNum);
    }
}
fibonacci(1, 1);
</script>
```

Notice that all variables are demarcated by a preceding var. This is similar to the $ sign in PHP, or the type declaration (int, String, List, etc.) in Java or C++. Python is unusual in that it doesn't have this sort of explicit variable declaration.

JavaScript is also extremely good at passing around functions just like variables:

```
<script>
var fibonacci = function() {
    var a = 1;
    var b = 1;
    return function () {
        var temp = b;
        b = a + b;
        a = temp;
        return b;
    }
}
var fibInstance = fibonacci();
console.log(fibInstance()+" is in the Fibonacci sequence");
console.log(fibInstance()+" is in the Fibonacci sequence");
console.log(fibInstance()+" is in the Fibonacci sequence");
</script>
```

This might seem daunting at first, but it becomes simple if you think in terms of lambda expressions (covered in Chapter 2). The variable fibonacci is defined as a function. The value of its function returns a function that prints increasingly large values in the Fibonacci sequence. Each time it is called, it returns the Fibonacci-calculating function, which executes again and increases the values in the function.

Although it might seem convoluted at first glance, some problems, such as calculating Fibonacci values, tend to lend themselves to patterns like this. Passing around functions as variables is also extremely useful when it comes to handling user actions and callbacks, and it is worth getting comfortable with this style of programming when it comes to reading JavaScript.

Common JavaScript Libraries

Although the core JavaScript language is important to know, you can't get very far on the modern Web without using at least one of the language's many third-party libraries. You might see one or more of these commonly used libraries when looking at page source code.

Executing JavaScript using Python can be extremely time consuming and processor intensive, especially if you're doing it on a large scale. Knowing your way around JavaScript and being able to parse it directly (without needing to execute it to acquire the information) can be extremely useful and save you a lot of headaches.

jQuery

jQuery is an extremely common library, used by 70% of the most popular Internet sites and about 30% of the rest of the Internet.[1] A site using jQuery is readily identifiable because it will contain an import to jQuery somewhere in its code, such as:

```
<script src="http://ajax.googleapis.com/ajax/libs/jquery/1.9.1/jquery.min.js"></
  script>
```

If you find jQuery is found on a site, you must be careful when scraping it. jQuery is adept at dynamically creating HTML content that appears only after the JavaScript is executed. If you scrape the page's content using traditional methods, you will retrieve only the preloaded page that appears before the JavaScript has created the content (we'll cover this scraping problem in more detail in "Ajax and Dynamic HTML" on page 151).

In addition, these pages are more likely to contain animations, interactive content, and embedded media that might make scraping challenging.

---

[1] Dave Methvin's blog post, "The State of jQuery 2014 (*http://blog.jquery.com/2014/01/13/the-stateof-jquery-2014/*)," January 13, 2014, contains a more detailed breakdown of the statistics.

Google Analytics

Google Analytics is used by about 50% of all websites,[2] making it perhaps the most common JavaScript library and the most popular user tracking tool on the Internet. In fact, both *http://pythonscraping.com* and *http://www.oreilly.com/* use Google Analytics.

It's easy telling whether a page is using Google Analytics. It will have JavaScript at the bottom similar to the following (taken from the O'Reilly Media site):

```
<!-- Google Analytics -->
<script type="text/javascript">

var _gaq = _gaq || [];
_gaq.push(['_setAccount', 'UA-4591498-1']);
_gaq.push(['_setDomainName', 'oreilly.com']);
_gaq.push(['_addIgnoredRef', 'oreilly.com']);
_gaq.push(['_setSiteSpeedSampleRate', 50]);
_gaq.push(['_trackPageview']);

(function() { var ga = document.createElement('script'); ga.type =
'text/javascript'; ga.async = true; ga.src = ('https:' ==
document.location.protocol ? 'https://ssl' : 'http://www') +
'.google-analytics.com/ga.js'; var s =
document.getElementsByTagName('script')[0];
s.parentNode.insertBefore(ga, s); })();

</script>
```

This script handles Google Analytics, specific cookies used to track your visit from page to page. This can sometimes be a problem for web scrapers that are designed to execute JavaScript and handle cookies (such as those that use Selenium, discussed later in this chapter).

If a site uses Google Analytics or a similar web analytics system and you do not want the site to know that it's being crawled or scraped, make sure to discard any cookies used for analytics or discard cookies altogether.

Google Maps

If you've spent any time on the Internet, you've almost certainly seen Google Maps embedded in a website. Its API makes it extremely easy to embed maps with custom information on any site.

If you're scraping any sort of location data, understanding how Google Maps works makes it easy to obtain well-formatted latitude/longitude coordinates and even

---

2 W3Techs, "Usage Statistics and Market Share of Google Analytics for Websites" (*http://w3techs.com/technologies/details/ta-googleanalytics/all/all*).

addresses. One of the most common ways to denote a location in Google Maps is through a *marker* (also known as a pin).

Markers can be inserted into any Google Map using code such as the following:

```
var marker = new google.maps.Marker({
    position: new google.maps.LatLng(-25.363882,131.044922),
    map: map,
    title: 'Some marker text'
});
```

Python makes it easy to extract all instances of coordinates that occur between `google.maps.LatLng(` and `)` to obtain a list of latitude/longitude coordinates.

Using Google's "reverse Geocoding" API (*http://bit.ly/1AGLnqI*), you can resolve these coordinate pairs to addresses that are well formatted for storage and analysis.

Ajax and Dynamic HTML

Until now the only way we've had of communicating with a web server is to send it some sort of HTTP request via the retrieval of a new page. If you've ever submitted a form or retrieved information from a server without reloading the page, you've likely used a website that uses *Ajax*.

Contrary to what some believe, Ajax is not a language but a group of technologies used to accomplish a certain task (much like web scraping, come to think of it). Ajax stands for Asynchronous JavaScript and XML, and is used to send information to and receive from a web server without making a separate page request. Note: you should never say, "This website will be written in Ajax." It would be correct to say, "This form will use Ajax to communicate with the web server."

Like Ajax, *dynamic HTML* or DHTML is a collection of technologies used for a common purpose. DHTML is HTML code, CSS language, or both that change due to client-side scripts changing HTML elements on the page. A button might appear only after the user moves the cursor, a background color might change on a click, or an Ajax request might trigger a new block of content to load.

Note that although the word "dynamic" is generally associated with words like "moving," or "changing," the presence of interactive HTML components, moving images, or embedded media does not necessarily make a page DHTML, even though it might look dynamic. In addition, some of the most boring, static-looking pages on the Internet can have DHTML processes running behind the scenes that depend on the use of JavaScript to manipulate the HTML and CSS.

If you scrape a large number of different websites, you will soon run into a situation in which the content you are viewing in your browser does not match the content you see in the source code you're retrieving from the site. You might view the output of your scraper and scratch your head, trying to figure out where everything you're see-ing on the exact same page in your browser has disappeared to.

The web page might also have a loading page that appears to redirect you to another page of results, but you'll notice that the page's URL never changes when this redirect happens.

Both of these are caused by a failure of your scraper to execute the JavaScript that is making the magic happen on the page. Without the JavaScript, the HTML just sort of sits there, and the site might look very different than what it looks like in your web browser, which executes the JavaScript without problem.

There are several giveaways that a page might be using Ajax or DHTML to change/load the content, but in situations like this there are only two solutions: scrape the content directly from the JavaScript, or use Python packages capable of executing the JavaScript itself, and scrape the website as you view it in your browser.

Executing JavaScript in Python with Selenium

Selenium (*http://www.seleniumhq.org/*) is a powerful web scraping tool developed originally for website testing. These days it's also used when the accurate portrayal of websites—as they appear in a browser—is required. Selenium works by automating browsers to load the website, retrieve the required data, and even take screenshots or assert that certain actions happen on the website.

Selenium does not contain its own web browser; it requires integration with third-party browsers in order to run. If you were to run Selenium with Firefox, for exam-ple, you would literally see a Firefox instance open up on your screen, navigate to the website, and perform the actions you had specified in the code. Although this might be neat to watch, I prefer my scripts to run quietly in the background, so I use a tool called PhantomJS (*http://phantomjs.org/*) in lieu of an actual browser.

PhantomJS is what is known as a "headless" browser. It loads websites into memory and executes JavaScript on the page, but does it without any graphic rendering of the website to the user. By combining Selenium with PhantomJS, you can run an extremely powerful web scraper that handles cookies, JavaScript, headers, and every-thing else you need with ease.

You can download the Selenium library from its website (*http://bit.ly/1GehgJU*) or use a third-party installer such as pip to install it from the command line.

PhantomJS can be downloaded from its website (*http://bit.ly/1eKiBfg*). Because Phan-tomJS is a full (albeit headless) browser and not a Python library, it does require a download and installation to use and cannot be installed with pip.

Although there are plenty of pages that use Ajax to load data (notably Google), I've created a sample page at *http://bit.ly/1HYuH0L* to run our scrapers against. This page contains some sample text, hardcoded into the page's HTML, that is replaced by Ajax-generated content after a two-second delay. If we were to scrape this page's data using traditional methods, we'd only get the loading page, without actually getting the data that we want.

The Selenium library is an API called on the a *WebDriver*. The WebDriver is a bit like a browser in that it can load websites, but it can also be used like a BeautifulSoup object to find page elements, interact with elements on the page (send text, click, etc.), and do other actions to drive the web scrapers.

The following code retrieves text behind an Ajax "wall" on the test page:

```
from selenium import webdriver
import time

driver = webdriver.PhantomJS(executable_path='')
driver.get("http://pythonscraping.com/pages/javascript/ajaxDemo.html")
time.sleep(3)
print(driver.find_element_by_id("content").text)
driver.close()
```

Selenium Selectors

In previous chapters, we've selected page elements using BeautifulSoup selectors, such as find and findAll. Selenium uses an entirely new set of selectors to find an element in a WebDriver's DOM, although they have fairly straightforward names.

In the example, we used the selector find_element_by_id, although the following other selectors would have worked as well:

```
driver.find_element_by_css_selector("#content")
driver.find_element_by_tag_name("div")
```

Of course, if you want to select multiple elements on the page, most of these element selectors can return a Python list of elements simply by using elements (i.e., make it plural):

```
driver.find_elements_by_css_selector("#content")
driver.find_elements_by_css_selector("div")
```

Of course, if you still want to use BeautifulSoup to parse this content you can, by using WebDriver's page_source function, which returns the page's source, as viewed by the DOM at that current time, as a string:

```
pageSource = driver.page_source
bsObj = BeautifulSoup(pageSource)
print(bsObj.find(id="content").get_text())
```

This creates a new Selenium WebDriver, using the PhantomJS library, which tells the WebDriver to load a page and then pauses execution for three seconds before looking at the page to retrieve the (hopefully loaded) content.

Depending on the location of your PhantomJS installation, you might also need to explicitly point Selenium in the right direction when creating a new PhantomJS Web-Driver:

```
driver = webdriver.PhantomJS(executable_path='/path/to/download/
                              phantomjs-1.9.8-macosx/bin/phantomjs')
```

If everything is configured correctly the script should take a few seconds to run and result in the following text:

```
Here is some important text you want to retrieve!
A button to click!
```

Note that although the page itself contains an HTML button, Selenium's `.text` function retrieves the text value of the button in the same way that it retrieves all other content on the page.

If the `time.sleep` pause is changed to one second instead of three, the text returned changes to the original:

```
This is some content that will appear on the page while it's loading.
 You don't care about scraping this.
```

Although this solution works, it is somewhat inefficient and implementing it could cause problems on a large scale. Page load times are inconsistent, depending on the server load at any particular millisecond, and natural variations occur in connection speed. Although this page load should take just over two seconds, we're giving it an entire three seconds to make sure that it loads completely. A more efficient solution would repeatedly check for the existence of some element on a fully loaded page and return only when that element exists.

This code uses the presence of the button with id `loadedButton` to declare that the page has been fully loaded: from selenium import webdriver.

```
from selenium.webdriver.common.by import By
from selenium.webdriver.support.ui import WebDriverWait
from selenium.webdriver.support import expected_conditions as EC

driver = webdriver.PhantomJS(executable_path='')
driver.get("http://pythonscraping.com/pages/javascript/ajaxDemo.html")
try:
    element = WebDriverWait(driver, 10).until(
                    EC.presence_of_element_located((By.ID, "loadedButton")))
finally:
    print(driver.find_element_by_id("content").text)
    driver.close()
```

There are several new imports in this script, most notably `WebDriverWait` and `expected_conditions`, both of which are combined here to form what Selenium calls an *implicit wait*.

An implicit wait differs from an explicit wait in that it waits for some state in the DOM to occur before continuing, while an explicit wait defines a hardcoded time like in the previous example, which has a wait of three seconds. In an implicit wait, the triggering DOM state is defined by `expected_condition` (note that the import is cast to `EC` here, a common convention used for brevity). Expected conditions can be many things in the Selenium library, among them:

- An alert box pops up
- An element (such as a text box) is put into a "selected" state
- The page's title changes, or some text is now displayed on the page or in a specific element
- An element is now visible to the DOM, or an element disappears from the DOM

Of course, most of these expected conditions require that you specify an element to watch for in the first place. Elements are specified using *locators*. Note that locators are not the same as selectors (see previous sidebar for more on selectors). A locator is an abstract query language, using the `By` object, which can be used in a variety of ways, including to make selectors.

In the following example code, a locator is used to find elements with the id `loaded Button`:

```
EC.presence_of_element_located((By.ID, "loadedButton"))
```

Locators can also be used to create selectors, using the `find_element` WebDriver function:

```
print(driver.find_element(By.ID, "content").text)
```

Which is, of course, functionally equivalent to the line in the example code:

```
print(driver.find_element_by_id("content").text)
```

If you do not need to use a locator, don't; it will save you an import. However, it is a very handy tool that is used for a variety of applications and has a great degree of flexibility.

The following locator selection strategies can used with the `By` object:

ID

Used in the example; finds elements by their HTML id attribute.

CLASS_NAME

Used to find elements by their HTML class attribute. Why is this function CLASS_NAME and not simply CLASS? Using the form object.CLASS would create problems for Selenium's Java library, where .class is a reserved method. In order to keep the Selenium syntax consistent between different languages, CLASS_NAME was used instead.

CSS_SELECTOR

Find elements by their class, id, or tag name, using the #idName, .className, tagName convention.

LINK_TEXT

Finds HTML <a> tags by the text they contain. For example, a link that says "Next" can be selected using (By.LINK_TEXT, "Next").

PARTIAL_LINK_TEXT

Similar to LINK_TEXT, but matches on a partial string.

NAME

Finds HTML tags by their name attribute. This is handy for HTML forms.

TAG_NAME

Finds HTML tags by their tag name.

XPATH

Uses an XPath expression (the syntax of which is described in the upcoming sidebar) to select matching elements.

XPath Syntax

XPath (short for XML Path) is a query language used for navigating and selecting portions of an XML document. It was founded by the W3C in 1999 and is occasionally used in languages such as Python, Java, and C# when dealing with XML documents.

Although BeautifulSoup does not support XPath, many of the other libraries in this book do. It can often be used in the same way as CSS selectors (such as `mytag#idname`), although it is designed to work with more generalized XML documents rather than HTML documents in particular.

There are four major concepts in the XPath syntax:

- *Root nodes versus non-root nodes*
  - `/div` will select the div node only if it is at the root of the document
  - `//div` selects all divs anywhere in the document
- *Attribute selection*
  - `//@href` selects any nodes with the attribute `href`
  - `//a[@href='http://google.com']` selects all links in the document that point to Google
- *Selection of nodes by position*
  - `//a[3]` selects the third link in the document
  - `//table[last()]` selects the last table in the document
  - `//a[position() < 3]` selects the first three links in the document
- *Asterisks (*) match any set of characters or nodes, and can be used in a variety of situations*
  - `//table/tr/*` selects all children of `tr` tags in all tables (this is good for selecting cells using both `th` and `td` tags)
  - `//div[@*]` selects all `div` tags that have any attributes

Of course, there are many advanced features of the XPath syntax. Over the years it has developed into a relatively complicated query language, with boolean logic, functions (such as `position()`), and a variety of operators not discussed here.

If you have an HTML or XML selection problem that cannot be addressed by the functions shown here, see Microsoft's XPath syntax page (*http://bit.ly/1HEMbd3*).

Handling Redirects

Client-side redirects are page redirects that are executed in your browser by Java-Script, rather than a redirect performed on the server, before the page content is sent. It can sometimes be tricky to tell the difference when visiting a page in your web browser. The redirect might happen so fast that you don't notice any delay in loading time and assume that a client-side redirect is actually a server-side redirect.

However, when scraping the Web, the difference is obvious. A server-side redirect, depending on how it is handled, can be easily traversed by Python's urllib library without any help from Selenium (for more information on doing this, see Chapter 3). Client-side redirects won't be handled at all unless something is actually executing the JavaScript.

Selenium is capable of handling these JavaScript redirects in the same way that it handles other JavaScript execution; however, the primary issue with these redirects is when to stop page execution—that is, how to tell when a page is done redirecting. A demo page at *http://bit.ly/1SOGCBn* gives an example of this type of redirect, with a two-second pause.

We can detect that redirect in a clever way by "watching" an element in the DOM when the page initially loads, then repeatedly calling that element until Selenium throws a StaleElementReferenceException; that is, the element is no longer attached to the page's DOM and the site has redirected:

```
from selenium import webdriver
import time
from selenium.webdriver.remote.webelement import WebElement
from selenium.common.exceptions import StaleElementReferenceException

def waitForLoad(driver):
    elem = driver.find_element_by_tag_name("html")
    count = 0
    while True:
        count += 1
        if count > 20:
            print("Timing out after 10 seconds and returning")
            return
        time.sleep(.5)
        try:
            elem == driver.find_element_by_tag_name("html")
        except StaleElementReferenceException:
            return

driver = webdriver.PhantomJS(executable_path='<Path to Phantom JS>')
driver.get("http://pythonscraping.com/pages/javascript/redirectDemo1.html")
waitForLoad(driver)
print(driver.page_source)
```

This script checks the page every half second, with a timeout of 10 seconds, although the times used for the checking time and timeout can be easily adjusted up or down as needed.

Image Processing and Text Recognition

From Google's self-driving cars to vending machines that recognize counterfeit currency, machine vision is a huge field with far-reaching goals and implications. In this chapter, we will focus on one very small aspect of the field: text recognition, specifically how to recognize and use text-based images found online by using a variety of Python libraries.

Using an image in lieu of text is a common technique when you don't want text to be found and read by bots. This is often seen on contact forms when an email address is partially or completely rendered as an image. Depending on how skillfully it is done, it might not even be noticeable to human viewers but bots have a very difficult time reading these images and the technique is enough to stop most spammers from acquiring your email address.

CAPTCHAs, of course, take advantage of the fact that users can read security images but most bots can't. Some CAPTCHAs are more difficult than others, an issue we'll tackle later in this book.

But CAPTCHAs aren't the only place on the Web where scrapers need image-to-text translation assistance. Even in this day and age, many documents are simply scanned from hard copies and put on the Web, making these documents inaccessible as far as much of the Internet is concerned, although they are "hiding in plain sight." Without image-to-text capabilities, the only way to make these documents accessible is for a human to type them up by hand—and nobody has time for that.

Translating images into text is called *optical character recognition*, or *OCR*. There are a few major libraries that are able to perform OCR, and many other libraries that support them or are built on top of them. This system of libraries can get fairly complicated at times, so I recommend you read the next section before attempting any of the exercises in this chapter.

Overview of Libraries

Python is a fantastic language for image processing and reading, image-based machine-learning, and even image creation. Although there are a large number of libraries that can be used for image processing, we will focus on two: Pillow and Tesseract.

Either can be installed by downloading from their websites and installing from source (*http://bit.ly/1FVNpnq* and *http://bit.ly/1Fnm6yt*) or by using a third-party Python installer such as pip and using the keywords "pillow" and "pytesseract," respectively.

Pillow

Although Pillow might not be the most fully featured image-processing library, it has all of the features you are likely to need and then some unless you are doing research or rewriting Photoshop in Python, or something like that. It is also a very well-documented piece of code that is extremely easy to use.

Forked off the Python Imaging Library (PIL) for Python 2.x, Pillow adds support for Python 3.x. Like its predecessor, Pillow allows you to easily import and manipulate images with a variety of filters, masks, and even pixel-specific transformations:

```
from PIL import Image, ImageFilter

kitten = Image.open("kitten.jpg")
blurryKitten = kitten.filter(ImageFilter.GaussianBlur)
blurryKitten.save("kitten_blurred.jpg")
blurryKitten.show()
```

In the preceding example, the image *kitten.jpg* will open in your default image viewer with a blur added to it and will also be saved in its blurrier state as *kitten_blurred.jpg* in the same directory.

We will use Pillow to perform preprocessing on images to make them more machine readable but as mentioned before, there are many other things you can do with the library aside from these simple manipulations. For more information, check out the Pillow documentation (*http://pillow.readthedocs.org/*).

Tesseract

Tesseract is an OCR library. Sponsored by Google (a company obviously well known for its OCR and machine learning technologies), Tesseract is widely regarded to be the best, most accurate, open source OCR system available.

In addition to being accurate, it is also extremely flexible. It can be trained to recognize any number of fonts (as long as those fonts are relatively consistent within themselves, as we will see soon) and it can be expanded to recognize any Unicode character.

Unlike libraries we've used so far in this book, Tesseract is a command-line tool written in Python, rather than a library used with an `import` statement. After installation, it must be run with the `tesseract` command, from outside of Python.

Installing Tesseract

For Windows users there is a convenient executable installer (*http://bit.ly/ 1ELAwHk*). As of this writing, the current version is 3.02, although newer versions should be fine as well.

Linux users can install Tesseract with `apt-get`:

```
$sudo apt-get tesseract-ocr
```

Installing Tesseract on a Mac is slightly more complicated, although it can be done easily with many third-party installers such as Homebrew (*http://brew.sh/*), which was used in Chapter 5 to install MySQL. For example, you can install Homebrew and use it to install Tesseract in two lines:

```
$ruby -e "$(curl -fsSL https://raw.githubusercontent.com/Homebrew/ \
        install/master/install)"
$brew install tesseract
```

Tesseract also can be installed from the source, on the project's download page (*http:// bit.ly/1ELAwHk*).

To use some features of Tesseract, such as training the software to recognize new characters later in this section, you will also need to set a new environment variable, `$TESSDATA_PREFIX`, to let it know where data files are stored.

You can do this in most Linux system and on Mac OS X using:

```
$export TESSDATA_PREFIX=/usr/local/share/
```

Note that `/usr/local/share/` is the default data location for Tesseract, although you should check to make sure that this is the case for your own installation.

Similarly, on Windows, you can use the following to use the environment variable:

```
#setx TESSDATA_PREFIX C:\Program Files\Tesseract OCR\
```

NumPy

Although NumPy is not required for straightforward OCR, you will need it if you want to train Tesseract to recognize additional character sets or fonts introduced later in this chapter. NumPy is a very powerful library used for linear algebra and other large-scale math applications. NumPy works well with Tesseract because of its ability to mathematically represent and manipulate images as large arrays of pixels.

As always, NumPy can be installed using any third-party Python installer such as pip:

```
$pip install numpy
```

Processing Well-Formatted Text

With any luck, most of the text that you'll need to process will be relatively clean and well formatted. Well-formatted text generally meets several requirements, although the line between what is "messy" and what is "well formatted" can be subjective.

In general, well-formatted text:

- Is written in one standard font (excluding handwriting fonts, cursive fonts, or excessively "decorative" fonts)
- If copied or photographed has extremely crisp lines, with no copying artifacts or dark spots
- Is well-aligned, without slanted letters
- Does not run off the image, nor is there cut-off text or margins on the edges of the image

Some of these things can be fixed in preprocessing. For instance, images can be converted to grayscale, brightness and contrast can be adjusted, and the image can be cropped and rotated as needed. However, there are some fundamental limitations that might require more extensive training. See "Reading CAPTCHAs and Training Tesseract" on page 169.

Figure 11-1 an ideal example of well-formatted text.

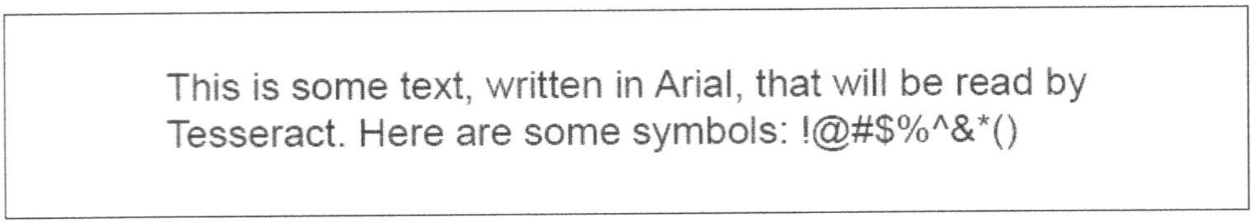

This is some text, written in Arial, that will be read by Tesseract. Here are some symbols: !@#$%^&*()

Figure 11-1. Sample text saved as a .tiff file, to be read by Tesseract

You can run Tesseract from the command line to read this file and write the results to a text file:

```
$tesseract text.tif textoutput | cat textoutput.txt
```

The output is a line of information about the Tesseract library to indicate that it is running, followed by the contents of the newly created *textoutput.txt*:

```
Tesseract Open Source OCR Engine v3.02.02 with Leptonica
This is some text, written in Arial, that will be read by
Tesseract. Here are some symbols: !@#$%"&'()
```

You can see that the results are mostly accurate, although the symbols "^" and "*" were interpreted as a double quote and single quote, respectively. On the whole, though, this lets you read the text fairly comfortably.

After blurring the image text, creating some JPG compression artifacts, and adding a slight background gradient, the results get much worse (see Figure 11-2).

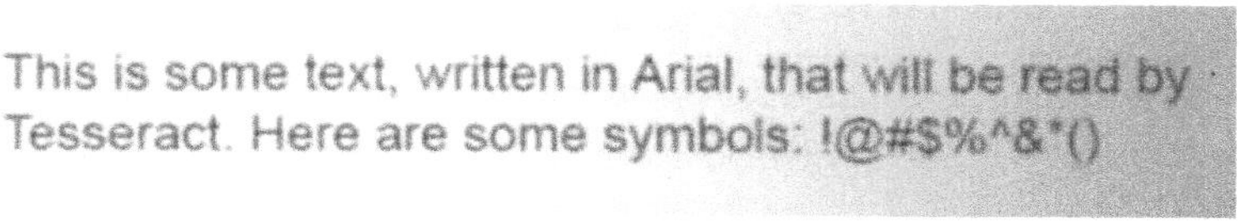

This is some text, written in Arial, that will be read by
Tesseract. Here are some symbols: !@#$%^&'()

Figure 11-2. Unfortunately, many of the documents you will encounter on the Internet will look more like this than the previous example

Tesseract is not able to deal with this image nearly as well mainly due to the background gradient and produces the following output:

```
This is some text, written In Arlal, that"
Tesseract. Here are some symbols: _
```

Notice that the text is cut off as soon as the background gradient makes the text more difficult to distinguish, and that the last character from each line is wrong as Tesseract tries futilely to make sense of it. In addition, the JPG artifacts and blurring make it difficult for Tesseract to distinguish between a lowercase "i" and an uppercase "I" and the number "1".

This is where using a Python script to clean your images first comes in handy. Using the Pillow library, we can create a threshold filter to get rid of the gray in the background, bring out the text, and make the image clearer for Tesseract to read:

```
from PIL import Image
import subprocess

def cleanFile(filePath, newFilePath):
    image = Image.open(filePath)

    #Set a threshold value for the image, and save
```

```
image = image.point(lambda x: 0 if x<143 else 255)
image.save(newFilePath)

#call tesseract to do OCR on the newly created image
subprocess.call(["tesseract", newFilePath, "output"])

#Open and read the resulting data file
outputFile = open("output.txt", 'r')
print(outputFile.read())
outputFile.close()

cleanFile("text_2.png", "text_2_clean.png")
```

The resulting image, automatically created as *text_2_clean.png*, is shown in Figure 11-3:

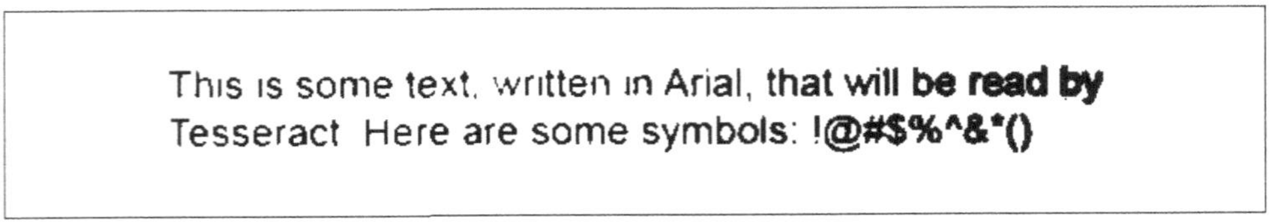

This is some text, written in Arial, that will be read by
Tesseract Here are some symbols: !@#$%^&*()

Figure 11-3. This image was created by passing the previous "messy" version of the image through a threshold filter

Apart from some barely legible or missing punctuation, the text is readable, at least to us. Tesseract gives it its best shot:

```
This us some text' written In Anal, that will be read by
Tesseract Here are some symbols: !@#$%"&'()
```

The periods and commas, being extremely small, are the first victims of this image wrangling and nearly disappear, both from our view and Tesseract's. There's also the unfortunate misinterpretation of "Arial" as "Anal," the result of Tesseract interpreting the "r" and the "i" as the single character "n."

Still, it's an improvement over the previous version in which nearly half of the text was cut off.

Tesseract's greatest weakness seems to be backgrounds with varying brightness. Tesseract's algorithms attempt to adjust the contrast of the image automatically before reading the text, but you can probably get better results doing this yourself with a tool like the Pillow library.

Images you should definitely fix before submitting to Tesseract are those that are tilted, have large areas of non-text, or have other problems.

Scraping Text from Images on Websites

Using Tesseract to read text from an image on your hard drive might not seem all that exciting, but it can be a very powerful tool when used with a web scraper. Images can inadvertently obfuscate text on websites (as with the JPG copy of a menu on a local restaurant site), but they can also purposefully hide the text, as I'll show in the next example.

Although Amazon's *robots.txt* file allows scraping of the site's product pages, book previews typically don't get picked up by passing bots. That's because the book previews are loaded via user-triggered Ajax scripts, and the images are carefully hidden under layers of divs; in fact, to the average site visitor they probably look more like a flash presentation than image files. Of course, even if we could get to the images, there's the not-so-small matter of reading them as text.

The following script accomplishes just this feat: it navigates to the large-print edition[1] of Tolstoy's *War and Peace*, opens the reader, collects image URLs, and then systematically downloads, reads, and prints the text from each one. Because this is relatively complex code that draws on multiple concepts from previous chapters, I've added comments throughout to make it a little easier to understand what's going on:

```
import time
from urllib.request import urlretrieve
import subprocess
from selenium import webdriver

#Create new Selenium driver
driver = webdriver.PhantomJS(executable_path='<Path to Phantom JS>')
driver.get(
        "http://www.amazon.com/War-Peace-Leo-Nikolayevich-Tolstoy/dp/1427030200")
time.sleep(2)

#Click on the book preview button
driver.find_element_by_id("sitbLogoImg").click()
imageList = set()

#Wait for the page to load
time.sleep(5)
#While the right arrow is available for clicking, turn through pages
while "pointer" in driver.find_element_by_id("sitbReaderRightPageTurner")
                                        .get_attribute("style"):
    driver.find_element_by_id("sitbReaderRightPageTurner").click()
    time.sleep(2)
```

---

1 When it comes to processing text it hasn't been trained on, Tesseract fares much better with large-format editions of books, especially if the images are small. In the next section we'll discuss how to train Tesseract on different fonts, which can help it read much smaller font sizes, including previews for non-large print book editions!

```
    #Get any new pages that have loaded (multiple pages can load at once,
        #but duplicates will not be added to a set)
    pages = driver.find_elements_by_xpath("//div[@class='pageImage']/div/img")
    for page in pages:
        image = page.get_attribute("src")
        imageList.add(image)

driver.quit()

#Start processing the images we've collected URLs for with Tesseract
for image in sorted(imageList):
    urlretrieve(image, "page.jpg")
    p = subprocess.Popen(["tesseract", "page.jpg", "page"],
                        stdout=subprocess.PIPE,stderr=subprocess.PIPE)
    p.wait()
    f = open("page.txt", "r")
    print(f.read())
```

As we have experienced with the Tesseract reader before, this prints many long passages of the book perfectly, as seen in the preview of page 6:

```
6

"A word of friendly advice, mon
cher. Be off as soon as you can,
that's all I have to tell you. Happy
he who has ears to hear. Good-by,
my dear fellow. Oh, by the by!" he
shouted through the doorway after
Pierre, "is it true that the countess
has fallen into the clutches of the
holy fathers of the Society of je-
sus?"

Pierre did not answer and left Ros-
topchin's room more sullen and an-
gry than he had ever before shown
himself.
```

However, when the text appears on a colored background on the front and back covers of the book, it becomes incomprehensible:

```
WEI' nrrd Peace
Len Nlkelayevldu Iolfluy

Readmg shmdd be ax
wlnvame asnossxble Wenfler
an mm m our cram: Llhvary

— Leo Tmsloy was a Russian rwovelwst
I and moval phflmopher med lur
A ms Ideas 01 nonviolenx reswslance m 5 We range 0, "and"
```

Of course, you can use the Pillow library to selectively clean images, but this can be extremely labor intensive for a process that was designed to be as human-free as possible.

The next section discusses another approach to solving the problem of mangled text, particularly if you don't mind investing a little time up front in training Tesseract. By providing Tesseract with a large collection of text images with known values, Tesseract can be "taught" to recognize the same font in the future with far greater precision and accuracy, even despite occasional background and positioning problems in the text.

Reading CAPTCHAs and Training Tesseract

Although the word "CAPTCHA" is familiar to most, far fewer people know what it stands for: Computer Automated Public Turing test to tell Computers and Humans Apart. Its unwieldy acronym hints at its rather unwieldy role in obstructing otherwise perfectly usable web interfaces, as both humans and nonhuman robots often struggle to solve CAPTCHA tests.

The Turing test was first described by Alan Turing in his 1950 paper, "Computing Machinery and Intelligence." In the paper, he described a setup in which a human being could communicate with both humans and artificial intelligence programs through a computer terminal. If the human was unable to distinguish the humans from the AI programs during a casual conversation, the AI programs would be considered to have passed the Turing test, and the artificial intelligence, Turing reasoned, would be genuinely "thinking" for all intents and purposes.

It's ironic that in the last 60 years we've gone from using these tests to test machines to using them to test ourselves, with mixed results. Google's notoriously difficult reCAPTCHA, currently the most popular among security-conscious websites, blocks as many as 25% of legitimate human users from accessing a site.[2]

Most other CAPTCHAs are somewhat easier. Drupal, a popular PHP-based content management system, for example, has a popular CAPTCHA module (*http://bit.ly/1QjuSmk*), that can generate CAPTCHA images of varying difficulty. The default image looks like Figure 11-4.

---

2 See *http://bit.ly/1HGTbGf*.

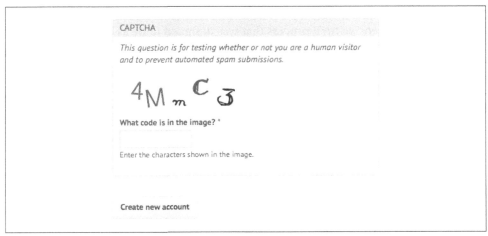

Figure 11-4. An example of the default text CAPTCHA for Drupal's CAPTCHA project

What makes this CAPTCHA so easy for both humans and machines to read, compared to other CAPTCHAs?

- Characters do not overlap each other, nor do they cross into each other's space horizontally. That is, it is possible to draw a neat rectangle around each character without overlapping any other character.
- There are no background images, lines, or other distracting garbage that could confuse an OCR program.
- It is not obvious from this image, but there are few variations on the font that the CAPTCHA uses. It alternates between a clean sans-serif font (as seen in the characters "4" and "M") and a handwriting-style font, (as seen in the characters "m," "C," and "3").
- There is a high contrast between the white background and the dark-colored characters.

This CAPTCHA does throw a few curves, though, that make it challenging for OCR programs to read:

- Both letters and numbers are used, increasing the number of potential characters.
- The randomized tilt of the letters might confuse OCR software, but remains very easy for humans to read.
- The relatively strange handwriting font presents particular challenges, with extra lines in the "C" and "3" and an unusually small lowercase "m" requiring extra training for computers to get the hang of.

When we run Tesseract over this image using the command:

```
$tesseract captchaExample.png output
```

we get this *output.txt* file:

```
4N\,,,C<3
```

It got the 4, C, and 3 right, but it's clearly not going to be able to fill out a CAPTCHA-protected field any time soon.

Training Tesseract

In order to train Tesseract to recognize writing, whether it's an obscure and difficult-to-read font or a CAPTCHA, you need to give it multiple examples of each character.

This is the part where you might want to queue up a good podcast or movie because it's going to be a couple of hours of fairly boring work. The first step is to download multiple examples of your CAPTCHA into a single directory. The number of examples you compile will depend on the complexity of the CAPTCHA; I used 100 sample files (a total of 500 characters, or about 8 examples per symbol, on average) for my CAPTCHA training, and that seems to work fairly well.

Tip: I recommend naming the image after the CAPTCHA solution it represents (i.e., *4MmC3.jpg*). I've found that this helps to do quick error-checking across large numbers of files at once—you can view all files as thumbnails and compare the image against its image name easily. This helps greatly in error checking in subsequent steps, as well.

The second step is to tell Tesseract exactly what each character is and where it is in the image. This involves creating box files, one for every CAPTCHA image. A box file looks like this:

```
4 15 26 33 55 0
M 38 13 67 45 0
m 79 15 101 26 0
C 111 33 136 60 0
3 147 17 176 45 0
```

The first symbol is the character represented, the next four numbers represent coordinates for a rectangular box outlining the image, and the last number is a "page number" used for training with multipage documents (0 for us).

Obviously, these box files are not fun to create by hand, but there are a variety of tools to help you out. I like the online tool Tesseract OCR Chopper (*http://bit.ly/1JhYQa5*) because it requires no installation or additional libraries, runs on any machine that has a browser, and is relatively easy to use: upload the image, click the "add" button at the bottom if you need additional boxes, adjust the size of the boxes if necessary, and copy and paste your new box file text into a new file.

Box files must be saved in plain text, with the *.box* file extension. As with the image files, it's handy to name the box files by the CAPTCHA solutions they represent (e.g., *4MmC3.box*). Again, this makes it easy to double-check the contents of the *.box* file text against the name of the file, and then again against the image file it is paired with if you sort all of the files in your data directory by their filename.

Again, you'll need to create about 100 of these files to ensure that you have enough data. Also, Tesseract does occasionally discard files as being unreadable, so you might want some buffer room on top of that. If you find that your OCR results aren't quite as good as you'd like, or Tesseract is stumbling over certain characters, it's a good debugging step to create additional training data and try again.

After creating a data folder full of *.box* files and image files, copy this data into a backup folder before doing any further manipulation on it. Although running training scripts over the data is unlikely to delete anything, it's better safe than sorry when hours' worth of work put into *.box* file creation is involved. Additionally, it's good to be able to scrap a messy directory full of compiled data and try again.

There are half a dozen steps to performing all the data analysis and creating the training files required for Tesseract. There are tools that do this for you given corresponding source image and *.box* files, but none at the moment for Tesseract 3.02, unfortunately.

I've written a solution in Python (*http://bit.ly/1HYw4wk*) that operates over a file containing both image and box files and creates all necessary training files automatically.

The main settings and steps that this program takes can be seen in its `main` and `run All` methods:

```
def main(self):
    languageName = "eng"
    fontName = "captchaFont"
    directory = "<path to images>"

def runAll(self):
    self.createFontFile()
    self.cleanImages()
    self.renameFiles()
    self.extractUnicode()
    self.runShapeClustering()
    self.runMfTraining()
    self.runCnTraining()
    self.createTessData()
```

The only three variables you'll need to set here are fairly straightforward:

languageName
The three-letter language code that Tesseract uses to understand which language it's looking at. In most cases, you'll probably want to use "eng" for English.

`fontName`
> The name for your chosen font. This can be anything, but must be a single word without spaces.

The directory containing all of your image and box files
> I recommend you make this an absolute path, but if you use a relative path, it will need to be relative to where you are running the Python code from. If it is absolute, you can run the code from anywhere on your machine.

Let's take a look at the individual functions used.

`createFontFile` creates a required file, *font_properties*, that lets Tesseract know about the new font we are creating:

```
captchaFont 0 0 0 0 0
```

This file consists of the name of the font, followed by 1s and 0s indicating whether italic, bold, or other versions of the font should be considered (training fonts with these properties is an interesting exercise, but unfortunately outside the scope of this book).

`cleanImages` creates higher-contrast versions of all image files found, converts them to grayscale, and performs other operations that make the image files easier to read by OCR programs. If you are dealing with CAPTCHA images with visual garbage that might be easy to filter out in post-processing, here would be the place to add that additional processing.

`renameFiles` renames all of your *.box* files and their corresponding image files with the names required by Tesseract (the file numbers here are sequential digits to keep multiple files separate):

- *<languageName>.<fontName>.exp<fileNumber>.box*
- *<languageName>.<fontName>.exp<fileNumber>.tiff*

`extractUnicode` looks at all of the created *.box* files and determines the total set of characters available to be trained. The resulting Unicode file will tell you how many different characters you've found, and could be a good way to quickly see if you're missing anything.

The next three functions, `runShapeClustering`, `runMfTraining`, and `runCtTraining`, create the files `shapetable`, `pfftable`, and `normproto`, respectively. These all provide information about the geometry and shape of each character, as well as provide statistical information that Tesseract uses to calculate the probability that a given character is one type or another.

Finally, Tesseract renames each of the compiled data folders to be prepended by the required language name (e.g., *shapetable* is renamed to *eng.shapetable*) and compiles all of those files into the final training data file *eng.traineddata*.

The only step you have to perform manually is move the created *eng.traineddata* file to your *tessdata* root folder by using the following commands on Linux and Mac:

```
$cp /path/to/data/eng.traineddata $TESSDATA_PREFIX/tessdata
```

Following these steps, you should have no problem solving CAPTCHAs of the type that Tesseract has now been trained for. Now when I ask Tesseract to read the example image, I get the correct response:

```
$ tesseract captchaExample.png output;cat output.txt
4MmC3
```

Success! A significant improvement over the previous interpretation of the image as "4N\,,,C<3"

This is just a quick overview of the full power of Tesseract's font training and recognition capabilities. If you are interested in extensively training Tesseract, perhaps starting your own personal library of CAPTCHA training files, or sharing new font recognition capabilities with the world, I recommend checking out the documentation (*https://code.google.com/p/tesseract-ocr/wiki/TrainingTesseract3*).

Retrieving CAPTCHAs and Submitting Solutions

Many popular content management systems are frequently spammed with registrations by bots that are preprogrammed with the well-known location of these user registration pages. On *http://pythonscraping.com*, for instance, even a CAPTCHA (admittedly, weak) does little to put a damper on the influx of registrations.

So how do these bots do it? We've successfully solved CAPTCHAs in images sitting around on our hard drive, but how do we make a fully functioning bot? This section ties together many techniques covered in previous chapters. If you haven't already, you should at least skim the chapters on submitting forms and downloading files.

Most image-based CAPTCHAs have several properties:

- They are dynamically generated images, created by a server-side program. They might have image sources that do not look like traditional images, such as <img src="WebForm.aspx?id=8AP85CQKE9TJ">, but can be downloaded and manipulated like any other image.
- The solution to the image is stored in a server-side database.
- Many CAPTCHAs time out if you take too long to solve them. This usually isn't a problem for bots, but queuing CAPTCHA solutions for later use, or other practi-

ces that may delay the time between when the CAPTCHA was requested, and when the solution is submitted, may not be successful.

The general approach to this is to download the CAPTCHA image file to your hard drive, clean it, use Tesseract to parse the image, and return the solution under the appropriate form parameter.

I've created a page at *http://pythonscraping.com/humans-only* with a CAPTCHA-protected comment form for the purpose of writing a bot to defeat. The bot looks like the following:

```
from urllib.request import urlretrieve
from urllib.request import urlopen
from bs4 import BeautifulSoup
import subprocess
import requests
from PIL import Image
from PIL import ImageOps

def cleanImage(imagePath):
    image = Image.open(imagePath)
    image = image.point(lambda x: 0 if x<143 else 255)
    borderImage = ImageOps.expand(image,border=20,fill='white')
    borderImage.save(imagePath)

html = urlopen("http://www.pythonscraping.com/humans-only")
bsObj = BeautifulSoup(html)
#Gather prepopulated form values
imageLocation = bsObj.find("img", {"title": "Image CAPTCHA"})["src"]
formBuildId = bsObj.find("input", {"name":"form_build_id"})["value"]
captchaSid = bsObj.find("input", {"name":"captcha_sid"})["value"]
captchaToken = bsObj.find("input", {"name":"captcha_token"})["value"]

captchaUrl = "http://pythonscraping.com"+imageLocation
urlretrieve(captchaUrl, "captcha.jpg")
cleanImage("captcha.jpg")
p = subprocess.Popen(["tesseract", "captcha.jpg", "captcha"], stdout=
    subprocess.PIPE,stderr=subprocess.PIPE)
p.wait()
f = open("captcha.txt", "r")

#Clean any whitespace characters
captchaResponse = f.read().replace(" ", "").replace("\n", "")
print("Captcha solution attempt: "+captchaResponse)

if len(captchaResponse) == 5:
    params = {"captcha_token":captchaToken, "captcha_sid":captchaSid,
            "form_id":"comment_node_page_form", "form_build_id": formBuildId,
                "captcha_response":captchaResponse, "name":"Ryan Mitchell",
                "subject": "I come to seek the Grail",
                "comment_body[und][0][value]":
                                    "...and I am definitely not a bot"}
```

```
    r = requests.post("http://www.pythonscraping.com/comment/reply/10",
                     data=params)
    responseObj = BeautifulSoup(r.text)
    if responseObj.find("div", {"class":"messages"}) is not None:
        print(responseObj.find("div", {"class":"messages"}).get_text())
else:
    print("There was a problem reading the CAPTCHA correctly!")
```

Note there are two conditions on which this script fails: if Tesseract did not extract exactly five characters from the image (because we know that all valid solutions to this CAPTCHA must have five characters), or if it submits the form but the CAPTCHA was solved incorrectly. The first case happens approximately 50% of the time, at which point it does not bother submitting the form and fails with an error message. The second case happens approximately 20% of the time, for a total accuracy rate of about 30% (or about 80% accuracy for each character encountered, over 5 characters).

Although this may seem low, keep in mind that there is usually no limit placed on the number of times users are allowed to make CAPTCHA attempts, and that most of these incorrect attempts can be aborted without needing to actually send the form. When a form is actually sent, the CAPTCHA is accurate most of the time. If that doesn't convince you, also keep in mind that simple guessing would give you an accuracy rate of .0000001%. Running a program three or four times rather than guessing 900 million times is quite the time saver!

Avoiding Scraping Traps

There are few things more frustrating than scraping a site, viewing the output, and not seeing the data that's so clearly visible in your browser. Or submitting a form that should be perfectly fine but gets denied by the web server. Or getting your IP address blocked by a site for unknown reasons.

These are some of the most difficult bugs to solve, not only because they can be so unexpected (a script that works just fine on one site might not work at all on another, seemingly identical, site), but because they purposefully don't have any tell tale error messages or stack traces to use. You've been identified as a bot, rejected, and you don't know why.

In this book, I've written about a lot of ways to do tricky things on websites (submitting forms, extracting and cleaning difficult data, executing JavaScript, etc.). This chapter is a bit of a catchall in that the techniques stem from a wide variety of subjects (HTTP headers, CSS, and HTML forms, to name a few). However, they all have something in common: they are meant to overcome an obstacle put in place for the sole purpose of preventing automated web scraping of a site.

Regardless of how immediately useful this information is to you at the moment, I highly recommend you at least skim this chapter. You never know when it might help you solve a very difficult bug or prevent a problem altogether.

A Note on Ethics

In the first few chapters of this book, I discussed the legal gray area that web scraping inhabits, as well as some of the ethical guidelines to scrape by. To be honest, this chapter is, ethically, perhaps the most difficult one for me to write. My websites have been plagued by bots, spammers, web scrapers, and all manner of unwanted virtual guests, as perhaps yours have been. So why teach people how to build better bots?

There are a few reasons why I believe this chapter is important to include:

- There are perfectly ethical and legally sound reasons to scrape some websites that do not want to be scraped. In a previous job I had as a web scraper, I performed an automated collection of information from websites that were publishing clients' names, addresses, telephone numbers, and other personal information to the Internet without their consent. I used the scraped information to make formal requests to the websites to remove this information. In order to avoid competition, these sites guarded this information from scrapers vigilantly. However, my work to ensure the anonymity of my company's clients (some of whom had stalkers, were the victims of domestic violence, or had other very good reasons to want to keep a low profile) made a compelling case for web scraping, and I was grateful that I had the skills necessary to do the job.
- Although it is almost impossible to build a "scraper proof" site (or at least one that can still be easily accessed by legitimate users), I hope that the information in this chapter will help those wanting to defend their websites against malicious attacks. Throughout, I will point out some of the weaknesses in each web scraping technique, which you can use to defend your own site. Keep in mind that most bots on the Web today are merely doing a broad scan for information and vulnerabilities, and employing even a couple of simple techniques described in this chapter will likely thwart 99% of them. However, they are getting more sophisticated every month, and it's best to be prepared.
- Like most programmers, I simply don't believe that withholding any sort of educational information is a net positive thing to do.

While you're reading this chapter, keep in mind that many of these scripts and described techniques should not be run against every site you can find. Not only is it not a nice thing to do, but you could wind up receiving a cease-and-desist letter or worse. But I'm not going to pound you over the head with this every time we discuss a new technique. So, for the rest of this book—as the philosopher Gump once said— "That's all I have to say about that."

Looking Like a Human

The fundamental challenge for sites that do not want to be scraped is figuring out how to tell bots from humans. Although many of the techniques sites use (such as CAPTCHAs) can be difficult to fool, there are a few fairly easy things you can do to make your bot look more human.

Adjust Your Headers

In Chapter 9, we used the `requests` module to handle forms on a website. The `requests` module is also excellent for setting headers. HTTP headers are a list of attributes, or preferences, sent by you every time you make a request to a web server. HTTP defines dozens of obscure header types, most of which are not commonly used. The following seven fields, however, are consistently used by most major browsers when initiating any connection (shown with example data from my own browser):

Host	https://www.google.com/
Connection	keep-alive
Accept	text/html,application/xhtml+xml,application/xml;q=0.9,image/webp,*/*;q=0.8
User-Agent	Mozilla/5.0 (Macintosh; Intel Mac OS X 10_9_5) AppleWebKit/537.36 (KHTML, like Gecko) Chrome/39.0.2171.95 Safari/537.36
Referrer	https://www.google.com/
Accept-Encoding	gzip, deflate, sdch
Accept-Language	en-US,en;q=0.8

And here are the headers that a typical Python scraper using the default `urllib` library might send:

Accept-Encoding	identity
User-Agent	Python-urllib/3.4

If you're a website administrator trying to block scrapers, which one are you more likely to let through?

Installing Requests

We installed the Requests module in Chapter 9, but if you haven't done so, you can find download links and instructions on the module's website (*http://bit.ly/1FVNZl6*) or use any third-party Python module installer.

Fortunately, headers can be completely customized using the `requests` module. The website *https://www.whatismybrowser.com* is great for testing browser properties viewable by servers. We'll scrape this website to verify our cookie settings with the following script:

```
import requests
from bs4 import BeautifulSoup

session = requests.Session()
headers = {"User-Agent":"Mozilla/5.0 (Macintosh; Intel Mac OS X 10_9_5)
                        AppleWebKit 537.36 (KHTML, like Gecko) Chrome",
          "Accept":"text/html,application/xhtml+xml,application/xml;
                    q=0.9,image/webp,*/*;q=0.8"}
url = "https://www.whatismybrowser.com/
      developers/what-http-headers-is-my-browser-sending"
req = session.get(url, headers=headers)

bsObj = BeautifulSoup(req.text)
print(bsObj.find("table",{"class":"table-striped"}).get_text())
```

The output should show that the headers are now the same ones set in the `headers` dictionary object in the code.

Although it is possible for websites to check for "humanness" based on any of the properties in HTTP headers, I've found that typically the only setting that really matters is the `User-Agent`. It's a good idea to keep this one set to something more inconspicuous than `Python-urllib/3.4`, regardless of what project you are working on. In addition, if you ever encounter an extremely suspicious website, populating one of the commonly used but rarely checked headers such as `Accept-Language` might be the key to convincing it you're a human.

Headers Change the Way You See the World

Let's say you want to write a machine learning language translator for a research project, but lack large amounts of translated text to test with. Many large sites present different translations of the same content, based on the indicated language preferences in your headers. Simply changing `Accept-Language:en-US` to `Accept-Language:fr` in your headers might get you a "Bonjour" from websites with the scale and budget to handle translation (large international companies are usually a good bet).

Headers also can prompt websites to change the format of the content they are presenting. For instance, mobile devices browsing the Web often see a very pared-down version of sites, lacking banner ads, Flash, and other distractions. If you try changing your `User-Agent` to something like the following, you might find that sites get a little easier to scrape!

> User-Agent:Mozilla/5.0 (iPhone; CPU iPhone OS 7_1_2 like Mac OS X) AppleWebKit/537.51.2 (KHTML, like Gecko) Version/7.0 Mobile/11D257 Safari/9537.53

Handling Cookies

Handling cookies correctly can alleviate many of scraping problems, although cookies can also be a double-edged sword. Websites that track your progression through a site using cookies might attempt to cut off scrapers that display abnormal behavior, such as completing forms too quickly, or visiting too many pages. Although these behaviors can be disguised by closing and reopening connections to the site, or even changing your IP address (see Chapter 14 for more information on how to do that), if your cookie gives your identity away, your efforts of disguise might be futile.

Cookies can also be very necessary to scrape a site. As shown in Chapter 9, staying logged in on a site requires that you be able to hold and present a cookie from page to page. Some websites don't even require that you actually log in and get a new version of a cookie every time—merely holding an old copy of a "logged in" cookie and visiting the site is enough.

If you are scraping a single targeted website or a small number of targeted sites, I recommend examining the cookies generated by those sites and considering which ones you might want your scraper to handle. There are a number of browser plug-ins that can show you how cookies are being set as you visit and move around a site. Edit-ThisCookie (*http://www.editthiscookie.com/*), a Chrome extension, is one of my favorites.

Check out the code samples in "Handling Logins and Cookies" on page 142 in Chapter 9 for more information about handling cookies using the `requests` module. Of course, because it is unable to execute JavaScript, the `requests` module will be unable to handle many of the cookies produced by modern tracking software, such as Google Analytics, which are set only after the execution of client-side scripts (or, sometimes, based on page events, such as button clicks, that happen while browsing the page). In order to handle these, you need to use the Selenium and PhantomJS packages (we covered their installation and basic usage in Chapter 10).

You can view cookies by visiting any site (*http://pythonscraping.com*, in this example) and calling `get_cookies()` on the webdriver:

```
from selenium import webdriver
driver = webdriver.PhantomJS(executable_path='<Path to Phantom JS>')
driver.get("http://pythonscraping.com")
driver.implicitly_wait(1)
print(driver.get_cookies())
```

This provides the fairly typical array of Google Analytics cookies:

```
[{'value': '1', 'httponly': False, 'name': '_gat', 'path': '/', 'expi
ry': 1422806785, 'expires': 'Sun, 01 Feb 2015 16:06:25 GMT', 'secure'
: False, 'domain': '.pythonscraping.com'}, {'value': 'GA1.2.161952506
2.1422806186', 'httponly': False, 'name': '_ga', 'path': '/', 'expiry
': 1485878185, 'expires': 'Tue, 31 Jan 2017 15:56:25 GMT', 'secure':
```

```
      False, 'domain': '.pythonscraping.com'}, {'value': '1', 'httponly': F
      alse, 'name': 'has_js', 'path': '/', 'expiry': 1485878185, 'expires':
       'Tue, 31 Jan 2017 15:56:25 GMT', 'secure': False, 'domain': 'pythons
      craping.com'}]
```

To manipulate cookies, you can call the `delete_cookie()`, `add_cookie()`, and `delete_all_cookies()` functions. In addition, you can save and store cookies for use in other web scrapers. Here's an example to give you an idea how these functions work together:

```
from selenium import webdriver

driver = webdriver.PhantomJS(executable_path='<Path to Phantom JS>')
driver.get("http://pythonscraping.com")
driver.implicitly_wait(1)
print(driver.get_cookies())

savedCookies = driver.get_cookies()

driver2 = webdriver.PhantomJS(executable_path='<Path to Phantom JS>')
driver2.get("http://pythonscraping.com")
driver2.delete_all_cookies()
for cookie in savedCookies:
    driver2.add_cookie(cookie)

driver2.get("http://pythonscraping.com")
driver.implicitly_wait(1)
print(driver2.get_cookies())
```

In this example, the first webdriver retrieves a website, prints the cookies, and then stores them in the variable `savedCookies`. The second webdriver loads the same website (technical note: it must load the website first so that Selenium knows which website the cookies belong to, even if the act of loading the website does nothing useful for us), deletes all of its cookies and replaces them with the saved cookies from the first webdriver. When loading the page again, the timestamps, codes, and other information in both cookies should be identical. According to Google Analytics, this second webdriver is now identical to the first one.

Timing Is Everything

Some well-protected websites might prevent you from submitting forms or interacting with the site if you do it too quickly. Even if these security features aren't in place, downloading lots of information from a website significantly faster than a normal human might is a good way to get yourself noticed, and blocked.

Therefore, although multithreaded programming might be a great way to load pages faster—allowing you to process data in one thread while repeatedly loading pages in another—it's a terrible policy for writing good scrapers. You should always try to keep individual page loads and data requests to a minimum. If possible, try to space them out by a few seconds, even if you have to add in an extra:

```
time.sleep(3)
```

Although web scraping often involves rule breaking and boundary pushing in order to get data, this is one rule you don't want to break. Not only does consuming inordinate server resources put you in a legally vulnerable position, but you might cripple or take down smaller sites. Bringing down websites is not an ethically ambiguous situation: it's just wrong. So watch your speed!

Common Form Security Features

There are many litmus tests that have been used over the years, and continue to be used, with varying degrees of success, to separate web scrapers from browser-using humans. Although it's not a big deal if a bot downloads some articles and blog posts that were available to the public anyway, it is a big problem if a bot creates thousands of user accounts and starts spamming all of your site's members. Web forms, especially forms that deal with account creation and logins, pose a significant threat to security and computational overhead if they're vulnerable to indiscriminate use by bots, so it's in the best interest of many site owners (or at least they think it is) to try to limit access to the site.

These anti-bot security measures centered on forms and logins can pose a significant challenge to web scrapers.

Keep in mind that this is only a partial overview of some of the security measures you might encounter when creating automated bots for these forms. Review Chapter 11, on dealing with CAPTCHAs and image processing, as well as Chapter 14, on dealing with headers and IP addresses, for more information on dealing with well-protected forms.

Hidden Input Field Values

"Hidden" fields in HTML forms allow the value contained in the field to be viewable by the browser but invisible to the user (unless they look at the site's source code). With the increase in use of cookies to store variables and pass them around on websites, hidden fields fell out of a favor for a while before another excellent purpose was discovered for them: preventing scrapers from submitting forms.

Figure 12-1 shows an example of these hidden fields at work on a Facebook login page. Although there are only three visible fields in the form (username, password, and a submit button), the form conveys a great deal of information to the server behind the scenes.

```
Q  ⧉  | Elements  Network  Sources  Timeline  Profiles  Resources  Audits  Console  EditThisCookie
         ▸ <a class="lfloat _ohe" href="/" title="Go to Facebook Home">_</a>
         ▾ <div class="menu_login_container rfloat _ohf">
            ▾ <form id="login_form" action="https://www.facebook.com/login.php?login_attempt=1" method="post" onsubmit="retu
                 <input type="hidden" name="lsd" value="AVoG5ZxZ" autocomplete="off">
               ▾ <table cellspacing="0" role="presentation">
                  ▾ <tbody>
                     ▸ <tr>_</tr>
                     ▸ <tr>_</tr>
                     ▸ <tr>_</tr>
                     </tbody>
                 </table>
                 <input type="hidden" autocomplete="off" name="timezone" value="300" id="u_0_m">
                 <input type="hidden" name="lgnrnd" value="072721_xhYS">
                 <input type="hidden" id="lgnjs" name="lgnjs" value="1414942041">
                 <input type="hidden" autocomplete="off" id="locale" name="locale" value="en_US">
                 <input type="hidden" name="qsstamp" value=
                 "W1tbNywxNCw0Nyw1NCw3MCw4NCwxMTEsMTMwLDE0MSwxNTYsMTY4LDE5NywyMDMsMjA0LDIxNSwyMjAsMjI3LDIzNiwyNjYsMjcyLDI3Cw
                 </form>
            </div>
```

Figure 12-1. The Facebook login form has quite a few hidden fields

There are two main ways hidden fields are used to prevent web scraping: a field can be populated with a randomly generated variable on the form page that the server is expecting to be posted to the form processing page. If this value is not present in the form, then the server can reasonably assume that the submission did not originate organically from the form page, but was posted by a bot directly to the processing page. The best way to get around this measure is to scrape the form page first, collect the randomly generated variable and then post to the processing page from there.

The second method is a "honey pot" of sorts. If a form contains a hidden field with an innocuous name, such as "username" or "email address," a poorly written bot might fill out the field and attempt to submit it, regardless of whether it is hidden to the user or not. Any hidden fields with actual values (or values that are different from their defaults on the form submission page) should be disregarded, and the user may even be blocked from the site.

In short: It is sometimes necessary to check the page that the form is on to see if you missed anything that the server might be expecting. If you see several hidden fields, often with large, randomly generated string variables, it is likely that the web server will be checking for their existence on form submission. In addition, there might be other checks to ensure that the form variables have been used only once, are recently generated (this eliminates the possibility of simply storing them in a script and using them over and over again over time), or both.

Avoiding Honeypots

Although CSS for the most part makes life extremely easy when it comes to differentiating useful information from nonuseful information (e.g., by reading the id and class tags), it can occasionally be problematic for web scrapers. If a field on a web form is hidden from a user via CSS, it is reasonable to assume that the average user visiting the site will not be able to fill it out because it doesn't show up in the browser. If the form *is* populated, there is likely a bot at work and the post will be discarded.

This applies not only to forms but to links, images, files, and any other item on the site that can be read by a bot but is hidden from the average user visiting the site through a browser. A page visit to a "hidden" link on a site can easily trigger a server-side script that will block the user's IP address, log that user out of the site, or take some other action to prevent further access. In fact, many business models have been based on exactly this concept.

Take for example the page located at *http://bit.ly/1GP4sbz*. This page contains two links, one hidden by CSS and another visible. In addition, it contains a form with two hidden fields:

```
<html>
<head>
    <title>A bot-proof form</title>
</head>
<style>
    body {
        overflow-x:hidden;
    }
    .customHidden {
        position:absolute;
        right:50000px;
    }
</style>
<body>
    <h2>A bot-proof form</h2>
    <a href=
     "http://pythonscraping.com/dontgohere" style="display:none;">Go here!</a>
    <a href="http://pythonscraping.com">Click me!</a>
    <form>
        <input type="hidden" name="phone" value="valueShouldNotBeModified"/><p/>
        <input type="text" name="email" class="customHidden"
                value="intentionallyBlank"/><p/>
        <input type="text" name="firstName"/><p/>
        <input type="text" name="lastName"/><p/>
        <input type="submit" value="Submit"/><p/>
    </form>
</body>
</html>
```

These three elements are hidden from the user in three different ways:

- The first link is hidden with a simple CSS `display:none` attribute
- The phone field is a hidden input field
- The email field is hidden by moving it 50,000 pixels to the right (presumably off the screen of everyone's monitors) and hiding the tell tale scroll bar

Fortunately, because Selenium actually renders the pages it visits, it is able to distinguish between elements that are visually present on the page and those that aren't.

Whether the element is present on the page can be determined by the `is_dis` `played()` function.

For example, the following code retrieves the previously described page and looks for hidden links and form input fields:

```
from selenium import webdriver
from selenium.webdriver.remote.webelement import WebElement

driver = webdriver.PhantomJS(executable_path='')
driver.get("http://pythonscraping.com/pages/itsatrap.html")
links = driver.find_elements_by_tag_name("a")
for link in links:
    if not link.is_displayed():
        print("The link "+link.get_attribute("href")+" is a trap")

fields = driver.find_elements_by_tag_name("input")
for field in fields:
    if not field.is_displayed():
        print("Do not change value of "+field.get_attribute("name"))
```

Selenium catches each hidden field, producing the following output:

```
The link http://pythonscraping.com/dontgohere is a trap
Do not change value of phone
Do not change value of email
```

Although you probably don't want to visit any hidden links you find, you will want to make sure that you submit any pre-populated hidden form values (or have Selenium submit them for you) with the rest of the form. To sum up, it is dangerous to simply ignore hidden fields, although you must be very careful when interacting with them.

The Human Checklist

There's a lot of information in this chapter, and indeed in this book, about how to build a scraper that looks less like a scraper and more like a human. If you keep getting blocked by websites and you don't know why, here's a checklist you can use to remedy the problem:

- First, if the page you are receiving from the web server is blank, missing information, or is otherwise not what you expect (or have seen in your own browser), it is likely caused by JavaScript being executed on the site to create the page. Review Chapter 10.
- If you are submitting a form or making a POST request to a website, check the page to make sure that everything the website is expecting you to submit is being submitted and in the correct format. Use a tool such as Chrome's Network inspector to view an actual POST command sent to the site to make sure you've got everything.

- If you are trying to log into a site and can't make the login "stick," or the website is experiencing other strange "state" behavior, check your cookies. Make sure that cookies are being persisted correctly between each page load and that your cookies are sent to the site for every request.
- If you are getting HTTP errors from the client, especially 403 Forbidden errors, it might indicate that the website has identified your IP address as a bot and is unwilling to accept any more requests. You will need to either wait until your IP address is removed from the list, or obtain a new IP address (either move to a Starbucks or see Chapter 14). To make sure you don't get blocked again, try the following:
  — Make sure that your scrapers aren't moving through the site too quickly. Fast scraping is a bad practice that places a heavy burden on the web administrator's servers, can land you in legal trouble, and is the number-one cause of scrapers getting blacklisted. Add delays to your scrapers and let them run overnight. Remember: Being in a rush to write programs or gather data is a sign of bad project management; plan ahead to avoid messes like this in the first place.
  — The obvious one: change your headers! Some sites will block anything that advertises itself as a scraper. Copy your own browser's headers if you're unsure about what some reasonable header values are.
  — Make sure you're not clicking on or accessing anything that a human normally would not be able to (refer back to "Avoiding Honeypots" on page 184 for more information).
  — If you find yourself jumping through a lot of difficult hoops to gain access, consider contacting the website administrator to let them know what you're doing. Try emailing *webmaster@<domain name>* or *admin@<domain name>* for permission to use your scrapers. Admins are people, too!

## CHAPTER 13

Testing Your Website with Scrapers

When working with web projects that have a large development stack, it's often only the "back" of the stack that ever gets tested regularly. Most programming languages today (including Python) have some type of test framework, but the front end of websites are often left out of these automated tests, although they might be the only customer-facing part of the project.

Part of the problem is that websites are often a mishmash of many markup languages and programming languages. You can write unit tests for sections of your JavaScript, but it's useless if the HTML it's interacting with has changed in such away that the JavaScript doesn't have the intended action on the page, even if it's working correctly.

The problem of front-end website testing has often been left as an afterthought, or delegated to lower-level programmers armed with, at most, a checklist and a bug tracker. However, with just a little more up-front effort, we can replace this checklist with a series of unit tests, and replace human eyes with a web scraper.

Imagine: test-driven development for web development. Daily tests to make sure all parts of the web interface are functioning as expected. A suite of tests run every time someone adds a new website feature, or changes the position of an element. In this chapter, we'll cover the basics of testing and how to test all sorts of websites, from simple to complicated, with Python-based web scrapers.

An Introduction to Testing

If you've never written tests for your code before, there's no better time to start than now. Having a suite of tests that can be run to ensure that your code performs as expected (at least, as far as you've written tests for) saves you time and worry and makes releasing new updates easy.

What Are Unit Tests?

The words *test* and *unit test* are often used interchangeably. Often, when programmers refer to "writing tests" what they really mean is "writing unit tests." On the other hand, when some programmers refer to writing unit tests, they're really writing some other kind of test.

Although definitions and practices tend to vary from company to company, a unit test generally has the following characteristics:

- Each unit test tests one aspect of the functionality of a component. For example, it might ensure that the appropriate error message is thrown if a negative number of dollars is withdrawn from a bank account.

  Often, unit tests are grouped together in the same class, based on the component they are testing. You might have the test for a negative dollar value being withdrawn from a bank account, followed by a unit test for the behavior of an overdrawn bank account.

- Each unit test can be run completely independently, and any setup or teardown required for the unit test must be handled by the unit test itself. Similarly, unit tests must not interfere with the success or failure of other tests, and they must be able to run successfully in any order.

- Each unit test usually contains at least one *assertion*. For example, a unit test might assert that the answer to 2+2 is 4. Occasionally, a unit test might contain only a failure state. For example, it might fail if an exception is not thrown, but pass by default if everything goes smoothly.

- Unit tests are separated from the bulk of the code. Although they necessarily need to import and use the code they are testing, they are generally kept in separate classes and directories.

Although there are many other types of tests that can be written—integration tests and validation tests, for example—we will primarily focus on unit testing in this chapter. Not only have unit tests become extremely popular, with recent pushes toward test-driven development, but their length and flexibility make them easy to work with as examples, and Python has some built-in unit testing capabilities as we'll see in the next section.

Python unittest

Python's unit testing module, `unittest`, comes packaged with all standard Python installations. Just import and extend `unittest.TestCase`, and it will do the following:

- Provide `setUp` and `tearDown` functions that run before and after each unit test
- Provide several types of "assert" statements to allow tests to pass or fail

- Run all functions that begin with `test_` as unit tests, and ignore functions that are not prepended as tests.

The following provides a very simple unit test for ensuring that 2+2 = 4, according to Python:

```python
import unittest

class TestAddition(unittest.TestCase):
    def setUp(self):
        print("Setting up the test")

    def tearDown(self):
        print("Tearing down the test")

    def test_twoPlusTwo(self):
        total = 2+2
        self.assertEqual(4, total);

if __name__ == '__main__':
    unittest.main()
```

Although `setUp` and `tearDown` don't provide any useful functionality here, they are included for the purposes of illustration. Note that these functions are run before and after each individual test, not before and after all the tests in the class.

Testing Wikipedia

Testing the front end of your website (excluding JavaScript, which we'll cover next) is as simple as combining the Python `unittest` library with a web scraper:

```python
from urllib.request import urlopen
from bs4 import BeautifulSoup
import unittest

class TestWikipedia(unittest.TestCase):
    bsObj = None
    def setUpClass():
        global bsObj
        url = "http://en.wikipedia.org/wiki/Monty_Python"
        bsObj = BeautifulSoup(urlopen(url))

    def test_titleText(self):
        global bsObj
        pageTitle = bsObj.find("h1").get_text()
        self.assertEqual("Monty Python", pageTitle);

    def test_contentExists(self):
        global bsObj
        content = bsObj.find("div",{"id":"mw-content-text"})
        self.assertIsNotNone(content)
```

```
if __name__ == '__main__':
    unittest.main()
```

There are two tests this time: the first tests whether the title of the page is the expected "Monty Python," and the second makes sure that the page has a content div.

Note that the content of the page is loaded only once, and that the global object bsObj is shared between tests. This is accomplished by using the unittest-specified function setUpClass, which is run only once at the start of the class (unlike setUp, which is run before every individual test). Using setUpClass instead of setUp saves unnecessary page loads; we can grab the content once and run multiple tests on it.

Although testing a single page at a time might not seem all that powerful or interesting, if you recall from Chapter 3, it is relatively easy to build web crawlers that can iteratively move through all pages of a website. What happens when we combine a web crawler with a unit test that makes some assertion about each page?

There are many ways to run a test repeatedly, but we must be careful only to load each page once for each set of tests we want to run on the page, and we must also avoid holding large amounts of information in memory at once. The following setup does just that:

```
class TestWikipedia(unittest.TestCase):
    bsObj = None
    url = None

    def test_PageProperties(self):
        global bsObj
        global url

        url = "http://en.wikipedia.org/wiki/Monty_Python"
        #Test the first 100 pages we encounter
        for i in range(1, 100):
            bsObj = BeautifulSoup(urlopen(url))
            titles = self.titleMatchesURL()
            self.assertEquals(titles[0], titles[1])
            self.assertTrue(self.contentExists())
            url = self.getNextLink()
        print("Done!")

    def titleMatchesURL(self):
        global bsObj
        global url
        pageTitle = bsObj.find("h1").get_text()
        urlTitle = url[(url.index("/wiki/")+6):]
        urlTitle = urlTitle.replace("_", " ")
        urlTitle = unquote(urlTitle)
        return [pageTitle.lower(), urlTitle.lower()]
```

```
    def contentExists(self):
        global bsObj
        content = bsObj.find("div",{"id":"mw-content-text"})
        if content is not None:
            return True
        return False

    def getNextLink(self):
        #Returns random link on page, using technique from Chapter 5

if __name__ == '__main__':
    unittest.main()
```

There are a few things to notice. First, there is only one actual test in this class. The other functions are technically only helper functions, even though they're doing the bulk of the computational work to determine whether a test passes. Because the test function performs the assertion statements, the results of the test are passed back to the test function where the assertions happen.

Also, while `contentExists` returns a boolean, `titleMatchesURL` returns the values themselves back for evaluation. To see why we would want to pass values back rather than just a boolean, compare the results of a boolean assertion:

```
======================================================================
FAIL: test_PageProperties (__main__.TestWikipedia)
----------------------------------------------------------------------
Traceback (most recent call last):
  File "15-3.py", line 22, in test_PageProperties
    self.assertTrue(self.titleMatchesURL())
AssertionError: False is not true
```

with the results of an `assertEquals` statement:

```
======================================================================
FAIL: test_PageProperties (__main__.TestWikipedia)
----------------------------------------------------------------------
Traceback (most recent call last):
  File "15-3.py", line 23, in test_PageProperties
    self.assertEquals(titles[0], titles[1])
AssertionError: 'lockheed u-2' != 'u-2 spy plane'
```

Which one is easier to debug?

In this case, the error is occurring because of a redirect, when the article *http://bit.ly/1JccOqF* redirects to an article titled "Lockheed U-2"

Testing with Selenium

As with Ajax scraping in Chapter 10, JavaScript presents particular challenges when doing website testing. Fortunately, Selenium has an excellent framework in place for handling particularly complicated websites; in fact, the library was originally designed for website testing!

Although obviously written in the same language, the syntax of Python unittests and Selenium unit tests have surprisingly little in common. Selenium does not require that its unit tests be contained as functions within classes; its "assert" statements do not require parentheses; and tests pass silently, only producing some kind of message on a failure:

```
driver = webdriver.PhantomJS()
driver.get("http://en.wikipedia.org/wiki/Monty_Python")
assert "Monty Python" in driver.title
driver.close()
```

When run, this test should produce no output.

In this way, Selenium tests can be written more casually than Python unittests, and assert statements can even be integrated into regular code, where it is desirable for code execution to terminate if some condition is not met.

Interacting with the Site

Recently, I wanted to contact a local small business through its website's contact form but found that the HTML form was broken; nothing happened when I clicked the submit button. After a little investigation, I saw they were using a simple mailto form that was designed to send them an email with the form's contents. Fortunately, I was able to use this information to send them an email, explain the problem with their form, and hire them, despite the technical issue.

If I were to write a traditional scraper that used or tested this form, my scraper would likely just copy the layout of the form and send an email directly—bypassing the form altogether. How could I test the functionality of the form and ensure that it was working perfectly through a browser?

Although previous chapters have discussed navigating links, submitting forms, and other types of interaction-like activity, at its core everything we've done is designed to *bypass* the browser interface, not use it. Selenium, on the other hand, can literally enter text, click buttons, and do everything through the browser (in this case, the headless PhantomJS browser), and detect things like broken forms, badly coded JavaScript, HTML typos, and other issues that might stymie actual customers.

Key to this sort of testing is the concept of Selenium `elements`. This object was briefly encountered in Chapter 10, and is returned by calls like:

```
usernameField = driver.find_element_by_name('username')
```

Just as there are a number of actions you can take on various elements of a website in your browser, there are many actions Selenium can perform on any given element. Among these are:

```
myElement.click()
myElement.click_and_hold()
myElement.release()
myElement.double_click()
myElement.send_keys_to_element("content to enter")
```

In addition to performing a one-time action on an element, strings of actions can be combined into *action chains*, which can be stored and executed once or multiple times in a program. Action chains are useful in that they can be a convenient way to string long sets of multiple actions, but they are functionally identical to calling the action explicitly on the element, as in the preceding examples.

To see this difference, take a look at the form page at *http://bit.ly/1AGKPRU* (which was previously used as an example in Chapter 9). We can fill out the form and submit it in the following way:

```
from selenium import webdriver
from selenium.webdriver.remote.webelement import WebElement
from selenium.webdriver.common.keys import Keys
from selenium.webdriver import ActionChains


driver = webdriver.PhantomJS(executable_path='<Path to Phantom JS>')
driver.get("http://pythonscraping.com/pages/files/form.html")

firstnameField = driver.find_element_by_name("firstname")
lastnameField = driver.find_element_by_name("lastname")
submitButton = driver.find_element_by_id("submit")

### METHOD 1 ###
firstnameField.send_keys("Ryan")
lastnameField.send_keys("Mitchell")
submitButton.click()
################

### METHOD 2 ###
actions = ActionChains(driver).click(firstnameField).send_keys("Ryan")
                        .click(lastnameField).send_keys("Mitchell")
                        .send_keys(Keys.RETURN)
actions.perform()
################

print(driver.find_element_by_tag_name("body").text)

driver.close()
```

Method 1 calls send_keys on the two fields, then clicks the submit button, while method 2 uses a single action chain to click on and enter text in each field, which happens in a sequence after the perform method is called. This script will operate in the same way if either the first method or the second method is used and will print the line:

```
Hello there, Ryan Mitchell!
```

There is another variation in the two methods, in addition to the objects they use to handle the commands: notice that the first method clicks the "submit" button, while the second uses the "return" keystroke to submit the form while the text box is submitted. Because there are many ways to think about the sequence of events that complete the same action, there are many ways to complete the same action using Selenium.

Drag and drop

Clicking on buttons and entering text is one thing, but where Selenium really shines is in its ability to deal with relatively novel forms of web interaction. Selenium allows for the manipulation of drag-and-drop interfaces with ease. Using its drag-and-drop function requires you to specify a "source" element (the element to be dragged) and either an offset to drag it across, or a target element to drag it to.

The demo page located at *http://bit.ly/1GP52py* presents an example of this type of interface:

```
from selenium import webdriver
from selenium.webdriver.remote.webelement import WebElement
from selenium.webdriver import ActionChains

driver = webdriver.PhantomJS(executable_path='<Path to Phantom JS>')
driver.get('http://pythonscraping.com/pages/javascript/draggableDemo.html')

print(driver.find_element_by_id("message").text)

element = driver.find_element_by_id("draggable")
target = driver.find_element_by_id("div2")
actions = ActionChains(driver)
actions.drag_and_drop(element, target).perform()

print(driver.find_element_by_id("message").text)
```

Two messages are printed out from the message div on the demo page. The first says:

```
Prove you are not a bot, by dragging the square from the blue area to the red
area!
```

Then, very quickly, after the task is completed, the content is printed out again, which now reads:

```
You are definitely not a bot!
```

Of course, like the demo page suggests, dragging elements to prove you're not a bot is a common theme in many CAPTCHAs. Although bots have been able to drag objects around for a long time (it's just a matter of clicking, holding, and moving), somehow the idea of using "drag this" as a verification of humanity just won't die.

In addition, these draggable CAPTCHA libraries rarely use any difficult-for-bots tasks, like "drag the picture of the kitten onto the picture of the cow" (which requires you to identify the pictures as "a kitten" and "a cow," while parsing instructions); instead, they often involve number ordering or some other fairly trivial task like the one in the preceding example.

Of course, their strength lies in the fact that there are so many different variations, and they are so infrequently used—no one will likely bother making a bot that can defeat all of them. At any rate, this example should be enough to illustrate why you should never use this technique for large-scale websites.

Taking screenshots

In addition to the usual testing capabilities, Selenium has an interesting trick up its sleeve that might make your testing (or impressing your boss) a little easier: screenshots. Yes, photographic evidence can be created from unit tests run without the need for actually pressing the PrtScn key:

```
driver = webdriver.PhantomJS()
driver.implicitly_wait(5)
driver.get('http://www.pythonscraping.com/')
driver.get_screenshot_as_file('tmp/pythonscraping.png')
```

This script navigates to *http://pythonscraping.com*, waits five seconds for any Java-Script to execute, then stores a screenshot of the home page in the local *tmp* folder (the folder must already exist for this to store correctly).

Unittest or Selenium?

The syntactical rigor and verboseness of a Python unittest might be desirable for most large test suites, while the flexibility and power of a Selenium test might be your only option for testing some website features. So which to use?

Here's the secret: you don't have to choose. Selenium can easily be used to obtain some information about a website, while unittest can evaluate whether that information meets the criteria for passing the test. There is no reason you can't import Selenium tools into a Python unittest, combining the best of both worlds.

For example, the following script creates a unit test for a website's draggable interface, asserting that it correctly says, "You are not a bot!" after one element has been dragged to another:

```
from selenium import webdriver
from selenium.webdriver.remote.webelement import WebElement
from selenium.webdriver import ActionChains
import unittest

class TestAddition(unittest.TestCase):
    driver = None
    def setUp(self):
        global driver
        driver = webdriver.PhantomJS(executable_path='<Path to Phantom JS>')
        url = 'http://pythonscraping.com/pages/javascript/draggableDemo.html'
        driver.get(url)

    def tearDown(self):
        print("Tearing down the test")

    def test_drag(self):
        global driver
        element = driver.find_element_by_id("draggable")
        target = driver.find_element_by_id("div2")
        actions = ActionChains(driver)
        actions.drag_and_drop(element, target).perform()

        self.assertEqual("You are definitely
                        not a bot!", driver.find_element_by_id(
                        "message").text)

if __name__ == '__main__':
    unittest.main()
```

Virtually anything on a website can be tested with the combination of Python's unittest and Selenium. In fact, combined with some of the image-processing libraries from Chapter 11, you can even take a screenshot of the website and test on a pixel-by-pixel basis what it should contain!

## CHAPTER 14

Scraping Remotely

That this chapter is the last in the book is somewhat appropriate. Up until now we have been running all the Python applications from the command line, within the confines of our home computers. Sure, you might have installed MySQL in an attempt to replicate the environment of a real-life server. But it's just not the same. As the saying goes: "If you love something, set it free."

In this chapter, I'll cover several methods for running scripts from different machines, or even just different IP addresses on your own machine. Although you might be tempted to put this step off as something you don't *need* right now, you might be surprised at how easy it is to get started with the tools you already have (such as a personal website on a paid hosting account), and how much easier your life becomes once you stop trying to run Python scrapers from your laptop.

Why Use Remote Servers?

Although using a remote server might seem like an obvious step when launching a web app intended for use by a wide audience, more often than not the tools we build for our own purposes are just left running locally. People who decide to push onto a remote platform usually base their decision on two primary motivations: the need for greater power and flexibility, and the need to use an alternative IP address.

Avoiding IP Address Blocking

When building web scrapers, the rule of thumb is: everything can be faked. You can send emails from addresses you don't own, automate mouse movement data from a command line, or even horrify web administrators by sending their website traffic from Internet Explorer 5.0.

The one thing that cannot be faked is your IP address. Anyone can send you a letter with the return address: "The President, 1600 Pennsylvania Avenue Northwest, Washington, DC 20500." However, if the letter is postmarked from Albuquerque, N.M., you can be fairly certain you're not corresponding with the President of the United States.[1]

Most efforts to stop scrapers from accessing websites focus on detecting the difference between humans and bots. Going so far as to block IP addresses is a little like a farmer giving up spraying pesticides in favor of just torching the field. It's a last-ditch but very effective method of simply discarding packets sent from troublesome IP addresses. However, there are problems with this solution:

- IP address access lists are painful to maintain. Although large websites most often have their own programs automating some of the routine management of these lists (bots blocking bots!), someone has to at least occasionally check them, or at least monitor their growth for problems.
- Each address adds a tiny amount of processing time to receive packets, as the server must check received packets against the list to decide whether to approve them. Many addresses multiplied by many packets can add up quickly. To save on processing time and complexity, admins often group these IP addresses into blocks and make rules such as "all 256 addresses in this range are blocked" if there are a few tightly clustered offenders. Which leads us to the third point.
- IP address blocking can lead to unintended consequences. For example, while I was an undergrad at Olin College of Engineering, one student wrote some software that attempted to rig votes for popular content on *http://digg.com* (this was before Reddit was in vogue). A single IP address blocked led to an entire dormitory being unable to access the site. The student simply moved his software to another server; in the meantime, Digg lost page visits from many regular users in its prime target demographic.

Despite its drawbacks, IP address blocking remains an extremely common method for server administrators to stop suspected web scrapers from accessing servers.

Portability and Extensibility

Some tasks are simply too large for a home computer and Internet connection. Although you don't want to put a large load on any single website, you might be collecting data across a wide range of sites, and require a lot more bandwidth and storage than your current setup can provide.

---

1 Technically, IP addresses can be spoofed in outgoing packets, which is a technique used in distributed denial-of-service attacks, where the attackers don't care about receiving return packets (which, if sent, will be sent to the wrong address). But web scraping is by definition an activity in which a response from the web server is required, so we think of IP addresses are one thing that can't be faked.

Moreover, by offloading computationally intensive processing, you can free up your home machine's cycles for more important tasks (*World of Warcraft*, anyone?). You don't have to worry about maintaining power and an Internet connection (launch your app at a Starbucks, pack up your laptop, and leave, knowing that everything's still running safely), and you can access your collected data anywhere there's an Internet connection.

If you have an application that requires so much computing power that a single Amazon extra-large computing instance won't satisfy you, you can also look into *distributed computing*. This allows multiple machines to work in parallel to accomplish your goals. As a simple example, you might have one machine crawl one set of sites and another crawl a second set of sites, and have both of them store collected data in the same database.

Of course, as noted in previous chapters, many can replicate what Google search does, but very few can replicate the scale at which Google search does it. Distributed computing is a very large field of computer science that is outside the scope of this book. However, learning how to launch your application onto a remote server is a necessary first step, and you might be surprised at what computers are capable of these days.

Tor

The Onion Router network, better known by the acronym *Tor*, is a network of volunteer servers set up to route and reroute traffic through many layers (hence the onion reference) of different servers in order to obscure its origin. Data is encrypted before it enters the network so that if any particular server is eavesdropped on the nature of the communication cannot be revealed. In addition, although the inbound and outbound communications of any particular server can be compromised, one would need to know the details of inbound and outbound communication for *all* the servers along the path of communication in order to decipher the true start and endpoints of a communication—a near-impossible feat.

Tor is commonly used by human rights workers and political whistleblowers to communicate with journalists, and receives much of its funding from the U.S. government. Of course, it is also commonly used for illegal activities as well, and so remains a constant target for government surveillance (although to date the surveillance has had only mixed success).

Limitations of Tor Anonymity

Although the reason we are using Tor in this book is to change our IP address, not achieve complete anonymity per se, it is worth taking a moment to address some of the strengths and limitations of Tor's ability to anonymize traffic.

Although you can assume when using Tor that the IP address you are coming from, according to a web server, is not an IP address that can be traced back to you, any information you share with that web server might expose you. For instance, if you log into your own Gmail account and then make incriminating Google searches, those searches can now be tied back to your identity.

Beyond the obvious, however, even the act of logging into Tor might be hazardous to your anonymity. In December 2013, a Harvard undergraduate student, in an attempt to get out of final exams, emailed a bomb threat to the school through the Tor network, using an anonymous email account. When the Harvard IT team looked at their logs, they found traffic going out to the Tor network from only a single machine, registered to a known student, during the time that the bomb threat was sent. Although they could not identify the eventual destination of this traffic (only that it was sent across Tor), the fact that the times matched up and there was only a single machine logged in at the time was damning enough to prosecute the student.

Logging into Tor is not an automatic invisibility cloak, nor does it give you free reign to do as you please on the Internet. Although it is a useful tool, be sure to use it with caution, intelligence, and, of course, morality.

Having Tor installed and running is a requirement for using Python with Tor, as we will see in the next section. Fortunately, the Tor service is extremely easy to install and start running with. Just go to the Tor downloads page (*http://bit.ly/1eLkRmv*) and download, install, open, and connect! Keep in mind that your Internet speed might appear to be slower while using Tor. Be patient—it might be going around the world several times!

PySocks

PySocks is a remarkably simple Python module that is capable of routing traffic through proxy servers and that works fantastically in conjunction with Tor. You can download it from its website (*http://bit.ly/1eLkTea*) or use any number of third-party module managers to install it.

Although not much in the way of documentation exists for this module, using it is extremely straightforward. The Tor service must be running on port 9150 (the default port) while running this code:

```
import socks
import socket
from urllib.request import urlopen

socks.set_default_proxy(socks.SOCKS5, "localhost", 9150)
socket.socket = socks.socksocket
print(urlopen('http://icanhazip.com').read())
```

The website *http://icanhazip.com* displays only the IP address for the client connecting to the server and can be useful for testing purposes. When this script is run, it should display an IP address that is not your own.

If you want to use Selenium and PhantomJS with Tor, you don't need PySocks at all—just make sure that Tor is currently running and add the optional `service_args` parameters, specifying that Selenium should connect through port 9150:

```
from selenium import webdriver
service_args = [ '--proxy=localhost:9150', '--proxy-type=socks5', ]
driver = webdriver.PhantomJS(executable_path='<path to PhantomJS>', \
                             service_args=service_args)

driver.get("http://icanhazip.com")
print(driver.page_source)
driver.close()
```

Again, this should print out an IP address that is not your own but the one that your running Tor client is currently using.

Remote Hosting

Although complete anonymity is lost once you pull out your credit card, hosting your web scrapers remotely dramatically improves their speed. This is both because you're able to purchase time on much larger machines than you likely own, but also because the connection no longer has to bounce through layers of a Tor network in order to reach its destination.

Running from a Website Hosting Account

If you have a personal or business website, you might already likely have the means to run your web scrapers from an external server. Even with relatively locked-down web servers, where you have no access to the command line, it is possible to trigger scripts to start and stop through a web interface.

If your website is hosted on a Linux server, it likely already runs Python. If you're hosting on a Windows server, you might be out of luck; you'll need to check specifically to see if Python is installed, or if the server administrator is willing to install it.

Most small web hosting providers come with software called *cPanel*, used to provide basic administration services and information about your website and related services. If you have access to cPanel, you can make sure that Python is set up to run on your server by going to "Apache Handlers" and adding a new handler (if it is not already present):

```
Handler: cgi-script
Extension(s): .py
```

This tells your server that all Python scripts should be executed as a *CGI-script*. CGI, which stands for *Common Gateway Interface*, is simply any program that can be run on a server and dynamically generate content that is displayed on a website. By explicitly defining Python scripts as CGI scripts, you're giving the server permission to execute them, rather than just display them in a browser or send the user a download.

Simply write your Python script, upload it to the server, and set the file permissions to 755 to allow it to be executed. To execute the script, simply navigate to the place you uploaded it to through your browser (or even better, write a scraper to do it for you). If you're worried about the general public accessing and executing the script, you have two options:

- Store the script at an obscure or hidden URL and make sure to never link to the script from any other accessible URL to avoid search engines indexing it.
- Protect the script with a password, or require that a password or secret token be sent to it before it can execute.

Of course, running a Python script from a service that is specifically designed to display websites is a bit of a hack. For instance, you'll probably notice that your web scraper-cum-website is a little slow to load. In fact, the page doesn't actually load (complete with the output of all "print" statements you might have written in) until the entire scrape is complete. This might take minutes, hours, or never complete at all, depending on how it is written. Although it certainly gets the job done, you might want more real-time output. For that you'll need an actual server.

Running from the Cloud

Back in the olden days of computing, programmers paid for or reserved time on computers in order to execute their code. With the advent of personal computers, this became unnecessary—you simply write and execute code on your own computer. Now, the ambitions of the applications have outpaced the development of the microprocessor to such a degree that programmers are once again moving to pay-per-hour computing instances.

This time around, however, users aren't paying for time on a single, physical machine but on its equivalent computing power, often spread among many machines. The nebulous structure of this system allows computing power to be priced according to times of peak demand. For instance, Amazon allows for bidding on "spot instances" when low costs are more important than immediacy.

Compute instances are also more specialized, and can be selected based on the needs of your application, with options like "high memory," "fast computing," and "large storage." Although web scrapers don't usually use much in the way of memory, you may want to consider large storage or fast computing in lieu of a more general-purpose instance for your scraping application. If you're doing large amounts of natural language processing, OCR work, or path finding (such as with the "Six Degrees of Wikipedia" problem), a fast computing instance might work well. If you're scraping large amounts of data, storing files, or large-scale analytics, you might want to go for an instance with storage optimization.

Although the sky is the limit as far as spending goes, at the time of this writing, instances start at just 1.3 cents an hour (for an Amazon EC2 micro instance), and Google's cheapest instance is 4.5 cents an hour, with a minimum of just 10 minutes. Thanks to the economies of scale, buying a small compute instance with a large company is about the same as buying your own physical, dedicated, machine—except that now, you don't need to hire an IT guy to keep it running.

Of course, step-by-step instructions for setting up and running cloud computing instances are somewhat outside of the scope of this book, but you will likely find that step-by-step instructions are not needed. With both Amazon and Google (not to mention the countless smaller companies in the industry) vying for cloud computing dollars, they've made setting up new instances as easy as following a simple prompt, thinking of an app name, and providing a credit card number. As of this writing, both Amazon and Google also offer hundreds of dollars worth of free computing hours to further tempt new clients.

Once you have an instance set up, you should be the proud new owner of an IP address, username, and public/private keys that can be used to connect to your instance through SSH. From there, everything should be literally the same as working with a server that you physically own—except, of course, you no longer have to worry about hardware maintenance or running your own plethora of advanced monitoring tools.

Additional Resources

Many years ago, running "in the cloud" was mostly the domain of those who felt like slogging through the documentation and already had some server administration experience. However, today, the tools have improved dramatically, due to increased popularity and competition among cloud computing providers.

Still, for building large-scale or more-complex scrapers and crawlers, you might want a little more guidance on creating a platform for collecting and storing data.

Google Compute Engine by Marc Cohen, Kathryn Hurley, and Paul Newson is a straightforward resource on using Google Cloud Computing with both Python and JavaScript. Not only does it cover Google's user interface, but also the command-line and scripting tools that you can use to give your application greater flexibility.

If you prefer to work with Amazon, Mitch Garnaat's *Python and AWS Cookbook* is a brief but extremely useful guide that will get you started with Amazon Web Services and show you how to get a scalable application up and running.

Moving Forward

The Web is constantly changing. The technologies that bring us images, video, text, and other data files are constantly being updated and reinvented. To keep pace, the collection of technologies used to scrape data from the Internet must also change.

Future versions of this text omit JavaScript entirely as an obsolete and rarely used technology and instead focus on HTML8 hologram parsing. However, what won't change is the mindset and general approach needed to successfully scrape any website. When encountering any web scraping project, now and into the distant future, you should always ask yourself:

- What is the question I want answered, or the problem I want solved?
- What data will help me achieve this, and where is it?
- How is the website displaying this data? Can I identify exactly which part of the website's code contains this information?
- How can I isolate the data and retrieve it?
- What processing or analysis needs to be done to make it more useful?
- How can I make this process better, faster, and more robust?

In addition, you will need to understand not just how to use the tools presented in this book in isolation, but how they can work together to solve a larger problem. Sometimes the data is easily available and well formatted, allowing a simple scraper to do the trick. Other times you have to put some thought into it.

In Chapter 10, for example, I combined the Selenium library to identify Ajax-loaded images on Amazon, and Tesseract to use optical character recognition to read them.

In the "Six Degrees of Wikipedia" problem, I used regular expressions to write a crawler that stored link information in a database, and then used a graph-solving algorithm in order to answer the question, "What is the shortest path of links between Kevin Bacon and Eric Idle"?

There is rarely an unsolvable problem when it comes to automated data collection on the Internet. Just remember: the Internet is one giant API with a somewhat poor user interface.

Python at a Glance

According to the Association for Computing Machinery (*http://acm.org*), Python is the top teaching language in the United States, with it being more commonly taught in introductory programming classes than BASIC, Java, and even C. This section will cover the basics of installing, using, and running Python 3.x and Python programs.

Installation and "Hello, World!"

If you have OS X or almost any flavor of Linux, you likely already have Python installed. If in doubt, type the following into your command line:

```
$python --version
```

We will be using Python 3.x throughout this book. If you see that you have Python 2.x installed, you upgrade on Linux simply by calling `apt-get`:

```
$sudo apt-get install python3
```

Note this might involve needing to execute your Python code by typing `$python3 myScript.py` into the command line, rather than `$python myScript.py`.

The OS X operating system, as of this writing, has Python 2.7 installed by default. To install Python 3.x, download an installer (*http://bit.ly/1KwxHPr*) from the Python website. Again, if you are running both Python 2.x and Python 3.x simultaneously, you might need to explicitly call Python 3.x using `$python3`.

For Windows users without Python installed, there are precompiled installers available for download (*http://bit.ly/1RCJ7VR*). Simply download, open, and install. You might also need to set the Windows system path to the directory in which you install Python in order to tell the operating system where it's at, but the website and installers have fairly straightforward instructions for doing so.

For more complete information about installing and upgrading Python on all platforms, visit the Python downloads page (*https://www.python.org/downloads/*).

Unlike Java, Python can be used as a scripting language without creating any new classes or functions. Opening up a new text file, writing:

```
print("Hello, Internet!")
```

and saving it as *hello.py* is perfectly legitimate. If you want to get a little more elaborate, you can create a new function, and use it to do the same thing:

```
def hello():
    print("Hello, Internet!")
hello()
```

There are a few things to notice here:

Python does not use semicolons to indicate the end of a line, nor does it use braces to indicate the beginning and ending of a loop or function. Instead, it relies on line breaks and tabs to control execution. Opening a line with def, followed by a function name, arguments (in this case, we have a (), indicating that there are no arguments), and a colon indicates that the body of a function will follow. Each line of a function following a function declaration *must* be indented, and outdenting indicates the end of the function body.

If the idea of using whitespace in this way seems a little pedantic (or insane) at first, keep at it. In my experience, writing Python actually improves the readability of my code writing in other languages. Just remember to add semicolons when you switch back over to something like Java or C!

Python is a weakly typed language, meaning that variable types (string, integer, object, etc.) do not need to be explicitly declared when the variables are initialized. As with other weakly typed languages, this can occasionally cause debugging issues, but it does make variable declaration a breeze:

```
greeting = "Hello, Internet!"
print(greeting)
```

And that's it! You're a Pythoneer!

Obviously, this isn't quite the truth, but one of the great things about Python is that it is such a simple language, programmers of other languages can read and interpret it without much prior exposure. This aspect of the language can probably be best summed up in Python's most famous "Easter Egg":

```
import this
```

The output of which is:

The Zen of Python, by Tim Peters

Beautiful is better than ugly.
Explicit is better than implicit.
Simple is better than complex.
Complex is better than complicated.
Flat is better than nested.
Sparse is better than dense.
Readability counts.
Special cases aren't special enough to break the rules.
Although practicality beats purity.
Errors should never pass silently.
Unless explicitly silenced.
In the face of ambiguity, refuse the temptation to guess.
There should be one-- and preferably only one --obvious way to do it.
Although that way may not be obvious at first unless you're Dutch.[1]
Now is better than never.
Although never is often better than *right* now.
If the implementation is hard to explain, it's a bad idea.
If the implementation is easy to explain, it may be a good idea.
Namespaces are one honking great idea -- let's do more of those!

---

1 This line might be a reference to the Dutch computer scientist Edsger Dijkstra, who said in a 1978 talk: "I thought that it was a firm principle of language design...that in all respects equivalent programs should have few possibilities for different representations... Otherwise completely different styles of programming arise unnecessarily, thereby hampering maintainability, readability and what have you" (*http://www.cs.utexas.edu/ ~EWD/transcriptions/EWD06xx/EWD660.html*). Or it may simply be due to the fact that the original creator of Python, Guido van Rossum, is Dutch. No one seems to be entirely sure on this subject, however.

The Internet at a Glance

As the types of transactions the Internet is required to handle become increasingly complex, the terms and technologies used to describe these transactions also increases in complexity. Far removed from its roots as a way to exchange research messages, the Internet must now handle large file uploads, streaming video, secure banking transactions, credit card purchases, and the transmission of sensitive corporate documents.

Despite these extra layers of complexity, however, the Internet remains, at its core, a series of messages. Some messages contain requests for information, some contain messages intended for a distant recipient, some contain file information or instructions for a particular application on the machine it's being sent to. These requests are sent from a client (desktop or mobile device) machine to a server, and vice versa. They can also be sent between servers themselves, perhaps in order to gather more information requested by a client.

Figure B-1 depicts a few common types of Internet transactions: a request for the location of a server at a particular domain name, the request of a web page and its associated image file across two servers, and uploading an image file.

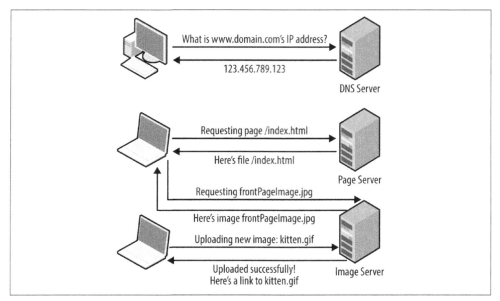

Figure B-1. A few types of common Internet transactions between clients and servers

There are many different protocols, or languages, that govern these communications between clients and servers. You might receive your mail via the SMTP protocol while making a phone call over VOIP and uploading files via FTP. All of these protocols define different fields for headers, data encodings, sending and receiving addresses or names, and other types of things. The protocol used for requesting, sending, and receiving websites is the Hypertext Transfer Protocol (HTTP).

For the vast majority of the scrapers in this book (and, likely, the majority of the scrapers you will write), HTTP is used to communicate with remote web servers. For this reason, it's important to examine the protocol in a little more detail.

An HTTP message contains two main parts: header fields and a data field. Each header field contains a title and a value. The possible titles for these fields are predefined by the HTTP standard. For instance, you might have a header field like:

```
Content-Type: application/json
```

indicating that the data in the HTTP packet will use the JSON format. There are 60+ possible header fields that might be found in an HTTP packet, but we will only use a small set of them in this book. The following table shows a few of the HTTP header fields you should be familiar with:

Name	Description	Example
User-Agent	A string indicating which browser and operating system you are making the request from.	Mozilla/5.0 (X11; Ubuntu; Linux x86_64; rv:28.0) Gecko/20100101 Firefox/28.0
Cookie	Variables used by the web application to hold session data and other information.	"__utma: 20549163.147923691.1398729710.1398729710.1398858679.2"
Status	A code indicating the success or failure of the page request.	"200" (Okay), "404" (Not Found)

Once a packet, carried by HTTP, reaches your browser, the contents of the packet must be interpreted as a website. The structure of websites are governed by HTML, or *HyperText Markup Language*. Although HTML is often referred to as a programming language, HTML is a *markup* language. It defines the structure of a document using tags in order to demarcate items such as title, content, sidebar, footer, and more.

All HTML pages (at least all well-formatted ones) are surrounded by opening and closing <html></html> tags, with <head> and <body> tags in between. Other tags populate these page headers and page bodies to form the structure and content of the page:

```
<html>
<head>
<title>An Example Page</title>
</head>
<body>
<h1>An Example Page</h1>
<div class="body">
Some example content is here
</div>
</body>
</html>
```

In this example, the page title (this is the text that is seen in a tab in your browser) is "An Example Page", with that same title echoed in the header <h1> tag. Immediately below that is a div ("divider") tag of the class "body," containing what might be a main article or longer piece of text.

CSS, or *Cascading Style Sheets*, go hand in hand with HTML in order to define the look of a website. CSS defines things like the color, position, size, and background of various objects on a website.

Using the HTML in the previous example, this might look something like:

```
h1{
    color:'red';
    font-size:1.5em;
},
div.body{
    border:2px solid;
}
```

This creates a medium-size red title, with a border around the content text on the site.

Unfortunately, going into greater detail about HTTP, HTML, or CSS is outside the scope of this book. However, if you're not familiar with the subjects, I recommend you take a look at W3Schools (*http://www.w3schools.com/*) to look up unfamiliar terms or lines of HTML/CSS as you read through the book. Using your browser's "view source" feature is a great help to start getting familiar with the syntax as well.

The Legalities and Ethics of Web Scraping

In 2010, software engineer Pete Warden built a web crawler to gather data from Face-book. He collected data from approximately 200 million Facebook users—names, location information, friends, and interests. Of course, Facebook noticed and sent him cease-and-desist letters, which he obeyed. When asked why he complied with the cease and desist, he said: "Big data? Cheap. Lawyers? Not so much."

In this chapter, we'll look at U.S. laws (and some international ones) that are relevant to web scraping, and learn how to analyze the legality and ethics of a given web scraping situation.

Before you read this section, consider the obvious: I am a software engineer, not a lawyer. Do not interpret anything you read here or in any other chapter of the book as professional legal advice or act on it accordingly. Although I believe I'm able to discuss the legalities and ethics of web scraping knowledgeably, you should consult a lawyer (not a software engineer) before undertaking any legally ambiguous web scraping projects.

Trademarks, Copyrights, Patents, Oh My!

Time for some Intellectual Property 101! There are three basic types of IP: trademarks (indicated by a ™ or ® symbol), copyrights (the ubiquitous ©), and patents (sometimes indicated by text describing that the invention is patent protected, but often by nothing at all).

Patents are used to declare ownership over inventions only. You cannot patent images, text, or any information itself. Although some patents, such as software patents, are less tangible than what we think of as "inventions," keep in mind that it is the *thing* (or technique) that is patented—not the information contained in the patent. Unless you are either building things from scraped blueprints, or someone patents a method of web scraping, you are unlikely to inadvertently infringe on a patent by scraping the Web.

Trademarks also are unlikely to be an issue, but still something that must be considered. According to the U.S Patent and Trademark Office:

> A **trademark** is a word, phrase, symbol, and/or design that identifies and distinguishes the source of the goods of one party from those of others. A **service mark** is a word, phrase, symbol, and/or design that identifies and distinguishes the source of a service rather than goods. The term "trademark" is often used to refer to both trademarks and service marks.

In addition to the traditional words/symbols branding that we think of when we think of trademarks, other descriptive attributes can be trademarked. This includes, for example, the shape of a container (think Coca-Cola bottles) or even a color (most notably, the pink color of Owens Corning's Pink Panther fiberglass insulation).

Unlike with patents, the ownership of a trademark depends heavily on the context in which it is used. For example, if I wish to publish a blog post with an accompanying picture of the Coca-Cola logo, I could do that (as long as I wasn't implying that my blog post was sponsored by, or published by, Coca-Cola). If I wanted to manufacture a new soft drink with the same Coca-Cola logo displayed on the packaging, that would clearly be a trademark infringement. Similarly, although I could package my new soft drink in Pink Panther pink, I could not use that same color to create a home insulation product.

Copyright Law

Both trademarks and patents have something in common in that they have to be formally registered in order to be recognized. Contrary to popular belief, this is not true with copyrighted material. What makes images, text, music, etc. copyrighted? It's not the "All Rights Reserved" warning at the bottom of the page, nor anything special about "published" versus "unpublished" material. Every piece of material you create is automatically subject to copyright law as soon as you bring it into existence.

The Berne Convention for the Protection of Literary and Artistic Works, named after Berne, Switzerland, where it was first adopted in 1886, is the international standard for copyright. This convention says, in essence, that all member countries must recognize the copyright protection of the works of citizens of other member countries as if they were citizens of their own country. In practice, this means that, as a U.S. citizen, you can be held accountable in the United States for violating the copyright of material written by someone in, say, France (and vice versa).

Obviously, copyright is a concern for web scrapers. If I scrape content from someone's blog and publish it on my own blog, I could very well be opening myself up to a lawsuit. Fortunately, there are several layers of protection that I have that might make my blog-scraping project defensible, depending on how it functions.

First, copyright protection extends to creative works only. It does not cover statistics or facts. Fortunately, much of what web scrapers are after *are* facts and statistics. Although a web scraper that gathers poetry from around the Web and displays that poetry on your own website might be violating copyright law, a web scraper that gathers information on the frequency of poetry postings over time is not. The poetry, in its raw form, is a creative work. The average word count of poems published on a website, by month, is not a creative work.

Even content that is posted verbatim (as opposed to aggregated/calculated content from raw scraped data) might not be violating copyright law if that data is prices, names of company executives, or some other factual piece of information.

Even copyrighted content can be used directly, within reason, under the Digital Millennium Copyright Act. The DMCA outlines some rules for the automated handling of copyrighted material. The DMCA is long, with many specific rules governing everything from ebooks to telephones. However, there are three main sections that are of particular interest:

- Under the "safe harbor" protection, if you scrape material from a source that you are led to believe contains only copyright-free material, but some user has submitted copyright material to, you are protected as long as you removed the copyrighted material when notified.
- You cannot circumvent security measures (such as password protection) in order to gather content.
- You can use content under the "fair use" rule, which takes into account the percentage of the copyrighted work used and the purpose it is being used for.

In short, you should never directly publish copyrighted material without permission from the original author or copyright holder. If you are storing copyrighted material that you have free access to in your own nonpublic database for the purposes of analysis, that is fine. If you are publishing that database to your website for viewing or download, that is not fine. If you are analyzing that database and publishing statistics about word counts, a list of authors by prolificacy, or some other meta-analysis of the data, that is fine. If you are accompanying that meta-analysis with a few select quotes, or brief samples of data to make your point, that is likely also fine, but you might want to examine the "fair use" clause of the DMCA to make sure.

Trespass to Chattels

Trespass to chattels is fundamentally different from what we think of as "trespassing laws" in that it applies not to real estate or land but to moveable property (such as a server). It applies when your access to property is interfered with in some way that does not allow you to access or use it.

In this era of cloud computing, it's tempting not to think of web servers as real, tangible, resources. However, not only do servers consist of expensive components, but they need to be stored, monitored, cooled, and supplied with vast amounts of electricity. By some estimates, 10% of global electricity usage is consumed by computers (if a survey of your own electronics doesn't convince you, consider Google's vast server farms, all of which need to be connected to large power stations).

Although servers are expensive resources, they're interesting from a legal perspective in that webmasters generally *want* people to consume their resources (i.e., access their websites); they just don't want them to consume their resources *too much*. Checking out a website via your browser is fine, launching a full-scale DDOS against it obviously is not.

There are three criteria that need to be met for a web scraper to violate trespass to chattels:

Lack of consent
> Because web servers are open to everyone, they are generally "giving consent" to web scrapers as well. However, many websites' Terms of Service agreements specifically prohibit the use of scrapers. In addition, any cease-and-desist notifications obviously revoke this consent.

Actual harm
> Servers are costly. In addition to server costs, if your scrapers take a website down, or limit its ability to serve other users, this can add to the "harm" you cause.

Intentionality
> If you're writing the code, you know what it does!

You must meet all three of these criteria for trespass to chattels to apply. However, if you are violating a Terms of Service agreement, but not causing actual harm, don't think that you're immune from legal action. You might very well be violating copyright law, the DMCA, the Computer Fraud and Abuse Act (more on that later), or one of the other myriad of laws that apply to web scrapers.

Throttling Your Bots

Back in the olden days, web servers were far more powerful than personal computers. In fact, part of the definition of "server" was "big computer." Now, the tables have turned somewhat. My personal computer, for instance, has a 3.5 GHz processor and 8 GB of RAM. An Amazon medium instance, in contrast (as of the writing of this book), has 4 GB of RAM and about 3 GHz of processing capacity.

With a decent Internet connection and a dedicated machine, even a single personal computer can place a heavy load on many websites, even crippling them or taking

---

them down completely. Unless there's a medical emergency and the only cure is aggregating all the data from Joe Schmo's website in two seconds flat, there's really no reason to hammer on a site.

A watched bot never completes. Sometimes it's better to leave crawlers running overnight than in the middle of the afternoon or evening for a few reasons:

- If you have about eight hours, even at the glacial pace of two seconds per page, you can crawl over 14,000 pages. When time is less of an issue, you're not tempted to push the speed of your crawlers.
- Assuming the target audience of the website is in your general location (adjust accordingly for remote target audiences), the website's traffic load is probably far lower during the night, meaning that your crawling will not be compounding peak traffic hour congestion.
- You save time by sleeping, instead of constantly checking your logs for new information. Think of how excited you'll be to wake up in the morning to brand-new data!

Consider the following scenarios:

- You have a web crawler that traverses Joe Schmo's website, aggregating some or all of its data
- You have a web crawler that traverses hundreds of small websites, aggregating some or all of their data.
- You have a web crawler that traverses a very large site, such as Wikipedia.

In the first scenario, it's best to leave the bot running slowly, and during the night.

In the second scenario, it's best to crawl each website in a round-robin fashion, rather than crawling them slowly, one at a time. Depending on how many websites you're crawling, this means that you can collect data as fast as your Internet connection and machine can manage, yet the load is reasonable for each individual remote server. You can accomplish this programatically, either using multiple threads (where each individual thread crawls a single site and pauses its own execution), or using Python lists to keep track of sites.

In the second scenario, the load your Internet connection and home machine can place on a site like Wikipedia is unlikely to be noticed, or cared much about. However, if you're using a distributed network of machines, this is obviously a different matter. Use caution, and ask a company representative whenever possible.

The Computer Fraud and Abuse Act

In the early 1980s, computers started moving out of academia and into the business world. For the first time, viruses and worms were seen as more than an inconvenience (or even a fun hobby) and as a serious criminal matter that could cause actual monetary damages. In response, the Computer Fraud and Abuse Act was created in 1986.

Although you might think that the act only applies to some stereotypical version of a malicious hacker unleashing viruses, the act has strong implications for web scrapers as well. Imagine a scraper that scans the web looking for login forms with easy-to-guess passwords, or collects government secrets accidentally left in a hidden but public location. All of these activities are illegal (and rightly so) under the CFAA.

The act defines seven main criminal offenses, which can be summarized as follows:

- The knowing unauthorized access of computers owned by the U.S. government and obtaining information from those computers.
- The knowing unauthorized access of a computer, obtaining financial information.
- The knowing unauthorized access of a computer owned by the U.S. government, affecting the use of that computer by the government.
- Knowingly accessing any protected computer with the attempt to defraud.
- Knowingly accessing a computer without authorization and causing damage to that computer.
- Shares or traffics passwords or authorization information for computers used by the U.S. government or computers that affect interstate or foreign commerce.
- Attempts to extort money or "anything of value" by causing damage, or threatening to cause damage, to any protected computer.

In short: stay away from protected computers, do not access computers (including web servers) that you are not given access to, and especially, stay away from government or financial computers.

robots.txt and Terms of Service

A website's terms of service and *robots.txt* files are in interesting territory, legally speaking. If a website is publicly accessible, the webmaster's right to declare what software can and cannot access it is debatable. Saying "it is fine if you use your browser to view this site, but not if you use a program you wrote to view it" is tricky.

Most sites have a link to their Terms of Service in the footer on every page. The TOS contains more than just the rules for web crawlers and automated access; it often has information about what kind of information the website collects, what it does with it, and usually a legal disclaimer that the services provided by the website come without any express or implied warranty.

If you are interested in search engine optimization (SEO) or search engine technology, you've probably heard of the *robots.txt* file. If you go to just about any large website and look for its *robots.txt* file, you will find it in the root web folder: *http://website.com/robots.txt*.

The syntax for *robots.txt* files was developed in 1994 during the initial boom of web search engine technology. It was about this time that search engines scouring the entire Internet, such as AltaVista and DogPile, started competing in earnest with simple lists of sites organized by subject, such as the one curated by Yahoo! This growth of search across the Internet meant an explosion in not only the number of web crawlers, but in the availability of information collected by those web crawlers to the average citizen.

While we might take this sort of availability for granted today, some webmasters were shocked when information they published deep in the file structure of their website became available on the front page of search results in major search engines. In response, the syntax for *robots.txt* files, called the Robots Exclusion Standard, was developed.

Unlike the TOS, which often talks about web crawlers in broad terms and in very human language, *robots.txt* can be parsed and used by automated programs extremely easily. Although it might seem like the perfect system to solve the problem of unwanted bots once and for all, keep in mind the following:

- There is no official governing body for the syntax of *robots.txt*. It is a commonly used and generally well-followed convention, but there is nothing to stop anyone from creating their own version of a *robots.txt* file (apart from the fact that no bot will recognize or obey it until it gets popular). That being said, it is a very widely accepted convention, mostly because it is relatively straightforward, and there is no incentive for companies to invent their own standard, or try to improve on it.
- There is no way to enforce a *robots.txt* file. It is merely a sign that says "Please don't go to these parts of the site." There are many web scraping libraries available that obey *robots.txt* (although this is often merely a default setting that can be overridden). Beyond that, there are often more barriers to following a *robots.txt* file (after all, you need to scrape, parse, and apply the contents of the page to your code logic) than there are to just going ahead and scraping whatever page you want to.

The Robot Exclusion Standard syntax is fairly straightforward. Like in Python (and many other languages), comments begin with a # symbol, end with a newline, and can be used anywhere in the file.

The first line of the file, apart from any comments, is started with `User-agent:`, which specifies the user that the following rules apply to. This is followed by a set of rules, either `Allow:` or `Disallow:`, depending on whether the bot is allowed on that section of the site or not. An asterisk (*), indicates a wildcard, and can be used to describe either a `User-agent` or a URL.

If a rule follows a rule that it seems to contradict, the last rule takes precedence. For example:

```
#Welcome to my robots.txt file!
User-agent: *
Disallow: *

User-agent: Googlebot
Allow: *
Disallow: /private
```

In this case, all bots are disallowed from anywhere on the site, except for the Googlebot, which is allowed anywhere except for the */private* directory.

In Twitter's *robots.txt* file, it has explicit instructions for the bots of Google, Yahoo!, Yandex (a popular Russian search engine), Microsoft, and other bots or search engines not covered by any of the preceding categories. The Google section (which looks identical to the permissions allowed to all other categories of bots) looks like:

```
#Google Search Engine Robot
User-agent: Googlebot
Allow: /?_escaped_fragment_

Allow: /?lang=
Allow: /hashtag/*?src=
Allow: /search?q=%23
Disallow: /search/realtime
Disallow: /search/users
Disallow: /search/*/grid

Disallow: /*?
Disallow: /*/followers
Disallow: /*/following
```

Notice that Twitter restricts access to the portions of its site that it has an API in place for. Because Twitter has a well-regulated API (and one that it can make money off of by licensing), it is in the company's best interest to disallow any "home-brewed APIs" that gather information by independently crawling its site.

Although a file telling your crawler where it can't go might seem restrictive at first, it can actually be a blessing in disguise for web crawler development. If you find a *robots.txt* file that disallows crawling in a particular section of the site, the webmaster is saying, essentially, that they are fine with crawlers in all other sections of the site (after all, if they weren't fine with it, they would have restricted access when they were writing *robots.txt* in the first place).

For example, the section of Wikipedia's *robots.txt* file that applies to general web scrapers (as opposed to search engines) is wonderfully permissive. It even goes as far as containing human-readable text to welcome bots (that's us!) and blocks access to only a few pages, such as the login page, search page, and "random article" page:

```
#
# Friendly, low-speed bots are welcome viewing article pages, but not
# dynamically generated pages please.
#
# Inktomi's "Slurp" can read a minimum delay between hits; if your bot supports
# such a thing using the 'Crawl-delay' or another instruction, please let us
# know.
#
# There is a special exception for API mobileview to allow dynamic mobile web &
# app views to load section content.
# These views aren't HTTP-cached but use parser cache aggressively and don't
# expose special: pages etc.
#
User-agent: *
Allow: /w/api.php?action=mobileview&
Disallow: /w/
Disallow: /trap/
Disallow: /wiki/Especial:Search
Disallow: /wiki/Especial%3ASearch
Disallow: /wiki/Special:Collection
Disallow: /wiki/Spezial:Sammlung
Disallow: /wiki/Special:Random
Disallow: /wiki/Special%3ARandom
Disallow: /wiki/Special:Search
Disallow: /wiki/Special%3ASearch
Disallow: /wiki/Spesial:Search
Disallow: /wiki/Spesial%3ASearch
Disallow: /wiki/Spezial:Search
Disallow: /wiki/Spezial%3ASearch
Disallow: /wiki/Specjalna:Search
Disallow: /wiki/Specjalna%3ASearch
Disallow: /wiki/Speciaal:Search
Disallow: /wiki/Speciaal%3ASearch
Disallow: /wiki/Speciaal:Random
Disallow: /wiki/Speciaal%3ARandom
Disallow: /wiki/Speciel:Search
Disallow: /wiki/Speciel%3ASearch
Disallow: /wiki/Speciale:Search
Disallow: /wiki/Speciale%3ASearch
Disallow: /wiki/Istimewa:Search
Disallow: /wiki/Istimewa%3ASearch
Disallow: /wiki/Toiminnot:Search
Disallow: /wiki/Toiminnot%3ASearch
```

Whether you choose to write web crawlers that obey *robots.txt* is up to you, but I highly recommend it, particularly if you have crawlers that indiscriminately crawl the Web.

Three Web Scrapers

Because web scraping is such a limitless field, there are a staggering number of ways to land yourself in legal hot water. In this section, we'll take a look at three cases that touched on some form of law that generally applies to web scrapers, and how it was used in that case.

eBay versus Bidder's Edge and Trespass to Chattels

In 1997, the Beanie Baby market was booming, the tech sector was bubbling, and online auction houses were the hot new thing on the Internet. A company called Bidder's Edge formed and created a new kind of meta-auction site. Rather than force you to go from auction site to auction site, comparing prices, it would aggregate data from all current auctions for a specific product (say, a hot new Furby doll or a copy of *Spice World*) and point you to the site that had the lowest price.

Bidder's Edge accomplished this with an army of web scrapers, constantly making requests to the web servers of the various auction sites in order to get price and product information. Of all the auction sites, eBay was the largest, and Bidder's Edge hit eBay's servers about 100,000 times a day. Even by today's standards, this is a lot of traffic. According to eBay, this was 1.53% of its total Internet traffic at the time, and it certainly wasn't happy about it.

eBay sent Bidder's Edge a cease-and-desist letter, coupled with an offer to license its data. However, negotiations for this licensing failed and Bidder's Edge continued to crawl eBay's site.

eBay tried blocking IP addresses used by Bidder's Edge, blocking 169 different IP addresses, although Bidder's Edge was able to get around this by using proxy servers (servers that forward requests on behalf of another machine, but using the proxy server's own IP address). As I'm sure you can imagine, this was a frustrating and unsustainable solution for both parties—Bidder's Edge was constantly trying to find new proxy servers and buy new IP addresses while old ones were blocked, while eBay was forced to maintain large firewall lists (and adding computationally expensive IP address-comparing overhead to each packet check).

Finally, in December of 1999, eBay sued Bidder's Edge under trespass to chattels.

Because eBay's servers were real, tangible resources that it owned, and it didn't appreciate Bidder's Edge's abnormal use of them, trespass to chattels seemed like the ideal law to use. In fact, in modern times, trespass to chattels goes hand in hand with web-scraping lawsuits, and is most often thought of as an IT law.

The courts ruled that in order for eBay to win its case using trespass to chattels, eBay had to show two things:

- Bidder's Edge did not have permission to use eBay's resources
- eBay suffered financial loss as a result of Bidder's Edge's actions

Given the record of eBay's cease-and-desist letters, coupled with IT records showing server usage and actual costs associated with the servers, this was relatively easy for eBay to do. Of course, no large court battles end easily: counter-suits were filed, many lawyers were paid, and the matter was eventually settled out of court for an undisclosed sum in March 2001.

So does this mean that any unauthorized use of another person's server is automatically a violation of trespass to chattels? Not necessarily. Bidder's Edge was an extreme case; it was using so many of eBay's resources that the company had to buy additional servers, pay more for electricity, and perhaps hire additional personnel (although 1.53% might not seem like a lot, in large companies, it can add up to a significant amount)

In 2003, the California Supreme Court ruled on another case, Intel Corp versus Hamidi, in which a former Intel employee (Hamidi) sent emails Intel didn't like, across Intel's servers, to Intel employees. The court said:

> Intel's claim fails not because e-mail transmitted through the Internet enjoys unique immunity, but because the trespass to chattels tort—unlike the causes of action just mentioned—may not, in California, be proved without evidence of an injury to the plaintiff's personal property or legal interest therein.

Essentially, Intel had failed to prove that the costs of transmitting the six emails sent by Hamidi to all employees (each one, interestingly enough, with an option to be removed from Hamidi's mailing list—at least he was polite!) contributed to any financial injury for them. It did not deprive Intel of any property or use of their property.

United States v. Auernheimer and The Computer Fraud and Abuse Act

If there is information readily accessible on the Internet to a human using a web browser, it's unlikely that accessing the same exact information in an automated fashion would land you in hot water with the Feds. However, as easy as it can be for a sufficiently curious person to find a small security leak, that small security leak can very quickly become a much larger and much more dangerous one when automated scrapers enter the picture.

In 2010, Andrew Auernheimer and Daniel Spitler noticed a nice feature of iPads: when you visited AT&T's website on them, AT&T would redirect you to a URL containing your iPad's unique ID number:

```
https://dcp2.att.com/OEPClient/openPage?ICCID=<idNumber>&IMEI=
```

This page would contain a login form, with the email address of the user whose ID number was in the URL. This allowed users to gain access to their accounts simply by entering their password.

Although there were a very large number of potential iPad ID numbers, it was possible, given enough web scrapers, to iterate through the possible numbers, gathering email addresses along the way. By providing users with this convenient login feature, AT&T, in essence, made its customer email addresses public to the Web.

Auernheimer and Spitler created a scraper that collected 114,000 of these email addresses, among them the private email addresses of celebrities, CEOs, and government officials. Auernheimer (but not Spitler) then sent the list, and information about how it was obtained, to Gawker Media, who published the story (but not the list) under the headline: "Apple's Worst Security Breach: 114,000 iPad Owners Exposed."

In June 2011, Auernheimer's home was raided by the FBI in connection with the email address collection, although they ended up arresting him on drug charges. In November 2012, he was found guilty of identity fraud and conspiracy to access a computer without authorization, and some time later sentenced to 41 months in federal prison and ordered to pay $73,000 in restitution.

His case caught the attention of civil rights lawyer Orin Kerr, who joined his legal team and appealed the case to the Third Circuit Court of Appeals. On April 11, 2014 (these legal processes can take quite a while), The Third Circuit agreed with the appeal, saying:

> Auernheimer's conviction on Count 1 must be overturned because visiting a publicly available website is not unauthorized access under the Computer Fraud and Abuse Act, 18 U.S.C. § 1030(a)(2)(C). AT&T chose not to employ passwords or any other protective measures to control access to the e-mail addresses of its customers. It is irrelevant that AT&T subjectively wished that outsiders would not stumble across the data or that Auernheimer hyperbolically characterized the access as a "theft." The company configured its servers to make the information available to everyone and thereby authorized the general public to view the information. Accessing the e-mail addresses through AT&T's public website was authorized under the CFAA and therefore was not a crime.

Thus, sanity prevailed in the legal system, Auernheimer was released from prison that same day, and everyone lived happily ever after.

Although it was ultimately decided that Auernheimer did not violate the Computer Fraud and Abuse Act, he had his house raided by the FBI, spent many thousands of dollars in legal fees, and spent three years in and out of courtrooms and prisons. As web scrapers, what lessons can we take away from this to avoid similar situations?

Scraping any sort of sensitive information, whether it's personal data (in this case, email addresses), trade secrets, or government secrets, is probably not something you want to do without having a lawyer on speed dial. Even if it's publicly available, think:

"Would the average computer user be able to easily access this information if they wanted to see it?" "Is this something the company wants users to see?"

I have on many occasions called companies to report security vulnerabilities in their websites and web applications. This line works wonders: "Hi, I'm a security professional who discovered a potential security vulnerability on your website. Could you direct me to someone so that I can report it, and get the issue resolved?" In addition to the immediate satisfaction of recognition for your (white hat) hacking genius, you might be able to get free subscriptions, cash rewards, and other goodies out of it!

In addition, Auernheimer's release of the information to Gawker Media (before notifying AT&T) and his showboating around the exploit of the vulnerability also made him an especially attractive target for AT&T's lawyers.

If you find security vulnerabilities in a site, the best thing to do is to alert the owners of the site, not the media. You might be tempted to write up a blog post and announce it to the world, especially if a fix to the problem is not put in place immediately. However, you need to remember that it is the company's responsibility, not yours. The best thing you can do is take your web scrapers (and, if applicable, your business) away from the site!

Field v. Google: Copyright and robots.txt

Blake Field, an attorney, filed a lawsuit against Google on the basis that its site-caching feature violated copyright law by displaying a copy of his book after he had removed it from his website. Copyright law allows the creator of an original creative work to have control over the distribution of that work. Field's argument was that Google's caching (after he had removed it from his website) removed his ability to control its distribution.

The Google Web Cache

When Google web scrapers (also known as "Google bots") crawl websites, they make a copy of the site and host it on the Internet. Anyone can access this cache, using the URL format:

```
http://webcache.googleusercontent.com/search?q=cache:http
://pythonscraping.com/
```

If a website you are searching for, or scraping, is unavailable, you might want to check there to see if a usable copy exists!

Knowing about Google's caching feature and not taking action did not help Field's case. After all, he could have prevented Google's bots from caching his website simply by adding the *robots.txt* file, with simple directives about which pages should and should not be scraped.

More importantly, the court found that the DMCS Safe Harbor provision allowed Google to legally cache and display sites such as Field's: "[a] service provider shall not be liable for monetary relief... for infringement of copyright by reason of the intermediate and temporary storage of material on a system or network controlled or operated by or for the service provider."

Index

Symbols

" (quotation marks), 17
$ (dollar sign), 27
() (parentheses), 25
* (asterisk), 25, 157
+ (plus sign), 25
- (hyphen), 113
. (period), 25
403 Forbidden error, 187
404 Page Not Found error, 9
500 Internal Server Error, 9
; (semicolon), 210
?! (does not contain), 27
[] (square brackets), 25
\ (forward slash), 27
^ (caret), 27
_ (underscore), 17
| (pipe), 25

A

a tag, 28, 156
Accept header, 179
Accept-Encoding header, 179
Accept-Language header, 179
action chains, 195
ActionScript , 147
add_cookie function, 182
Ajax (Asynchronous JavaScript and XML),
    151-152
API keys
    Echo Nest example, 52, 54
    Google example, 60-63
    Twitter example, 56
APIs

about, 49-50, 68
authentication and, 52
common conventions, 50-52
Echo Nest example, 52, 54-55
Google examples, 50, 60-63
HTTP methods and, 51
parsing JSON, 63
responses , 52
Twitter example, 55-60
Wikipedia example, 64-68
ASCII character encoding, 95-98
assertions (unit tests), 190
asterisk (*), 25, 157
Asynchronous JavaScript and XML (Ajax),
    151-152
AttributeError exception, 10
attributes
    accessing, 14, 28
    finding tags based on, 15-18
Auernheimer, Andrew, 227
auth module, 144
authentication
    about, 52
    handling logins, 142-144
    HTTP basic access, 144
    Twitter example, 57

B

backing up data, 172
BeautifulSoup library
    about, 6
    children() function, 20
    descendants() function, 20
    find() function, 16-18

findAll() function, 15-18, 28
get_text() function, 15
installing, 6
next_siblings() function, 21
previous_siblings() function, 21
regular expressions and, 27
running, 8
searching for tags, 14-22
XPath and, 157
BeautifulSoup object, 15, 18, 192
Berne Convention for the Protection of Literary
    and Artistic Works, 218
body tag, 215
.box file extension, 171
building web scrapers
    advanced HTML parsing, 13-29
    crawling across the Web, 31-48
    first web scraper, 3-11
    reading documents, 93
    storing data, 71-91
    using APIs, 49-69
By object, 155
BytesIO object, 103

C

CAPTCHA characters
    about, 161, 169-171
    dragging, 197
    machine training and, 135, 171-174
    retrieving, 174-176
caret (^), 27
Carroll , Lewis, 6
Cascading Style Sheets (CSS)
    about, 14, 216
    dynamic HTML and, 151
    hidden fields and, 184
CGI (Common Gateway Interface), 204
checklist, human, 186
children (tags), 20
children() function, 20
Chrome developer tool , 141
class attribute, 14, 17, 156
cleaning dirty data
    cleaning after the fact, 114-118
    cleaning in code, 109-113
client-side processing
    handling redirects, 44, 158
    scripting languages and, 147
cloud computing, 204

colorpickers, 140
comma-separated values (CSV) files
    reading, 98-100
    storing data to, 74-76
Comment object, 18
Common Gateway Interface (CGI), 204
Computer Fraud and Abuse Act , 221, 227-229
Connection header, 179
Connection object, 83
connection/cursor model, 83
context-free grammars, 135
cookies
    handling, 142-143, 181-182
    verifying settings, 179
copyright law, 218-219, 229
cPanel software, 204
crawling across the Web (see web crawlers)
CREATE DATABASE statement, 80
CREATE INDEX statement, 86
CREATE TABLE statement, 80
credentials
    Google accounts, 60
    Twitter accounts, 58
CSS (Cascading Style Sheets)
    about, 14, 216
    dynamic HTML and, 151
    hidden fields and, 184
CSV (comma-separated values) files
    reading , 98-100
    storing data to, 74-76
csv library, 98-100
Cursor object, 83

D

Dark Web, 36
data gathering, 36, 38-40
data management
    about, 71
    email and, 90-91
    MySQL and, 76-89
    storing data to CSV, 74-76
    storing media files, 71-74
data normalization, 112-113
data warehouses, 40
database size versus query time, 86
Davies, Mark, 121
deactivate command, 8
Deep Web, 36
DELETE method (HTTP), 51

DELETE statement, 82
delete_all_cookies function, 182
delete_cookie function, 182
delimiters, 74
descendants (tags), 20
descendants() function, 20
DESCRIBE statement, 80
DHTML (dynamic HTML), 151-152
dictionaries, 85
DictReader object, 100
Digital Millennium Copyright Act (DMCA), 219
directed graph problems, 126
display:none attribute, 185
distributed computing, 201
DMCA (Digital Millennium Copyright Act), 219
.doc format, 102
documents, reading (see reading documents)
.docx format, 102-105
dollar sign ($), 27
downloading files from Internet, 74
drag-and-drop interfaces, 196
dynamic HTML (DHTML), 151-152

E

Easter Egg, 210
eBay v. Bidder's Edge, 226
Echo Nest API, 52, 54-55
EditThisCookie Chrome extension, 181
elements (Selenium), 153, 194
email
    identifying addresses, 24
    sending and receiving, 90-91
email package, 90
encoding (document)
    about, 93
    text files and, 94-98
environment variables, 163
escape characters, 27, 110
ethical guidelines, 177-178, 217-230
exception handling
    external links, 43
    handling redirects, 158
    network connections, 9
    suggestions for, 35, 40
explicit wait, 155
eXtensible Markup Language (XML), 52
external links

cautions using, 41
crawling across the Internet, 40-45
crawling with Scrapy, 45-48
finding, 42

F

Facebook social media site, 217
fair use clause, 219
fast scraping, 182, 187
Fibonacci sequence, 149
Field v. Google, 229
file attribute, 141
File object, 142
file uploads, 141
filtering data, 115-116, 165
finally statement, 85
find() function , 16-18
findAll() function, 15-18, 28
for loops, 39
forms
    about, 137
    file uploads and, 141
    handling logins and cookies, 142-144
    hidden fields in, 183-186
    images in, 141, 161
    input fields supported, 140
    malicious bots, 144
    security considerations, 183-186
    submitting basic, 138-140
forward slash (\), 27
frequency distributions, 131-132
functions
    handling in JavaScript, 148
    lambda expressions and, 28

G

gathering data, 36, 38-40
GET method (HTTP)
    about, 51
    Google example, 62
    retrieving data , 53
    tracking requests, 140
get_cookies function, 181
get_text() function, 15
Google
    API examples, 50, 60-63
    building, 40
    Markov model example, 124
Google Analytics, 150, 181

Google Maps , 150
GREL (OpenRefine Expression Language), 116

H

h1 tag, 9, 39
head tag, 98, 215
headers (HTTP), 179-180, 187
hidden fields in forms, 183-186
Homebrew package manager, 78
homonyms, 133
honeypots, 184-186
Host header, 179
hotlinking, 72
href attribute, 28
HTML (HyperText Markup Language), 215
HTML Parser library, 29
HTML parsing
    accessing attributes, 28
    avoiding the need for, 13
    BeautifulSoup example, 14-22
    lambda expressions, 28
    regular expressions, 22-28
html tag, 215
HTTP (Hypertext Transfer Protocol)
    API functionality and, 50
    basic access authentication, 144
    error handling, 9, 187
    headers supported, 179-180
    methods supported, 51
HTTPBasicAuth object, 144
human checklist, 186
HyperText Markup Language (HTML), 215
Hypertext Transfer Protocol (see HTTP)
hyphen (-), 113

I

id attribute, 156
image processing
    scraping text from images, 167-169
    submitting image files, 141
    text recognition and, 161-176
img tag, 28
implicit wait, 155
indexing, 85
Innes, Nick, 101
input tag, 141
INSERT INTO statement, 81, 84
Intel Corp v. Hamidi, 227
intellectual property, 217-219

internal links
    crawling an entire site, 35-40
    crawling with Scrapy, 45-48
    traversing a single domain, 31-35
Internet
    about, 213-216
    cautions downloading files from, 74
    crawling across, 40-45
    moving forward, 206
IP address blocking, avoiding, 199-200
ISO character sets, 96-98
is_displayed function, 186
Item object, 46, 48
items.py file, 46

J

JavaScript
    about, 147-149
    common libraries, 149-151
    executing with Selenium, 152-156
    handling redirects, 158
    importing files, 14
JavaScript Object Notation (JSON)
    about, 52
    parsing, 63
jQuery library, 149
JSON (JavaScript Object Notation)
    about, 52
    parsing, 63

K

Kerr, Orin, 228
keywords, 17

L

lambda expressions, 28, 74
legalities of web scraping, 217-230
lexicographical analysis with NLTK, 132-136
libraries
    bundling with projects, 7
    OCR support, 161-164
logging with Scrapy, 48
logins
    about, 137
    handling, 142-143
    troubleshooting, 187
lxml library, 29

M

machine learning, 135, 180
machine training, 135, 171-174
Markov text generators, 123-129
media files, storing, 71-74
Mersenne Twister algorithm, 34
methods (HTTP), 51
Microsoft SQL Server, 76
Microsoft Word, 102-105
MIME (Multipurpose Internet Mail Extensions) protocol, 90
MIMEText object, 90
MySQL
    about, 76
    basic commands, 79-82
    database techniques, 85-87
    installing, 77-79
    integrating with Python, 82-85
    Wikipedia example, 87-89

N

name attribute, 140
natural language processing
    about, 119
    additional resources, 136
    Markov models, 123-129
    Natural Language Toolkit, 129-136
    summarizing data, 120-123
Natural Language Toolkit (NLTK)
    about, 129
    installation and setup, 129
    lexicographical analysis, 132-136
    statistical analysis, 130-132
NavigableString object, 18
navigating trees, 18-22
network connections
    about, 3-5
    connecting reliably, 9-11
    security considerations, 181
next_siblings() function, 21
ngrams module, 132
n-grams, 109-112, 120
NLTK (Natural Language Toolkit)
    about, 129
    installation and setup, 129
    lexicographical analysis, 132-136
    statistical analysis, 130-132
NLTK Downloader interface, 130
NLTK module, 129

None object, 10
normalizing data, 112-113
NumPy library, 164

O

OAuth authentication, 57
OCR (optical character recognition)
    about, 161
    library support, 162-164
OpenRefine Expression Language (GREL), 116
OpenRefine tool
    about, 114
    cleaning data, 116-118
    filtering data, 115-116
    installing, 114
    usage considerations, 114
optical character recognition (OCR)
    about, 161
    library support, 162-164
Oracle DBMS, 76
OrderedDict object, 112
os module, 74

P

page load times, 154, 182
parentheses (), 25
parents (tags), 20, 22
parsing HTML pages (see HTML parsing)
parsing JSON, 63
patents, 217
pay-per-hour computing instances, 205
PDF files, 100-102
PDFMiner3K library, 101
Penn Treebank Project, 133
period (.), 25
Peters, Tim, 211
PhantomJS tool, 152-155, 203
PIL (Python Imaging Library), 162
Pillow library
    about, 162
    processing well-formatted text, 165-169
pipe (|), 25
plus sign (+), 25
POST method (HTTP)
    about, 51
    tracking requests, 140
    troubleshooting, 186
    variable names and, 138
    viewing form parameters, 140

previous_siblings() function, 21
primary keys in tables, 85
programming languages, regular expressions
    and, 27
projects, bundling with libraries, 7
pseudorandom number generators, 34
PUT method (HTTP), 51
PyMySQL library, 82-85
PySocks module, 202
Python Imaging Library (PIL), 162
Python language, installing, 209-211

Q

query time versus database size, 86
quotation marks ("), 17

R

random number generators, 34
random seeds, 34
rate limits
    about, 52
    Google APIs, 60
    Twitter API, 55
reading documents
    document encoding, 93
    Microsoft Word, 102-105
    PDF files, 100
    text files, 94-98
recursion limit, 38, 89
redirects, 44, 158
Referrer header, 179
RegexPal website, 24
regular expressions
    about, 22-27
    BeautifulSoup example, 27
    commonly used symbols, 25
    programming languages and, 27
relational data, 77
remote hosting
    running from a website hosting account,
      203
    running from the cloud, 204
remote servers
    avoiding IP address blocking, 199-200
    extensibility and, 200
    portability and, 200
    PySocks and, 202
    Tor and, 201-202
Requests library

about, 137
auth module, 144
installing, 138, 179
submitting forms, 138
tracking cookies, 142-143
requests module, 179-181
responses, API calls and, 52
Robots Exclusion Standard, 223
robots.txt file, 138, 167, 222-225, 229

S

safe harbor protection, 219, 230
Scrapy library, 45-48
screenshots, 197
script tag, 147
search engine optimization (SEO), 222
searching text data, 135
security considerations
    copyright law and, 219
    forms and, 183-186
    handling cookies, 181
SELECT statement, 79, 81
Selenium library
    about, 143
    elements and, 153, 194
    executing JavaScript, 152-156
    handling redirects, 158
    security considerations, 185
    testing example, 193-198
    Tor support, 203
semicolon (;), 210
SEO (search engine optimization), 222
server-side processing
    handling redirects, 44, 158
    scripting languages and, 147
sets, 67
siblings (tags), 21
Simple Mail Transfer Protocol (SMTP), 90
site maps, 36
Six Degrees of Wikipedia, 31-35
SMTP (Simple Mail Transfer Protocol), 90
smtplib package, 90
sorted function, 113
span tag, 15
Spitler, Daniel, 227
SQL Server (Microsoft), 76
square brackets [], 25
src attribute, 28, 72, 74
StaleElementReferenceException, 158

statistical analysis with NLTK, 130-132
storing data (see data management)
StringIO object, 99
strings, regular expressions and, 22-28
stylesheets
    about, 14, 216
    dynamic HTML and, 151
    hidden fields and, 184
Surface Web, 36

T

tables
    creating in databases, 80
    inserting data into, 81
    primary keys and, 85
    Wikipedia example, 88
Tag object, 18
tags
    accessing attributes, 14, 28
    finding based on location in document,
        18-22
    finding based on name and attribute, 15-18
    preserving, 15
Terms of Service, 222-225
Tesseract library
    about, 163
    installing, 163
    processing well-formatted text, 165-169
    training, 171-174
Tesseract OCR Chopper tool, 171
testing
    about, 189
    Selenium example, 193-198
    unit tests, 190, 197
    unittest module, 190, 197
    Wikipedia example, 191-193
Text object, 130
text processing
    image-to-text translation, 161-176
    reading text files, 94-98
    scraping text from images, 167-169
    searching text data, 135
    strings and regular expressions, 22-28
    well-formatted text, 164-169
The Onion Network (Tor), 201-202
threshold filters, 165
timestamps, 87
tokens, 52, 58
Tor (The Onion Network), 201-202

trademarks, 218
traversing the Web (see web crawlers)
tree navigation, 18-22
trespass to chattels, 219-220, 226
trigrams module, 132
try...finally statement, 85
Twitov app, 123
Twitter API, 55-60

U

underscore (_), 17
undirected graph problems, 127
Unicode standard, 83, 95-98, 110
unit tests, 190, 197
United States v. Auernheimer, 227-229
unittest module, 190, 197
UPDATE statement, 82
urllib library, 5, 45
urllib.error module, 5
urllib.parse module, 5
urllib.request module, 5, 72
urllib2 library , 5
urlopen function, 5, 97
urlretrieve function, 72
USE statement, 80
User-Agent header, 179
UTF standards, 95, 110

V

variables
    environment, 163
    handling in JavaScript, 148
    lambda expressions and, 28
versions, multiple, 45
virtual environments, 7

W

Warden, Pete, 217
web crawlers
    about, 31
    cautions using, 41
    crawling across the Internet, 40-45
    crawling an entire site, 35-40
    crawling with Scrapy, 45-48
    traversing a single domain, 31-35
    usage considerations, 220
web scraping, viii-ix
WebDriver, 153-155, 181

websites
    analyzing for scraping, 216
    crawling entire, 35-40
    running from hosting accounts, 203
    scraping text from images on, 167-169
    testing with scrapers, 189-198
well-formatted text, 164-169
whitespace, 74, 210
Wikipedia
    cleaning dirty data, 109-112
    Markov model example, 126-129
    MySQL example, 87-89

revision history example, 64-68
robots.txt file, 224
testing example, 191-193
traversing a single domain example, 31-35
Word (Microsoft), 102-105
w:t tag, 104

X

XML (eXtensible Markup Language), 52
XPath (XML Path), 157

About the Author

Ryan Mitchell is a software engineer at LinkeDrive in Boston, where she develops the company's API and data analysis tools. She is a graduate of Olin College of Engineering, and is a master's degree student at Harvard University School of Extension Studies. Prior to joining LinkeDrive, she built web scrapers and bots at Abine Inc. and regularly consults on web scraping projects, primarily in the financial and retail industries.

Colophon

The animal on the cover of *Web Scraping with Python* is a ground pangolin *(Smutsia temminckii)*. The pangolin is a solitary, nocturnal mammal and closely related to armadillos, sloths, and anteaters. They can be found in southern and eastern Africa. There are three other species of pangolins in Africa and all are considered to be critically endangered.

Full-grown ground pangolins can average in size between 12-39 inches in length and weigh between a mere 3.5-73 pounds. They resemble armadillos, covered in protective scales that are either dark, light brown, or olive in color. Immature pangolin scales are more pink in color. When threatened, the scales on the tails can act more like an offensive weapon, as they are able to cut and wound attackers. The pangolin also has a defense strategy similar to skunks, in which they secrete a foul-smelling acid from glands located close to the anus. This serves as a warning to potential attackers, but also helps the pangolin mark territory. The underside of the pangolin is not covered in scales, but, instead, with little bits of fur.

Like their anteater relatives, pangolin diets consist of ants and termites. Their incredibly long tongues allow them to scavenge logs and anthills for their meals. The tongue is longer than their body and retracts into their chest cavity while at rest.

Though they are solitary animals, once matured, the ground pangolin lives in large burrows that run deep underground. In many cases, the burrows once belonged to aardvarks and warthogs and the pangolin has simply taken over the abandoned residence. With the three, long, curved claws found on their forefeet, however, pangolins don't have a problem digging their own burrows if necessary.

Many of the animals on O'Reilly covers are endangered; all of them are important to the world. To learn more about how you can help, go to *animals.oreilly.com*.

The cover image is from *Lydekker's Royal Natural History*. The cover fonts are URW Typewriter and Guardian Sans. The text font is Adobe Minion Pro; the heading font is Adobe Myriad Condensed; and the code font is Dalton Maag's Ubuntu Mono.

Get even more for your money.

Join the O'Reilly Community, and register the O'Reilly books you own. It's free, and you'll get:

- $4.99 ebook upgrade offer
- 40% upgrade offer on O'Reilly print books
- Membership discounts on books and events
- Free lifetime updates to ebooks and videos
- Multiple ebook formats, DRM FREE
- Participation in the O'Reilly community
- Newsletters
- Account management
- 100% Satisfaction Guarantee

Signing up is easy:

1. Go to: oreilly.com/go/register
2. Create an O'Reilly login.
3. Provide your address.
4. Register your books.

Note: English-language books only

To order books online:
oreilly.com/store

For questions about products or an order:
orders@oreilly.com

To sign up to get topic-specific email announcements and/or news about upcoming books, conferences, special offers, and new technologies:
elists@oreilly.com

For technical questions about book content:
booktech@oreilly.com

To submit new book proposals to our editors:
proposals@oreilly.com

O'Reilly books are available in multiple DRM-free ebook formats. For more information:
oreilly.com/ebooks

Have it your way.

Lightning Source UK Ltd.
Milton Keynes UK
UKOW07f2246150615

253523UK00003B/12/P